T0366537

The Metaphysical Demonstration of the Existence of God

Other Titles of Interest from St. Augustine's Press and Dumb Ox Books

Francisco Suarez, *On Creation, Conservation, & Concurrence: Metaphysical Disputations 20–22*

Thomas Aquinas, *Disputed Questions on Virtue*

Thomas Aquinas, *Commentary on Aristotle's De Anima*

Thomas Aquinas, *Commentary on Aristotle's Metaphysics*

Thomas Aquinas, *Commentary on Aristotle's Nicomachean Ethics*

Thomas Aquinas, *Commentary on Aristotle's Physics*

William of Ockham, *Ockham's Theory of Terms: Part I of the Summa Logicae*

William of Ockham, *Ockham's Theory of Terms: Part II of the Summa Logicae*

Roger Bacon, *Roger Bacon's Philosophy of Nature*. Translation of *De multiplicatione specierum and De speculis comburentibus*

Aristotle, *Aristotle – On Poetics*, translated by Seth Benardete and Michael Davis

Plato, *The Symposium of Plato: The Shelley Translation*, translated by Percy Bysshe Shelley, edited by David K. O'Connor

Leszek Kolakowski, *My Correct Views on Everything*, edited by Zbigniew Janowski

Leszek Kolakowski, *The Two Eyes of Spinoza and Other Essays on Philosophers*, edited by Zbigniew Janowski

Leszek Kolakowski, *Religion: If There Is No God . . . On God, the Devil, Sin, and Other Worries of the So-Called Philosophy of Religion*

Leszek Kolakowski, *Husserl and the Search for Certitude*

Leszek Kolakowski, *Bergson*

Zbigniew Janowski, *Augustinian-Cartesian Index*

Rémi Brague, *Eccentric Culture: A Theory of Western Civilization*

Mario Enrique Sacchi, *The Apocalypse of Being: The Esoteric Gnosis of Martin Heidegger*

Roger Scruton, *An Intelligent Person's Guide to Modern Culture*

Roger Scruton, *The Meaning of Conservatism*

Josef Pieper, *Leisure, the Basis of Culture*

Josef Pieper, *Scholasticism: Personalities and Problems*

Josef Pieper, *The Silence of St. Thomas*

Peter Kreeft, *Socratic Logic: A Logic Text Using Socratic Method, Platonic Questions, and Aristotelian Principles*

Jacques Maritain, *Natural Law: Reflections on Theory and Practice*

Gabriel Marcel, *The Mystery of Being* (in two volumes)

Yves R. Simon, *The Great Dialogue of Nature and Space*

The Metaphysical Demonstration of the Existence of God

Metaphysical Disputations 28-29

Francisco Suárez, S.J.

Translated and Edited by John P. Doyle

ST. AUGUSTINE'S PRESS
South Bend, Indiana
2004

1 2 3 4 5 6 10 09 08 07 06 05 04

Library of Congress Cataloging in Publication Data
Suárez, Francisco, 1548–1617.
[Disputationes metaphysicae. 28-29. English]
The metaphysical demonstration of the existence of God : metaphysical disputations 28 and 29 / Francisco Suárez ; translated from the Latin by John P. Doyle.
p. cm.
Includes bibliographical references and index.
ISBN 1-58731-501-7
1. Metaphysics. 2. God. I. Title.
B785.S823 D5713 2002
212'.1– dc21 2002012096

∞ *The paper used in this publication meets the minimum requirements of the American National Standard for Information Sciences – Permanence of Paper for Printed Materials, ANSI Z39.48-1984.*

TO MARY GALE

WITH LOVE

CONTENTS

INTRODUCTION

I. Suárez: the Man, his Career and Work:[1]

Born at Granada on January 5, 1548, 56 years after the expulsion of the Moors from Spain, Francisco Suárez enrolled in 1561 at the University of Salamanca, where he began his study of Law, an interest he would have for the rest of his life. In June of 1564 he entered the Society of Jesus, i.e. the Jesuits. In October 1566, after two intensive years of philosophical education, he went on to study theology, still at Salamanca. In this pursuit, the most important of his teachers was the Dominican, Juan Mancio (1497–1576), who was holding Salamanca's principal chair (*Cátedra de Prima*) of theology, fourth in the line of succession after the great Francisco de Vitoria, O.P (1492/3–1546)

In 1570 Suárez began to teach philosophy, first at Salamanca and then at Segovia. He was ordained a priest in March 1572 and he continued to lecture in philosophy until, in September 1574, at the Jesuit College, Valladolid, he began his life's work as a theology teacher for the Society. In years after, he taught his

---

1 For details of Suárez's life, see Raoul De Scorraille, S.J., *François Suarez de la Compagnie de Jésus, Paris*, 1911, I, 3. This work is still the chief source for Suárez's life. In English see Joseph Fichter, *Man of Spain, Francis Suarez*, New York, 1940. For a briefer but still accurate presentation, cf. P. Monnot, "Suarez, François. I. Vie et oeuvres," *Dictionnaire de Théologie Catholique*, XIV, 2_0 partie (Paris, 1941) cols. 2638–49. On Suárez's ancestry cf., José de Duenas, S.J., "Los Suárez de Toledo." *Razón y Fe*, numero extraordinario (Madrid, 1948), pp. 91–110. For more recent presentations of Suárez in his historical setting, cf. Jorge J.E. Gracia, "Francisco Suárez: The Man in History," *The American Catholic Philosophical Quarterly*, LXV (1991), pp. 259–66; Carlos Noreña, "Suárez and the Jesuits," *ibid.*, pp. 267–86, and John P. Doyle, "Suárez, Francisco," *Routledge Encyclopedia of Philosophy* (London/New York: Routledge, 1998), vol. 9, pp. 189–96.

subject at Avila (1575), Segovia (1575), Valladolid again (1576), Rome (1580),[2] Alcalá (1585), and Salamanca (1593). In 1597, he accepted the principal chair of theology at the University of Coimbra, where in 1612 he published the results of his legal teaching in his monumental treatise, "On Laws," (*De legibus*). He remained at Coimbra until his retirement in 1615. On 25 September 1617, he died in Lisbon.

In addition to his teaching, Suárez engaged in theological and political debates. The most famous of these was the controversy *De auxiliis* ("On the Helps [for Salvation]"). Raging between sixteenth-century Jesuits and Dominicans, this centered on God's Foreknowledge and Causality, Grace, and human freedom. Suárez, with his fellow Jesuits, Robert Bellarmine (1542–1621) and Luis Molina (1535–1600), allowed for Divine prerogatives but also championed human free will. Less metaphysical and more political was the dispute between the Republic of Venice and the papacy about the limits of papal jurisdiction. In the course of this dispute Suárez in 1607 composed (but did not actually publish[3]) a pro-papal treatise entitled, "On the ecclesiastical immunity violated by the Venetians." Praising his effort, Pope Paul V [Camillo Borghese (1552–1621), pope (1605–1621)], in the year of its composition, stated that the work showed its author to be "an outstanding and pious doctor" (*Doctor eximius ac pius*) Hence the honorific title Suárez has enjoyed in the history of Scholasticism – "*Doctor eximius*."

Tied to his teaching, Suárez's writings, which have been estimated to comprise approximately 21 million words[4] and which fill 26 volumes in the most accessible nineteenth-century edition,[5] were mainly theological and usually corresponded to some area of the *Summa Theologiae* of St. Thomas Aquinas (1225–1274). Outside this Thomistic framework were two controversial writings: the just mentioned treatise on ecclesiastical immunity and a long Latin work whose title translates as: "A Defense of the Catholic Faith against the Errors of the Anglican Sect, with a Reply to the 'Apology' for the 'Oath of Fidelity' and the 'Warning Preface' of James, the Most Serene King of England." Appearing at Coimbra in 1613, this work detailed Suárez's political philosophy. However,

2 It is worth mentioning that Suárez was in Rome at the time in which the great Jesuit mathematician, Christopher Clavius (1538–1612), was working there on the 1582 reform of the calendar under the auspices of Pope Gregory XIII.

3 The work was finally published by Mgr. J.-B. Malou, bishop of Bruges, as the 4th Treatise in a volume entitled: *R.P. Francisci Suarezii, Opuscula sex inedita* (Paris/Bruxelles: P. Gueau, 1859).

4 For this, cf. J. Fichter, *Man of Spain* ..., p. 327.

5 *Opera Omnia* (Paris: L. Vivès, 1856–1866); plus two volumes (27 and 28) of indices, 1878.

in the very year of its appearance it was by order of James I publicly burned in London, because in it Suárez had opposed the absolute right of kings and had defended the indirect power of the papacy over temporal rulers. This last was coupled with a legitimation of citizens' resistance against a tyrannical monarch – even to the point of tyrannicide in the case of a monarch deposed for heresy by the pope.

II. The Disputationes Metaphysicae:

Again outside the Thomistic framework are the two volumes of the *Disputationes metaphysicae* ("Metaphysical Disputations"), which were published at Salamanca in 1597. Without doubt Suárez's most important and influential enterprise, the volumes contain résumés of his own and previous Scholastic thought on countless questions, arranged in the form of fifty-four "Disputations" that deal in systematic fashion with topics in metaphysics. Even a casual reader will be struck by the work's tremendous display of its author's erudition. Again in the most accessible edition, it comprises almost 2000 quarto pages, which, from a computer word count of a representative page, I estimate to contain more than 1.4 million words. After stating each problem, Suárez has searched the history of philosophy and theology for solutions that have been offered to it. With as many as twenty-two opinions listed in connection with a single question, almost every available Greek, Arabic, Patristic, and especially Scholastic writer has been cited, often many times. As a rule, these citations are from original sources and exact references are given. One historian has counted 7709 citations, referring to 245 different authors.[6] Hardly surprising in a work on metaphysics, Aristotle (384–322 BC) was most mentioned, a total of 1735 times, while St. Thomas Aquinas was next, cited 1008 times.[7] But the *Doctor eximius* does not just assemble opinions. Much more does he show himself ever an independent thinker with a passion for fairness, faithfully reporting as many positions as he can and giving equitable treatment both to those he endorsed and to those he opposed.

In a preface addressed to the reader of the *Disputationes*, Suárez remarks that he is taking time out from theological preoccupations to author a systematic metaphysics. This metaphysics, which will be Christian and at the service of theology, will be divided into two parts, to which he says the two volumes of the printed work will correspond. In the twenty-seven Disputations, which make up the first volume, Suárez is concerned with being in general while, symmetrically, in the twenty-seven Disputations of the second volume he descends to

---

6 Cf. Jesús Iturrioz, S.J., "Fuentes de la metafísica de Suárez," *Pensamiento*, numero extraordinario (Madrid, 1948), pp. 31–89, esp. p. 39.

7 *Ibid.*, p. 40.

particular beings – in effect dividing metaphysics itself into a general and a special part.[8]

In the very first Disputation (*Opera omnia*, Paris: Vivès [1856]: vol. 25, pp. 1–64), he tells us that the object of metaphysics is "being insofar as it is real being." Explaining this, in Disputation 2 (pp. 64–102) he uses two distinctions already familiar to Scholastic authors. The first is between the *formal concept* as an act of the mind and the *objective concept* as what is immediately the object of that act. This latter may be an individual thing or some common feature (*ratio*) of things. It may, further, be something mind-independent, whether actual or possible, or it may be something merely objective or mind-dependent. The second distinction is between *being as a participle*, which refers to actual existents and *being as a noun*, which refers to whatever is not a simple fiction but is true in itself and apt really to exist. The object of metaphysics is then identified with the "common objective concept of being as a noun." This precise object, which reflects Avicenna's (980–1037) understanding of Aristotelian metaphysics, abstracts from existence and, as common, transcends all categories, genera, species and differences to embrace everything real. This last runs a range from extrinsic denominations (such as "being right," "being left," "being known," or "being willed"),[9] through mere possibles (which reduce to non-contradiction), to actual created substances and accidents, to the subsistent, purely actual, necessary, uncreated, and infinite reality of God. Over this range, the common concept of being as a noun is analogous with what Suárez will call "an analogy of intrinsic attribution." In this analogy, a unified concept of being is shared, in an order that is intrinsic to it, by different beings (God and creatures, substance and accidents) in such way that the being of what is posterior depends upon and indeed "demands" (*postulat*) the being of what is prior.[10]

Disputation 3 (pp. 102–115) offers a general treatment of the transcendental properties, namely unity, truth, and goodness, which belong to every being insofar as it is a being. The property of unity is as such treated in Disputation 4

8 On general and special metaphysics in Suárez, cf. Asa Goudriaan, *Philosophische Gotteserkenntnis bei Suárez und Descartes in Zusammenhang mit der niederländischen reformierten Theologie und Philosophie des 17. Jahrhunderts* (Leiden/Boston/Köln: Brill, 1999), pp. 14–20, esp. 14, note 4. Let me remark here that Goudriaan's volume overall will supply excellent background reading for the present translation.

9 On extrinsic denomination, cf. my article, "*Prolegomena* to a Study of Extrinsic Denomination in the Work of Francis Suarez, S.J.." *Vivarium*, 22 (1984), 2: pp. 121–60.

10 For Suárez's doctrine here, see my article: "Suarez on the Analogy of Being," *The Modern Schoolman*, 46 (1969): pp. 219–49; 323–41.

(pp. 115–45), following which questions are raised in Disputation 5 (pp. 145–201) about individuation, in Disputation 6 (pp. 201–50) about formal and universal unity, and in Disputation 7 (pp. 250–74) about different kinds of distinction. In the course of his discussion of unity, Suárez rejects the Aristotelian-Thomistic doctrine that traces individuation to "quantified matter." He also rejects Scotistic "thisness" (*haecceitas*) while coming close to nominalism with a view that every thing is individual by its very entity. On universals, again he inclines to nominalism with a denial of any real common nature independent of individuals. At the same time, he teaches that the universalizing activity of the mind has a foundation in the likenesses of things. Distinctions he divides as real, rational, and modal. Along the way, he opposes the "real formal distinction" (*distinctio formalis a parte rei*) that Duns Scotus had taught to be present between "formalities" (*formalitates*) prior to any operation of the intellect.

In succeeding Disputations: the discussion of truth, which Suárez understands as conformity between formal and objective concepts, in Disputation 8 (pp. 274–312) is balanced by discussion of falsity in Disputation 9 (pp. 312–28). Likewise, discussion of goodness in Disputation 10 (pp. 328–55) is balanced by that of evil in Disputation 11 (pp. 355–72). Disputation 12 (pp. 372–95) treats causes in general, while Disputations 13–25 (pp. 395–916) treat material, formal, efficient, and final causes in detail. Completing the first part as well as the first volume of the *Disputationes*, Disputation 26 (pp. 916–49) considers causes in relation to their effects, while Disputation 27 (pp. 949–61) deals with causes in relation one to another.

The second part and second volume of the *Disputationes* begins in Disputation 28 (Vivès: vol. 26, pp. 1–21) with the principal division and principal analogy of being between infinite and finite. In Disputation 29 (pp. 21–60), Suárez demonstrates the existence of God in an expressly "metaphysical" way, once more reflecting Avicenna. This way turns on the principle, "Everything which comes to be, comes to be by another" and scales the ladder of the common concept of being from lesser and lower being to a First Being. In the course of his reasoning, Suárez rejects any "physical" demonstration, such as that of Aristotle, adopted by Averroes (1126–1198) and also St. Thomas, which would turn on the principle, "Everything which is moved is moved by another," to pass from motion to a First Mover. These two Disputations are translated in the present volume.

Following demonstration of God's existence, Disputation 30, which is the longest Disputation (pp. 60–224), investigates the Divine nature and attributes. Disputation 31 (pp. 224–312) inaugurates treatment of finite being with a denial of the Thomistic distinction of essence and existence in creatures, which distinction the *Doctor eximius* understands as falling between two "things" (*res*). For Suárez the only distinction that can obtain here is one of reason with some basis in reality. In Disputation 32 (pp. 312–29), substance and accidents are considered in general, as well as the analogy of being between created substances and accidents. Over the next four Disputations (pp. 329–491) substance is treated in detail while the various categories of accident are treated in Disputations 37 to 53 (pp. 491–1014). The whole work concludes in Disputation 54 (pp. 1014–41) with an extremely important discussion of "beings of reason" (*entia rationis*) divided into negations (which include so-called impossible objects), privations, and mind-dependent relations – all of which are outside the real being that is the object of metaphysics.

III. A Summary of Disputation 28:[11]

As mentioned, the two Disputations that are translated in the present work open the second part of the *Disputationes metaphysicae* and mark the turn from being in general to particular beings. Their concern is with, first in Disputation 28, a comprehensive division of being in general, and after in Disputation 29, the existence of the principal member of this division, namely, that being which is God.

Disputation 28 is divided into three Sections, which ask about the legitimacy and the sufficiency of the division, as well as whether the dividend, i.e. being, is univocal or analogous between God and creatures. In the first Section (Vivès: vol. 26, pp. 1–8), the question is whether being is rightly divided into infinite and finite being? Doubts arise from the fact that "infinite" and "finite" on their face do not appear to cover the whole range of being but rather look to be restricted to accidental being in the category of quantity (§ 1). In addition, the terms of the proposed division seem obscure, especially the term "infinite" (§ 2). Suárez's answer is to analyze the terms (§ 3) and then to defend the division as one that is good and necessary (§ 4) as well as first and most evident (§ 5). It is equivalent to other divisions such as being by itself (*ens a se*) and being from another (*ens ab alio*) (§§ 6–7) or, with clarifications, necessary being and contingent being (§§ 8–12). It is also equivalent to: essential being and being by participation (§ 13), created being and uncreated being (§ 14), or being in act and being in potency (§§ 15–16). Suárez next compares the first division with the rest (§ 17), explains the terms of the first division by comparison with quantity (§ 17), and closes the first Section (§ 18) with a reply to objections raised at its beginning.

Section 2 (vol. 26, pp. 8–13) opens with reasons for doubting the sufficiency of the division. These include that fact that relations, because they are found both in creatures and in God, seem to be neither finite nor infinite and do not therefore fit the division (§ 1). Something akin to this occurs from the case of Christ who is both finite and infinite inasmuch as he is both God and man (§ 2).

11 What follows is meant to be little more than an outline. Readers are advised to look at what Suárez has to say for himself, albeit in the present poor English version, rather than rely upon any synopsis of that.

Again, there is question regarding the free acts of the Divine Will, which would apparently be at once both contingent and necessary (§ 3). Then there is an opinion of Duns Scotus to the effect that being should first be divided into quantified and non-quantified being, and that the division into finite and infinite is a subdivision of quantified being (§ 4). After addressing this last opinion (§§ 5–6), Suárez goes on to defend the sufficiency of the divisions proposed in Section 1, especially that in terms of being by itself and being from another (§ 7). He then gives extended expositions of and answers to the difficulties proposed about relations, Christ, and Divine free acts (§§ 8–16).

Section 3 of Disputation 28 (vol. 26, pp. 13–21) begins with a rejection of the view that the term *being* as used between God and creatures is simply equivocal (§ 1). A quite opposite view, which was held by Duns Scotus (1266–1308), is that *being* is said univocally of God and creatures (§ 2). After explaining the reasons for this view and for its opposition to analogy in this context (§§ 3–4), Suárez himself presents an opinion that the term *being* is indeed said analogously of God and creatures (§ 5), discusses arguments in support of this (§§ 6–8), and replies to objections that may be raised against these arguments (§ 9). Subsequently, he inquires about the kind of analogy that is present here (§ 10) and rejects Cajetan's doctrine that there is "a proper analogy of proportionality" between God and creatures (§ 11). Also rejecting any "analogy of attribution to a third thing," that is, any position that would affirm that God and creatures are called *being* only by reference to something else, he next affirms that there is here "an analogy of one to another," which is to say that creatures are being in reference to God and the term *being* is said more principally of God than of creatures (§ 12). At this point, he brings in the "Platonic" opinion that God is not being but rather above being, which occasions a brief explanation of the name of God in *Exodus* 3, 14 (§ 13). Following this, he explains and affirms that the analogy of being here is intrinsic inasmuch as creatures are designated *beings* from their own intrinsic being and not just extrinsically from God (§§ 14–17). Finally, his reply to objections and arguments in support of univocity closes the third Section and the Disputation itself (§§ 18–22).

IV. A Summary of Disputation 29:

Though almost twice as long, Disputation 29 like the one before is again divided into three Sections. Section 1 (vol. 26, pp. 21–34) begins after two introductory paragraphs (§§ 1–2) in which Suárez gives reasons for the location of the subject matter of the Disputation in this place and remarks how he will leave aside as much as possible items which depend for their understanding on Revelation. The first Section then asks whether and/or by what means the existence of God can be demonstrated. Among the Scholastic Doctors, Peter d'Ailly (1350–1420) has denied the possibility of such a demonstration. To this Suárez makes the brief but revealing reply that already by the various divisions of being that have been presented in the previous *Disputation* the existence of "some being which is uncreated or not produced" has been proven (§ 1). The obvious implication is that by now the existence of God has in effect been proven. But immediately the question arises: by what means, physical or metaphysical, is this properly done? On one side, the opinion of Averroes is that the means is physical, namely the motion of the heavens (§ 2). The contrary opinion, that of Avicenna and later of Duns Scotus among others, holds that the means must be metaphysical (§ 3) – that is, not motion but being itself. A third and a fourth opinion hold in different ways that the task must belong to both physics, that is natural philosophy, and metaphysics (§§ 4–5). In different ways the means would thus be both physical and metaphysical. In Suárez's judgment the second opinion is certainly the true one but there can be some probability in the fourth position, if it is rightly explained (§ 6).

At this juncture, he examines at length the physical argument that proceeds by the medium of motion and for various reasons he finds it wanting (§§ 7–17). Then he considers another physical argument, from the operations and the essence of the rational soul (§ 18). This too comes up short, unless we first pose a question about the soul's being, which is a metaphysical question (§ 19). Here Suárez gives the metaphysical argument that is based upon a broader and deeper principle than the physical one, "*Whatever is moved is moved by another*." The metaphysical principle is "*Whatever is made or produced is made by another*" and the argument itself concludes to an unmade Maker (§§ 20–21). An objection of a possibly circular chain of causes is dismissed as every bit as inadmissible as a thing's causing itself (§ 22). Other objections involve an infinite number of causes that would preclude any arriving at a first uncaused or unmade cause. There are different ways to conceive such an infinity of causes. Suárez explains such ways in detail and shows their insufficiencies (§§ 23–40). The first Section ends (§§ 41–42) with a brief rehearsal of and summary judgment upon the opinions listed at the beginning.

Section 2 (pp. 34–47) gets more exact and asks: whether one can show in an *a posteriori* way that there is only one uncreated being which will in fact be God? The thought here is that although the basic demonstration has been displayed in the previous Section or even in the previous Disputation, it needs precision. For it might be the case that while by now an unmade or uncreated being has been proven to exist, perhaps there is more than one such, which would mean that we have not reached the true God, who is unique (§§ 1–2).

In a totally opposite direction is a position, which has been associated with St. Anselm of Canterbury (1033–1109), to the effect that the existence of God is self-evident and therefore need not and in fact cannot be demonstrated (§ 3). Suárez's own view is that the existence of God can be demonstrated but it is necessary first to be clear about what we mean by God, that is to say what it is we are attempting to demonstrate (§ 4). This he tells us is "a certain most noble being which both surpasses all the rest and from which as from a first author all the rest depend, which, accordingly, should be worshipped and venerated as the supreme deity" (§ 5). There are, he says, two ways to prove the existence of such a God: "one is completely *a posteriori* and from effects; the other is immediately *a priori*, although remotely it also is *a posteriori*" (§ 7). In the first way, "the beauty of the whole universe and the wonderful connection and order of all things in it sufficiently declare that there is one first being, by whom all things are governed and from whom they draw their origin" (ibid). Four objections are that (1) this may prove that there is one governor of the world but not necessarily that there is one creator, (2) this proof does not rule out a number of rulers who might govern the world by consensus, (3) it says nothing about spiritual beings themselves or their connection with the present material world, and (4) this proof does not foreclose on there being another world besides this one (§ 8). Suárez goes on in paragraphs following to answer these objections in detail. In reply to the first, he draws from the ancient Christian writer, Lactantius (ca. 240–320), the lesson that "the universe can be governed only by him by whose counsel and power it has been created" (§ 9). He then devotes eleven paragraphs (§§ 10–20) to further explain this in the cases of the elements, mixed bodies (more or less perfect), and especially the heavens. In this last regard, he pays special attention to the causality between the heavens and sublunar natural things. The second objection is met through nine paragraphs (§§ 21–29) in which Suárez argues that a number of world rulers would require that such be at once intelligent but also imperfect and liable to disagreement among themselves. The third objection is presented in more detail (§ 30) and answered over six paragraphs (§§ 31–36) in which Suárez treats the Aristotelian separate substances. From the motion of the heavens their existence is at best only probable, and even if they do exist they must be creatures of God. Finally, in reply to the fourth objection, Suárez shows the reasonable character of the Christian doctrine that God is not limited to making only one world and could indeed be the creator of any number of worlds besides this one, with the result that the objection has no force (§ 37).

Nevertheless, at this point Suárez tells us: "from this and the preceding objection I am convinced that the reasoning made to prove that there is only one unproduced being and that all the rest of beings have been made by that being does not conclude absolutely about all beings, but only about those which can fall under human cognition by way of natural reasoning or philosophy. Therefore, in order that the argument conclude universally, there necessarily must be employed a demonstration *a priori*, which ... we will pursue in the following Section" (ibid.)

Section 3 (pp. 47–60) first affirms the impossibility of demonstrating the existence of God in *a priori* manner from cause to effect, since obviously God has no cause (§ 1). Nevertheless, once He has been, in an *a posteriori* way, demonstrated to exist, it is possible secondarily to use *a priori* demonstrations to arrive at some of his properties or attributes (§ 2). However, this is not easy to do, as Suárez shows by rejecting an argument which has been offered to prove God's unicity on the basis that being can belong first and through itself only to a single unproduced being (§§ 3–7). He then proposes two more arguments that purport to prove that there cannot be several beings that exist of themselves. However, objections can be made to both of these arguments (§§ 8–10). A fourth argument, which Suárez finds "very probative," is to the effect that singularity must belong by nature to an unproduced being; therefore such a being cannot be multiplied (§ 11). While objection may be made to this reasoning, Suárez thinks it can be defended (§ 12) and indeed, if it is rightly understood, it may strengthen the first argument offered (§ 13). He further infers that being can belong to other things only by way of efficient causality or effective emanation from the first unproduced being (§ 14). Suárez then considers at length a fifth argument, which he thinks is "enough by itself and also confirms the preceding argument" (§ 15) to the effect that two or more unproduced beings could be neither the same nor diverse in species (§§ 15–22). This leads to an explanation of a text from Aristotle that seems at variance with this (§ 23). At this point, a sixth argument is introduced to show that a first unproduced being which is supreme and infinite in its perfection and most powerful in its acting produces "all things that are" (§ 24). An objection is raised to the effect that if it were to produce all things it would produce itself (§ 25), which, of course, is absurd. Suárez answers that it belongs to the perfection of that being and subsequently to its power "that it is not itself producible by itself" while all else is produced by it (§ 26). Yet another argument can be taken, says the *Doctor eximius*, "from the causality of the ultimate end" (§ 27) and objections to this are raised and answered (§§ 28–31). Now Suárez states his conclusion – "From all of this, it has been sufficiently demonstrated that God exists" – and reaffirms its metaphysical character (§ 32). "Lastly," he says, "from all that has been said it can be clear by, so to speak, a certain most evident experience how far from truth is the opinion ... which asserted that the existence of God is so self-evident that, for that reason, it could not be demonstrated" (§ 33). This occasions a final discussion of self-evident propositions (§ 34) as well as of reasons that could motivate such an opinion (§§ 34–37).

V. Some Influence of Suárez:

Most scholars would agree with Martin Heidegger (1889–1976) that Suárez was the main source through which Greek ontology passed from the Middle Ages to usher in the metaphysics and the transcendental philosophy of modern times.[12]

12 *Sein und Zeit* (Halle: M. Niemeyer, 1941), p. 22, tr. J. McQuarrie and E. Robinson,

First of all, the authority of the *Doctor eximius* for post-Renaissance Catholic Scholasticism was profound. While just a glance will show his importance even for Catholic writers who disagree with him,[13] not surprisingly, he was most influential for succeeding Jesuits. Largely through the growth and activity of the Society of Jesus, his metaphysics spread from the Catholic schools of Spain, Portugal, and Italy to northern European countries.[14] Beyond Catholicism, it crossed religious lines to the Lutheran universities of Germany where the *Disputationes metaphysicae* (of which seventeen editions appeared between 1597 and 1636[15]) was studied, by those especially who embraced what had been Melanchthon's (1497–1560) attitude toward philosophy.[16] In a similar way,

---

Being and Time (New York: Harper, 1962), p. 43; also cf.: *Die Frage nach dem Ding* (Tübingen: M. Niemeyer, 1962), p. 77. For some of what is involved in this, see my article, "Heidegger and Scholastic Metaphysics," *The Modern Schoolman*, 49 (1972), pp. 201–20. On the question of the relation between Suárez's metaphysics and Heidegger's "onto-theo-logical" conception of metaphysics, cf. A. Goudriaan, *Philosophische Gotteserkenntnis* ..., esp. pp. 8–10.

13 For example, the Dominican, John of St. Thomas, in the three volumes of his *Cursus philosophicus* has explicitly cited Suárez 167 times; cf. Ioannis a Sancto Thoma, O.P., *Cursus philosophicus Thomisticus*, ed. B. Reiser, O.S.B. (Taurini: Marietti, 1930–37), tom. III, pp. 492–95. While John is usually at odds with Suárez, at virtually every one of these citations he gives extended serious consideration to the positions of the *Doctor eximius*.

14 On this northern expansion of the Jesuits, see Bernhard Duhr, *Geschichte der Jesuiten in den Ländern deutscher Zunge*, vols. 1 and 2, Freiburg im B.: Herder, 1907–1913.

15 For this, cf.: "Se trata de una verdadera aventura publicitaria, y por lo mismo, es un acontecimiento ello sólo. Entre la fecha acabada de mencionar, 1597, y la de 1636–39 años- tiene dicha Metafísica las siguientes ediciones, todas en el extranjero: En 1599, en Venecia; en 1600, en Maguncia; en 1605, tres: una en Maguncia, una en Venecia, una en Paris. Tres años mas tarde, el 1608, una en Colonia. El 1610, una en Venecia. El 1614, cuatro: dos en Ginebra, una en Colonia, una en Maguncia. El 1619, una en Paris, una en Venecia (la cuarta en esta ciudad). El 1620, una en Colonia y es la tercera. El 1630, una en Ginebra (la tercera en la ciudad de Calvino). Total: 17 ediciones en 39 anos," Joaquín Iriarte, S.J., "La proyección sobre Europa de una gran metafísica, o Suárez en la filosofía de los dias del barocco," *Razón y fe*, 138 (1948), pp. 229–65, esp. 236. Iriarte regards this astounding diffusion of Suarez's work as perhaps unique in the history of philosophy and he compares it with the early editions of Descartes's *Meditationes:* "Descartes, por ejemplo, en todo el siglo XVII alcanzó cuatro ediciones del conjunto total de sus Obras filosóficas. Y de sus 'Meditaciones Metafísicas,' por separado, en ese mismo siglo (1641–1700), nueve ediciones. Meditaciones que no son sino un folleto, después de todo," *ibid.,* n. 6.

16 For much of this, see: Karl Eschweiler, "Die Philosophie der spanischen

Suárez had major influence in the Calvinist tradition of German and Dutch[17] schools, for both metaphysics[18] and law.[19]

In all probability, it was Suarezian metaphysics that René Descartes (1596–1650) first imbibed from his Jesuit teachers at La Flèche.[20] While he is short on explicit citations, he has on at least one occasion referred to the *Disputationes*,[21] of which he is believed to have owned a copy.[22] Gottfried Wilhelm Leibniz (1649–1716) boasted that when he was young he had read

---

Spätscholastik auf der Universitäten des 17 Jahrhunderts," in *Spanische Forschungen der Gorresgesellschaft*, Münster i.W.: Aschendorff, 1928, 251–325; Ernst Lewalter, *Spanische-jesuitische und deutschlutherische Metaphysik des 17 Jahrhunderts*, Darmstadt: Wissenschaftliche Buchgesellschaft, 1967 (reprint of Hamburg, 1935), Max Wundt, *Die deutsche Schulmetaphysik des 17 Jahrhunderts*, Tubingen: J.C. Mohr, 1939, and J. Iriarte, "La proyección ...".

17 *Ibid.*. Also cf. the remarks of Paul Dibon, *La philosophie néerlandaise au siècle d'or, tome I: L'enseignment philosophique dans les universités à l'époque précartésienne (1575–1650)*, (Paris/Amsterdam/Londres/New York, 1954), p. 42: "La *Disputatio*, si florissante dans les universités médiévales, a survécu à la Renaissance et Suarez apparait, à la fin du 16e siècle, comme un maître incontesté en cet art traditionnel. Où trouverait-on en effet examen plus exhaustif des arguments et forme syllogistique plus rigoureuse dans la solution de la question que dans les *Disputationes metaphysicae* du jésuite espagnol?"

18 For Suárez's influence in the Netherlands with regard to the metaphysical demonstration of God's existence and further knowledge of Divine attributes, see A. Goudriaan, *Philosophische Gotteserkenntnis* ..., esp. pp. 1–167.

19 In the context of law: for Suárez as a forerunner of the famous Dutch jurisprudent, Hugo Grotius, see: Paola Negro, "Intorno alle fonti scolastiche in Hugo Grotius," in *Dalla prima alla seconda Scolastica*, a cura di A. Ghisalberti (Bologna: Edizioni Studio Domenicano, 2000), pp. 200–51, esp. 207–8, 217–18, 228–36, and 250–51.

20 Cf. E. Gilson, *Being and Some Philosophers*, 2nd edition (Toronto: Pontifical Institute of Mediaeval Studies, 1952), p. 109. Also cf.: "Descartes, who was educated by the Jesuits, certainly studied Suárez's work, and a considerable amount of the framework for the Meditations (particularly the reasoning in the Third Meditations) bears the clear imprint of Suárez's ideas." R. Ariew/J. Cottingham/T. Sorell (eds.), *Descartes' Meditations. Background Source Materials* (Cambridge, 1998), p. 29, as cited by A. Goudriaan, *Philosophische Gotteserkenntnis* ..., p. 1, note 2.

21 Cf. *Reply to the Fourth Objections*, where Descartes cites Suárez, *DM* IX, 2, 4; in *Oeuvres de Descartes*, ed. Adam-Tannery (1897 sq.), VII, p. 235; also see Leonard Gilen, S.J., "Über die Beziehungen Descartes' zur zeitgenössischen Scholastik," *Scholastik*, XXXII (1957), esp. p. 54, n. 71.

22 Gilson, *Being* ..., p. 109.

Suárez "like a novel."[23] Arthur Schopenhauer (1788–1860), in his principal work, *Die Welt als Wille und Vorstellung*, shows great familiarity with the *Disputationes* and values it as "an authentic compendium of the whole Scholastic tradition."[24] Again, Franz Brentano (1838–1917), in his 1862 work on the various meanings of being according to Aristotle, has recommended the *Disputationes metaphysicae* to anyone who wants to understand diverse medieval views on Aristotle.[25] But, to my mind most important for later philosophy, Christian Wolff (1679–1754), whose *Ontologia* was for Immanuel Kant (1724–1804) almost identical with pre-critical metaphysics,[26] is on record telling us about "Francisco Suárez, of the Society of Jesus, who among Scholastics pondered metaphysical questions with particular penetration."[27] And beyond all doubt Wolff was in his own metaphysics very much in debt to Suárez.[28]

For more details of Suárez's influence on the philosophy of the seventeenth century and after, I recommend to the reader the secondary sources that have been cited in the notes of the last three paragraphs. For my purposes now, I am

---

23 See *Vita Leibnitii a seipso*, in Foucher de Careil, *Nouvelles lettres et opuscles inédits de Leibnitz* (Paris, 1857), p. 382–83; as cited by L. Mahieu, *François Suarez, sa philosophie et les rapports qu'elle a avec sa théologie* (Paris, 1921), p. 517–18. Also cf. P. Mesnard, S.J., "Comment Leibniz se trouva placé dans le sillage de Suarez," *Archives de Philosophie*, XVIII, cahier 1 (Paris, 1949), pp. 7–32; Mesnard (esp. pp. 22–30) has much of interest to say about Suárez's *Disputationes* in the Protestant universities of Germany. For recent comment on the relation between Leibniz and Suárez with particular reference to the doctrine of individuation, see Jean-François Courtine, *Suarez et le système de la métaphysique* (Paris: Presses Universitaires de France, 1990), esp. pp. 496–519.

24 Cf. *Arthur Schopenhauers sämtliche Werke*, ed. P. Deussen, I (Munchen, 1911), pp. 134, 148, 181, 500; cited by Nikolaus Junk, *Die Bewegungslehre des Franz Suarez* (Innsbruck/Leipzig: F. Rauch, 1938), p. 13.

25 For this, see Brentano, *Von der mannigfachen Bedeutung des Seienden nach Aristoteles* (Freiburg im Breisgau: Herder, 1862, reprint: Hildesheim: G. Olms, 1960), p. 3, n. 6; translated by Rolf George: *On the Several Senses of Being in Aristotle* (Berkeley: University of California Press, 1975), p. 150, n. 6.

26 Cf. Gilson, *Being* ..., p. 119.

27 Cf. C. Wolff, *Philosophia prima sive ontologia*, I, 2, 3, n. 169 (Francofurti et Lipsiae, 1736), p. 138.

28 Cf. Gilson, *Being* ..., pp. 112–20. On Suarezian metaphysics as it passes through Wolff to Kant, see the excellent work of Ludger Honnefelder, *Scientia Transcendens: Die formale Bestimmung der Seiendheit und Realität in der Metaphysik des Mittelalters und der Neuzeit (Duns Scotus – Suárez – Wolff – Kant – Peirce)*, (Hamburg: Felix Meiner Verlag, 1990), esp. pp. 200–381.

satisfied to have said enough about his life, his work, and his influence, to lay a general foundation for the present translation.

Translator's Remarks

Although Francisco Suárez was a fine philosopher and normally a quite clear writer, his Scholastic Latin style was often wordy and repetitious while at other times too brief and cryptic. Yet my aim was to translate his work as literally as possible. This may account for an excess of run-on labyrinthine sentences in my English as well as awkward word order within those sentences. It definitely does account for the proliferation of words like "therefore" – although at times I relented and used "hence" or "accordingly" even where there was no change in Suárez's "*ergo*." While sometimes I changed his passive voice verbs to active voice or modified his impersonal constructions, generally I resisted "improving" on Suárez's expression for the sake of more readable English. For example, I fought the temptation in a number of places to substitute "consequent" for Suárez's "consequence." But on occasion I did resort to synonyms for a single word used by Suárez a number of times in close succession. Again, for clarity's sake, I supplied words that were not in the text. Usually I indicated this with the device of square brackets. Frequently, when I had to choose among different meanings of a Latin word, I gave the original word in parentheses. Something I did do generally was break Suárez's long paragraphs into smaller ones. My hope was to better convey his meaning. The reader should be aware that Suárez's own paragraphs equate with the numbers within the Sections.

I was undecided about capitalization of items like "First Maker" or "First Cause" as well as "He" or "His" in contexts that did, but not in an explicit way, refer to God. I tried to use small letters where Suárez was speaking more generally of divisions of being and capital letters, especially in Disputation 29, from Section 2 on, where the discussion was expressly about God and where the reference was unmistakable. However, I cannot claim that I was always consistent in this. Something similar occurred when Suárez, obviously speaking of Aristotelian "separate substances," wrote "*intelligentiae,*" which I translated with a capital letter as "Intelligences."

While as a rule Suárez's references are accurate, on occasion, where he was perhaps citing from a faulty memory, they are not. Where I found lapses, I have indicated them with "[sic]" and have attempted to give the correct references in footnotes. In deference to Suárez, it needs noting that apparent lapses may have occurred because editions of the works he cited were divided differently from editions that are available today. An example of this would be Fonseca's *Commentary* on Aristotle's *Metaphysics*, which Suárez used and which divides Aristotle's text sometimes at variance with present-day divisions. Nevertheless, I was very impressed by how good overall the *Doctor eximius*' citations were. In this regard, his attention to the Greek texts he was citing from Aristotle was particularly striking. He possessed at least three translations of the *Metaphysics*, those of Fonseca, Bessarion, and Argyropolous, and on the basis of his own reading of Aristotle's Greek he was not hesitant to choose among them.

I did have a problem with his often vague cross-references to his own text, both between the two Disputations translated as well as to places in other Disputations. While it now and then required imagination, as much as possible I identified the passages to which he was referring. For this and for verifying references to other writers, I have given footnotes that fix Suárez's citations more in detail. In doing so, I was fortunate to have access to the *Vatican Film Library*, and to the rare books in *The St. Louis Room*, here at *St. Louis University*. For references to early Christian writers, I used when I could the volumes of J.-P. Migne's Greek and Latin *Patrologies*. Even where other more critical texts may have replaced them, the Migne volumes continue to be accessible.

In addition, I have employed footnotes to give brief explanations of points Suárez is making in the text. Obviously, some things needed clarification while others on their face seemed plain enough. The problem was deciding which points to explain. More often than not, I was content to let Suárez explain himself without any help from me. That however did not obviate the fact that there were extended portions of his text in which he presupposes background which he does not identify and which if I had pursued would have taken me too far from the main task of presenting Suárez himself. The best example of such background that comes to mind is the geocentric astronomy, neither purely Aristotelian nor Ptolemaic, which the *Doctor eximius* accepts but never spells out. My best guess is that it is a hybrid system that reflects the medieval doctrine of Sacrobosco [i.e. John Holywood (fl. ca. 1230)],[29] which itself combined Aristotelian and Ptolemaic elements and which continued to be a standard text in Jesuit schools into the seventeenth century.[30] But then I cannot be certain in all places.

As the Latin source for the translation, I used C. Berton's edition of the *Disputationes Metaphysicae* from Suárez's *Opera Omnia* (Paris: Vivès,

29 For this, see: Lynn Thorndike, *The Sphere of Sacrobosco and its Commentators*, Chicago: The University of Chicago Press, 1949.

30 On this see especially the Commentary of Clavius: Christophori Clavii Bambergensis ex Societate Jesu, *In Speram Ioannis de Sacro Bosco commentarius, nunc quinto ab ipso auctore hoc anno 1606, recognitus, et plerisque in locis locupletatus. Accessit Geometrica, atque uberrima de crepusculis tractatio* (Romae: Sumptibus Io. Pauli Gellii, 1607). The first edition of this work of Clavius appeared in 1581, during Suárez's Roman teaching.

1856–1866). In places, I checked Berton's reading against a Mainz edition of 1605. This is mentioned in my bibliography along with the modern bilingual, Latin and Spanish, work of Sergio Rábade Romeo *et al*. For some passages, the Spanish version was helpful, but in overwhelming part the final English text is my own directly from the Latin.

DISPUTATION 28

On the First Division of Being into the Absolutely Infinite and the Finite, and Other Divisions Which Equate with This.

The connection of the present treatise with what has gone before.– This is the second principal part of this work. After, in the first part, treating the common concept of being and the properties that are reciprocally said of it, in this part our task is to descend to definite kinds of beings, insofar as the formal object and the abstraction proper to this science permit.[1] But this cannot be done any

---

1 For Suárez the *adequate object* of metaphysics is "being insofar as it is real being;" cf. *Disputationes metaphysicae* (henceforth DM), I, s. 1, n. 26, in *Opera omnia*, 26 vols. (Paris: L. Vivès, 1856–1866), vol. 25, p. 11. (Unless otherwise noted, later references to and citations of Suárez will be from this edition, to which two volumes of indices were added in 1878.) Within this object metaphysics proceeds by way of a consideration of things insofar as they abstract from all matter (sensible and intelligible) and fall under a common concept (*ratio formalis sub qua*) of being. This then constitutes the formal object (*objectum formale*) of the discipline. There needs only be added that the abstraction here is of two types: (1) according to being (*secundum esse*) and (2) according to concept (*secundum rationem*). In a case of abstraction according to being, we are dealing with beings (e.g. God and Aristotelian "Separate Substances") which are of themselves immaterial. When we speak of an abstraction according to concept, we are dealing not just with things which are immaterial in themselves, but also with everything else inasmuch as it falls under concepts like being, unity, truth, and goodness which in their application are not restricted to things which are immaterial in themselves but are common to these and to other things as well. For this, cf. esp. *DM* I, s. 2, n. 13, vol. 25, pp. 16–7.

better than through the various divisions of that [common concept of being] and its members, and through their precise consideration.

We have, however, said above in *Disputation* 4, section 4 [*sic*],[2] that the first and most essential division of being is into finite and infinite, [infinite, that is,] according to essence or in the character of being, which alone is properly and simply infinite. Accordingly, we are beginning this part from this division, under which we are including others that in fact coincide with this, although they are conceived and expressed by us with different words and concepts.[3] And because we have spoken in the first and second Disputations about what is divided in this division (for it is that being which indeed is the adequate object of metaphysics[4]), it remains only to see of what sort the mentioned division is, and whether as given it is correct and sufficient.

SECTION ONE

Whether Being Is Correctly Divided into Infinite and Finite, and What Divisions Are Equivalent to This.

1. *Reasons which make the issue doubtful.*– A possible first reason for doubting is that "finite" and "infinite" are relevant only to things which have some expanse or extension, and therefore they are ordinarily said with respect to quantity, since in their proper natures they include a relation to some endpoint. For that is called "finite" which is bounded by endpoints, whereas the "infinite" is what has no endpoint. Nothing, however, is related to an endpoint unless it has some expanse or extension that is to be ended. But it is not of the nature of being to have some expanse or extension. Therefore, it is not of the nature of being to be bounded, or not bounded, by endpoints, that is: to be finite or infinite. Hence, these members do not correctly divide being.

This is explained and confirmed, because infinite here is taken either privatively or in a merely negative way. But indeed nothing seems infinite in the first way, for only that being could be called privatively infinite, which, although it is apt to be bounded by endpoints, in fact is not so bounded. But manifestly there is no being of this kind, for not even God himself is infinite in this way, since he is not apt to be bound by endpoints. But if infinite is taken in the second way, then every indivisible being will be infinite, since no such being is bound by endpoints. For what in itself is entirely indivisible is not capable of any other ending.

2. *Second.*– A possible second difficulty with this division comes from the fact that it is presented through certain modes or attributes of being which are

2 For this, cf. *DM*, IV, s. 8, n. 10, vol. 25, p. 140.

3 For the same thought, cf. *DM* IV, s. 8, n. 9, vol. 25, p. 139.

4 Cf. *DM* I, s. 1, n. 26, vol. 25, p. 11.

very obscure and which can, at least on one side,[5] scarcely be explored by natural reason. However, the first division of being should be most clear and, if possible, composed of self-evident terms. The antecedent here is explained: for with respect to God, it can scarcely be shown, and perhaps it cannot be demonstrated, that he is absolutely infinite. In addition, it is more difficult to explain in what such infinity may consist. Therefore, the mentioned division is not properly posed, especially in the first place and as the foundation of others.

3. *What the terms of the division in question signify.*– With respect to this division, we must at the outset state what in fact it means, and then it will easily become clear that this division is the best and has been put in the right place and order. Thus, in point of fact, being is divided here into God and creatures. But because we cannot conceive – with positive concepts, which are simple and proper to God – things of God as they exist in themselves, we use negative concepts, in order to separate and distinguish that most excellent being, which is most distant from the rest and less agrees with them than they do among themselves. And in this way we contrive the aforesaid distinction: taking something in which all created or creatable things agree and removing it from a certain more noble being, for the reason that this has a more excellent degree of essence or entity.[6] Thus we reduce the whole range of being to these two members.

The Resolution of the Question.

4. *The stated division is good and most of all necessary.*– From what has been said, it is evident first that this division in actual fact is best and most necessary. This is clear first, because this division is commensurate with being. For, as we will make more clear in the following Section, no being can be conceived besides God and creatures. Second, because, as was stated above in the cited Disputation, Section Four [*sic*],[7] those [two] members are most of all removed from one another. Hence, also, the necessity of this division is evident. For, besides those things that have been treated above,[8] nothing is common between the first being and all others, although all those others have much in common among themselves. For the first being does not have a cause, but all the others do have a cause. Again, these latter can be divided into definite genera and species,

---

5 That is, the side of the infinite.

6 This paragraph should be noted as a partial presentation of Suárez's thoughts on the so-called "negative theology." For more, see A. Goudriaan, *Philosophische Gotteserkenntnis* ..., esp., pp. 148–55.

7 See note 2, above in this Section.

8 That is, in the first 27 Disputations dealing with the common concept of being, its transcendental properties, its principles and causes.

but that former exists outside every genus.[9] And in all these latter some kind of composition is found, whereas the former is completely simple and exists outside any composition. Therefore, it was necessary to separate that first being from the others, in order that once its nature was separately explained, what is common to the rest could be distinctly and clearly treated.

5. *The stated division is first and most known.*– Hence it is clear, second (what was proven in the previously mentioned *Disputation*, Section 4), that the aforementioned division by itself and by the order of teaching (*ordo doctrinae*)[10] is first and most known. And yet, perhaps as far as we are concerned, it is not known as well as the division of being into substance and accident, or others like this, which are nearer to the senses and are therefore more easily known by us.[11] However, from the side on which it includes the fact that God is and has an essence or an entity of a certain unlimited nature and perfection, the aforesaid division is harder for us to attain and explain. Because, however, in treating this science we are observing the order of teaching, we are rightly, therefore, setting up this distinction in the first place.

The Division of Being into Being by Itself and Being from Another.

6. Third, it is inferred from what has been said that this division into two members can be presented in many other ways, or under different words and concepts, which can clarify and illustrate it, although, as is clear from their terms, they all amount to the same thing. For example, being could be divided into that which has being by itself and that which has being from another. Augustine

---

9 On this, cf. St. Thomas Aquinas, *Summa Theologiae* I, q. 3, a. 5; and Suárez, *Tractatus de Divina Substantia ejusque attributis*, I, c. 4, n. 9, vol. 1, p. 15.

10 This is a phrase that Suárez uses frequently; but I do not know of any passage in which he has defined it. The closest I have found is in his "Most Ample Index to the Metaphysics of Aristotle" (*Index locupletissimus in Metaphysicam Aristotelis*), which is joined to the *Disputationes metaphysicae*, where he seems to equate it with "proceeding from things more known to those which are less known" and says "that method is everywhere repeated by Aristotle, and to explain it is the proper task of a logican;" cf. *Index*, VII, c. 4, vol. 25, p. xxxi. Within the century after the appearance of the *Disputationes metaphysicae*, the expression was used by other Scholastics. For example, see John of St. Thomas, *Naturalis philosophiae*, I, q. 1, a. 3, in *Ioannis a Sancto Thomae, O.P., Cursus philosophicus thomisticus*, nova editio a P. Beato Reiser, O.S.B. (Taurini: Ex Officina Domus Editorialis Marietti, 1933), tom. II, pp. 20–22, who, following Aristotle (in *Posterior Analytics* 1.2.72a1), regards it as an order in which we move from the more universal and confused (which are more known to us) to the more particular and distinct.

11 Note here that the order of teaching is evidently not entirely equivalent to the order in which things are known to us.

touched on this division, in chapter 7 of his *Book on the Knowledge of True Life*, and proposed it first in order to show that God exists.[12]

For, under these terms, it is a most known and most evident division, inasmuch as it is manifest that there are many beings which have being communicated from another, which beings, as experience itself well proves, would not exist unless they had received being from another. Furthermore, it is evident that not all beings could be of this kind. For, if all the individuals of any species are from another, it is also necessary that the whole species be from another, because a species exists only in an individual, and individuals do not have any other connatural way to receive existence apart from what the species requires. Therefore, if all individuals are such that they do not have being from themselves, but need causing by something else in order to receive being, the whole species also has need and a lack of perfection. It follows from this that a whole species cannot have being from some individual within that species, because the same thing cannot cause itself. It must, therefore, receive being from a superior being, about which one must again inquire whether it has being from itself or from another. For, if it has being from itself, with this the division we intend is complete; but if it has being from another, likewise it will be necessary for the whole species of such being to draw its origin from yet another which is superior.

However, we cannot proceed to infinity, because in that event the flowing forth of one thing from another would never have begun, or never, after infinite flowings forth of one thing from another, would it have come to the production of a present being. Again [we cannot proceed to infinity] because any whole collection of effects cannot be dependent unless we suppose that there is some independent thing or cause, as will be shown in the following *Disputation*,[13] Section One. Therefore, we must necessarily stop at some being which has its being from itself and from which all those which have only received being take their origin. And in this way the division in question is evident, whether that being which is not from another but rather by itself is one or many. For we are not now concerned with this, but only with the fact that all beings may be reduced to these two members, which have between them a manifest opposition or contradiction and which, therefore, must be both distinct and adequately dividing being.

7. Moreover, what is said to be from itself or by itself, although it seems to be positive, only adds a negation to being as such, since a being cannot be from itself by way of a positive origin or emanation. Therefore, it is said to be by itself, insofar as it has being which does not emanate from another. Through this nega-

---

12 For this, cf. Auctor incertus (Augustinus Hipponensis?), *Cognitio vitae seu de cognitione verae vitae liber unus*, c. 7, in *Patrologiae cursus completus, series Latina*, ed. J.-P. Migne (Paris: Migne, 1844–1891) [hereafter: *PL*], vol. 40, col. 1011.

13 That is, *Disputation* 29.

tion we state a positive and simple perfection of that being, which thus in itself and its own essence includes existence itself, in such way that it receives it from no other – which perfection that being does not have which has being only because it receives it from another.

And some of the Saints should be understood in this way when they say that God is for himself the cause of his own being, or his substance, or his wisdom. Thus, Jerome, [commenting on] *Ephesians*, chapter 3 [v. 14], says: "God is his own source and the cause of his own substance."[14] And Augustine, in his book, *On 83 Diverse Questions*, Questions 15 [*sic*] and 16, says that God is the cause of his own wisdom.[15] And in Book 7, Chapter 1, of *On the Trinity*, speaking of the Father, he says: "Because he is the cause of his own being, he is also the cause of his being wise."[16] For all these sayings should be interpreted in a negative way. However, Lactantius, who says, in his first book: *On False Religion*, that God has made himself,[17] does not seem to permit such interpretation. For he also says that God made himself at a moment in time (*ex tempore*), and as a basis for this, he assumes that what exists must at some time have begun to be;[18] which error is so absurd that it needs no refutation.[19]

The Division of Being into Necessary and Contingent.

8. Again, from this, other terms are easily stated by means of which this division can be presented. And in reality it is the same, although conceptually it is expressed with a different relation or negation. Thus, being can be divided into

14 Cf. S. Eusebii Hieronyimi Stridonensis presbyteri, *Commentariorum in epistolam ad Ephesios, libri tres*, II, c. 3, v. 14, in *PL*, vol. 26, col. 489a.

15 Cf. St. Augustine, *De diversis quaestionibus, 83*, q. 16, in *PL*, vol. 40, col. 15.

16 Cf. St. Augustine, *De Trinitate libri quindecim*, VII, c. 1, in *PL*, vol. 42, col. 936.

17 Cf. Lucii Caecilii Firmiani Lactantii, *Divinarum institutionum, liber primus: De falsa religione deorum*, c. 7, in *PL*, vol. 6, cols. 152b–53a, where Lactantius is with approval quoting Apollinus and Seneca.

18 *Ibid.*, col. 152a.

19 On this point in Scholasticism before Descartes, cf. "En effet, la scolastique n'a jamais envisagé, même à propos de Dieu, l'hypothèse d'une essence qui serait *causa sui*; elle connait donc des êtres qui possedent ou ne possedent pas certaines perfections, mais non des êtres qui se les donnent ou ne se les donnent pas." Étienne Gilson, *René Descartes: Discours de la méthode, texte et commentaire* (Paris: Vrin, 1947), p. 333. For much more detail, cf. J.-L. Marion, "Entre analogie et principe de raison: la *causa sui*," in J.-M. Beyssade and J.-L. Marion (eds), *Descartes. Objecter et répondre* (Paris: Presses Universitaires de France, 1994), pp. 305–34. On the relation between Suárez and Descartes here, see: Leonard Gilen, S.J., "Über die Beziehungen Descartes' zur zeitgenössichen Scholastik," *Scholastik*, vol. 32 (1957), pp. 41–66, esp. 58–60.

that which is simply necessary and that which is not necessary or what is broadly taken as contingent. In these terms, one should first note that necessary and contingent are not taken here as expressing the relation of an effect to a cause which is acting naturally or freely or which can or can not be impeded. We did speak of necessary and contingent in this way when we treated above of causes.[20] But necessary is now being taken absolutely in regard to existence, in which way a being is called necessary which has existence in such manner that it cannot lose it – to which is contrasted or opposed that being which is in such manner that it is able not to be, or which is not in such manner that it is able to be.[21]

From the preceding division, therefore, it is clear that there must be among beings one which is absolutely necessary. For that being which has its being from itself, and not from another, must be absolutely necessary, inasmuch as it evidently cannot deprive itself of its being, nor can it be deprived of it by another, since it does not depend on another. For what does not have being from another is not conserved in being by another, and in this sense it is said to be from itself and thus it is completely incompatible [with that] for it not to be.

Hence, it further results that, besides this being which is absolutely necessary, there are other beings which are not so necessary and which are thus contingent, if, broadly speaking, everything which is capable of not being is called

---

20 For this, see *DM* XIX, vol. 25, pp. 687–745.

21 It is worth noting that for St. Thomas Aquinas, as opposed to Suárez here, the terms "necessary" and "contingent" were not so radically divisive. Partly influenced by the doctrine of Aristotle and his Arab commentators, Aquinas accepted the notion of a necessary being which could be dependent; cf. e.g. *Summa Theologiae* I, q. 2, a. 3. Such in fact are all created beings which *in themselves* have no potency to non-being, for example, spiritual substances; cf. *Contra Gentiles* II, c. 55. The term "contingent" in this context is reserved to signify the manner of existence which is proper to a material, corruptible thing; cf. *Summa Theologiae* I, q. 86, a. 3 and *De Potentia* V, 3. Inasmuch as their matter can receive other forms, such things can radically change or be corrupted. But even in this instance there is no tendency to absolute nothing; *ibid.* For a more complete statement of the Thomistic doctrine of necessity and contingency, see: Cornelio Fabro, "Intorno alla nozione 'Tomista' di contingenza," *Rivista di filosofia neo-scolastica*, vol. 30 (1938), pp. 132–49; Thomas Wright, "Necessary and Contingent Being in St. Thomas," *The New Scholasticism*, 25 (1951), 439–56; and Armand Maurer, C.S.B., "Henry of Harclay's Questions on Immortality," *Mediaeval Studies*, vol. 19 (1957), pp. 79–107, reprinted in: Armand Maurer, *Being and Knowing: Studies in Thomas Aquinas and Later Medieval Philosophers* (Toronto: Pontifical Institute of Mediaeval Studies, 1990), pp. 229–71, esp. 230–38. Suárez was much aware of St. Thomas' doctrine on this matter (cf. *DM* XXXV, 3, nn. 53ff, vol. 26, pp. 457–58) and he even accepts it after a fashion (*ibid.*, n. 56; cf. also *DM* XXVIII, 1, n. 12 below). But despite that, in the present context, "necessary" and "contingent" are evidently opposed as God and creatures.

contingent. This is proven, because in addition to that being which exists by itself, there are beings which receive being from something else. Since these beings, then, do not have being from themselves, for this reason they have no aversion to not being. And, from another angle, just as they depend upon another from whom they receive being, so they can also not receive it and consequently not be.

9. *Two objections are met.*– You may say: if we imagine that God acts necessarily and without freedom, then things coming from him would be beings from another, and yet they would be necessary beings. Therefore, formally, and by virtue of the terms, these two members [i.e. "from itself" and "necessary"] would not be reciprocal. This is confirmed: for the [Divine] Word (or the Holy Spirit) can be called a being from another, inasmuch as it has being only by emanation from another [i.e. the Father]; and still it is an absolutely necessary being, inasmuch as it proceeds not by a free, but rather by a natural and necessary, production.

10. I answer, beginning from this confirmation, because it is theological: in the present context a being is called "from another" only because it is from another by way of a true causality. For the natural light [of reason], under which we are now philosophizing, does not recognize a true production and a real procession without a true causality, nor without a distinction in essence and being between the thing producing and the thing produced. However, in the case of Divine Persons this is not the way of emanation, because it is imperfect. And, therefore, just as all the Persons are the true and one God, so all are the one Being by itself, and all are essentially constituted by the essence which is its own uncaused and unproduced being. Thus, each Person is a necessary being, not only because it necessarily emanates, but also because it is necessarily constituted by a being and an essence that is entirely unproduced. For, although a Divine Person is produced, its Nature is not produced, but is communicated to that Person, through the production of that same Person. Hence, no argument with respect to created things may be taken from this Mystery.

11. *Even though God might act necessarily, there would be some non-necessary beings.– Scotus*, 1, *d.* 8, *q.* 4 [*sic*].[22] – Therefore, first in answer to the argument: granted that hypothesis [i.e. that God would act necessarily] it still would not follow that all beings would be necessary. For all beings might not be made immediately and with full power by the first being alone, or without the resistance or the hindrance of another cause – on all of which grounds it can result that something which is now receiving being might afterwards not receive it, and *vice versa*. Thus, even though some philosophers have erroneously assert-

---

22 Cf. Duns Scotus, *Ordinatio* I, d. 8, p. 2, q. 1, in *Joannis Duns Scoti Opera omnia*, IV (Civitas Vaticana: Typis Polyglottis Vaticanis, 1956), pp. 310–28, nn. 275–306.

ed that God acts of necessity, nevertheless, none has denied that there are many non-necessary beings, since, indeed from experience itself, that fact is most evident in corruptible and successive things. And, although from that hypothesis some produced being would be necessary, this would not be, like God, from an intrinsic and essential necessity, but only from the extrinsic necessity of an agent. Therefore, Avicenna, in Book 8, chapters 4 and 6 [*sic*], of his *Metaphysics*,[23] has said that only that being is necessary which exists of itself, but not other beings, even if they have a necessity of existing by another, [in which] he is perhaps referring not to an absolute necessity but to one which supposes the action of a First cause.

Finally, the supposed hypothesis is false for the following reason. For that being which exists of itself communicates itself to things outside not necessarily but freely. Hence, apart from that being, nothing is absolutely necessary. About this freedom in the action of the first being, we will speak later,[24] insofar as it is attainable either by the authority of the philosophers or by natural reason.

12. *The necessity by which incorruptible things are necessary.–* But you may still object: for incorruptible beings, even if they stem from a freely acting other, are called necessary beings by the Commentator [i.e. Averroes], in his book, *On the Substance of the Orb* [*of the Heavens*][25] and in his [Commentary on Aristotle's] *De Coelo*, Book 1, text 136,[26] and in his [Commentary on] Book 12, of the *Metaphysics*, text 41.[27] And St. Thomas, in [his work] *On the Power* [of God], question 5, article 3, accepts Averroes' opinion on this.[28]

The answer here, taken from St. Thomas himself, [in his *Summa Theologiae*] Part I, question 9, article 2[29] and in *Contra Gentiles*, Book III [*sic*],[30] chapters

---

23 Cf. Avicenna, *Liber de philosophia prima sive scientia divina*, V-X, édition critique de la traduction latine médiévale, par. S. Van Riet (Louvain: E. Peeters/ Leiden: E.J. Brill, 1980), Tractatus VII, c. 4, pp. 397–98 and c. 5, p. 406.

24 For this, see *DM* XXX, s. 9, vol. 26, pp. 116–36.

25 Cf. *Averrois Cordubensis Sermo de substantia orbis, nuper castigatus, et duobus capitulis auctus*, cap. 7, in *Aristotelis Opera cum Averrois commentariis* (Venetiis: Apud Junctas, 1562–1574), vol. 9, fol. 13v–14v.

26 Cf. *In Libros de Coelo Aristotelis* I, c. 2, pars 8, comm. 136, in *Aristotelis Opera ...* , vol. 5, fol. 92v.

27 Cf. *In Libros Metaphysicorum Aristotelis* XII, c. 3, comm. 41, in *Aristotelis Opera* ..., vol. 8, fol. 324v.

28 S. Thomae Aquinatis, *De Potentia*, q. 5, a. 3, in *Quaestiones disputatae*, vol. 2, cura et studio P. Bazzi, et al., editio VIII (Taurini: Marietti, 1949), p. 135.

29 Cf. *Summa Theologiae* I, q. 9, a. 2, in *Sancti Thomae Aquinatis Opera omnia*, vol. 4 (Romae: Ex Typographia Polyglotta, S.C. De Propaganda Fide, 1888), pp. 91–92.

30 Both the Vivès [vol. 26, p. 4] and the Mainz [i.e. R.P. Francisci Suarez e Societate Jeus, *Metaphysicarum disputationum*, tomus posterior (Moguntiae: Excudebat

30[31] and 35 [*sic*],[32] is that the word "necessity" is equivocal. For, in one way, it can be taken for incorruptibility, in which sense incorruptible creatures are sometimes said to be necessary beings. For, from the fact that they once exist they have no intrinsic potency to not exist. Instead, left to themselves, they endure forever, which without doubt is a certain necessity of being, since it excludes any intrinsic potency to not being. Nevertheless, such beings are not absolutely and in every way necessary. For neither from themselves, nor from their essence, do they have existence; nor do they receive it, or keep it, by an absolute necessity.

When, therefore, in the present case we distinguish a necessary from a non-necessary being, we are taking necessity in the first way. And for this reason no being which is by another is absolutely necessary. For, at least by a potency existing in that other, it can lose existence, even though in itself there is no intrinsic, true, and real potency to not exist – which potency is found only in those things which have a physical and passive potency for another being that is contradictory of and incompatible with their own being. But in other things, logical potency, if I may call it so, is enough, which on their part entails only non-contradiction,[33] while on the part of an extrinsic cause it implies a potency to suspend the action by which it imparts being. So therefore it is clear that this division is the same as the one preceding, although in the first way it is given under more known concepts, and it supposes fewer principles.

The Division of Being into Being by Essence and Being by Participation.

13. Again, the same division is usually given in the following terms, which indeed are equivalent to those above: one [kind of] being is by essence and a second is by participation. For that being is said to be by essence which has being essentially, by virtue of its essence, and not as received or participated from another. Oppositewise, a being by participation is one which has being only as communicated by and participated from another.

From this explanation of the terms, it is clear that this division is equivalent with those preceding. Hence, St. Thomas, in *Contra Gentiles*, Book 2, chapter 15, says that God is being by his essence, since He is Being Itself (*Ipsum Esse*).[34]

Balthasarus Lippius, Sumptib. Arnoldi Mylii, 1605), p. 7], editions have this, instead of the correct "II."

31 See *Summa contra Gentiles* II, c. 30, in *Opera*, vol. 13 (Romae: Typis Riccardi Garroni, 1918), pp. 338–40.

32 Cf. *ibid.*, c. 31, pp. 342–43.

33 On this, cf.: *DM* XLII, s. 3, n. 9, vol. 26, p. 613 and *DM* XLIII, s. 4, n. 2, p. 645. For general background and criticism, see my article: "Suarez on the Reality of the Possibles," *The Modern Schoolman*, XLVI (1967), pp. 29–40.

34 Cf. *Summa contra Gentiles* II, c. 15, in *Opera,* vol. 13, pp. 294–96.

And in [*Contra Gentiles*] Book 3, chapter 66, reason 6, he says that God alone is being by essence, while other things exist by participation.[35] For only in God is being [the same as] his essence, that is, belonging to his essence in such way that the essence of God, as it is proper to God, cannot be conceived by the mind if it is understood only as being in potency and not in act. Thus, to be a being by essence is the same as to have being from itself and from its own essence, to which a being by participation is in opposite fashion dissimilar.

Hence, this twofold grade or order of being should be proven by the same reasoning through which we have proven[36] that there is some being which is by itself and superior to all things that have being by another. For just as we should not proceed to infinity in beings which have being by another, so we should not thus proceed in beings by participation. Hence it is necessary that a being which exists by participation be reduced to something else which has being without such participation. But if that has another being also which is participated in another way, or by another kind of participation, then that will have to be referred to another. Therefore, so as not to proceed to infinity, we must stop at some being which is a being by essence.

Neither, on the other hand, can all beings be such by essence, first, because a being by essence is absolutely necessary, inasmuch as of its essence it actually exists, and clearly not all beings are necessary; and, second, because there is or can be only one being by essence, as we shall afterwards see.

A Division of Being into Uncreated and Created.

14. Further, this division is customarily given under these terms: *being is either uncreated or created* – which members manifest an immediate opposition to one another and coincide in reality with the members of the preceding divisions. They differ only, especially from those first members, namely *by itself* and *from another*, because those words are more general, since they are taken from a relation to dependence in general. But the words here are more specific, taken from the particular action or dependence of creation. Because, however, creation is the first emanation from another, with dependence on that other, and it is general in some way to all beings which depend on another, these members thus coincide in reality with those. For it is necessary that a being which is by itself and not from another be uncreated. For if dependence is without qualification denied of something, necessarily also that particular dependence which is creation is denied of it. Conversely, if a being is uncreated, it is necessary that it be by itself and not from another, because the first emanation with dependence on another, and as it were the basis of all other dependences, is creation. That, there-

35 *Ibid.*. III, c. 66, in *Opera*, vol. 14, p. 189.

36 See this Section, § 6, above.

fore, which has being without creation, necessarily has an entirely independent being, and it is thus a being by its essence, and not by something else.

Accordingly, the same reasoning which proves that there is some being which is by itself and independent also proves that there is some uncreated being, both because, as I have shown, these two are in reality the same and also because the same form of argument can be easily applied. For, if there are some created beings, unless we proceed to infinity, it is necessary to stop at some uncreated being, from which they have come forth. But that there are some created beings is proven from this that the first and fundamental dependence of all things is creation, which has been explained and proven [just] above. But because this is not by itself so known and evident as is the fact that there are beings which depend on something else, therefore, this division, under these terms [created and uncreated] is not so known as far as we are concerned, unless the word *creation* is taken not so much in the strict sense as a making from nothing, but more broadly for any true making or true dependence at all. And in this sense, these terms in almost no way differ from the first terms, as is immediately evident.

A Division of Being into Pure Act and Potential Being.

15. *The division under these terms can be suitably understood in two ways.– The first is explained.–* Moreover, the same division of being can be proposed under these terms: some being is entirely actual, but other being is potential, or some being is pure act while other includes potency or some potentiality. Under these terms, because of some obscurity in them, this division does not seem so appropriate, especially to be placed first in order. However, in reality it is very good and is the same as the preceding division.

For first of all it is clear that the members of this division have an immediate contradictory opposition to each other, because to be in act and to be in potency, taken as they should be with proportion and with regard to the same thing, entail a privative or a contradictory opposition.[37] However, being can be called

37 On the distinction between privative and contradictory opposition, cf. Suárez, "This can be explained through two affirmations, in which predicates, either contradictorily or privatively opposed, are predicated of the same subject. For those which are contradictorily opposed do not have any medium. But of any subject at all one of them is truly said, and it is impossible that both be simultaneously affirmed or denied without one proposition being true and the other being false. In this way, Aristotle everywhere teaches that there is no medium between contradictories; cf. *Metaphysics* X, chapters 6 [*sic*] and 10, and *Posterior Analytics* I, chapter 2. The reason is that no medium can be envisioned between being and non-being. .... a negation simply removes a form, i.e. that which it negates, and it requires no special condition in the subject. Therefore it is necessary that either the form or the negation of the form belong in the subject. However, in things privatively opposed a medium is given, not indeed through the participation of either extreme, but through a removal, because

actual and potential, either in relation to the being of actual existence or in relation to some passive potency, which properly is a potency that includes imperfection and is ordered to the composition of some imperfect being, which for that reason is called potential. For active potency as such does not include imperfection, nor is it of itself ordered to some composition of that whose potency it is, and therefore from that it is not denominated potential being. Therefore, the first relation of these terms[38] is most proper and it seems that the given division should be so understood; for in that way, from what has been said, it is clear and without difficulty.

For it is necessary that there be some being which is so actual in its existence that in this it is completely in act and not at all in potency. This is proven: because to be in act in this way is actually to exist; while to be in potency is to be able to exist, although actually [the thing in question] does not exist. But there must be some being by essence so necessary that it cannot for any reason not exist – neither by intrinsic nor extrinsic potency, nor by physical potency, nor by that which is called "logical" potency.[39] Therefore there must be such a being which is completely actual in existing, that is, a being which totally excludes every character and way of being only in potency.

Moreover, from this it is easy to conclude that all beings which are not in this way are in some way potential. For, although they sometimes exist in act, still it is not impossible for them sometimes to exist only in potency, either because of some intrinsic passive potency or because of only an extrinsic active potency together with a logical potency, or a non-contradiction, on their part. Therefore, it is clear that every being is either a completely actual being, or is somehow potential in the aforesaid sense.

16. *The second is explained.*– Hence it can be further inferred that even in the latter sense, this division is universal and equivalent to those preceding. For that being which is purely actual in its existence is also in itself without qualification pure act, that is, in itself, in its entity or make-up, admitting no mixture of passive potency, since wherever there is any kind of passive potency there is also some sort of material cause. But, corresponding to a material cause there is necessarily an efficient cause, which may operate from it or on it and reduce it to act, for passive potency as such cannot reduce itself to act. Since, however, to be subject to efficient causality is far removed from the first being, which as through

---

privation does not mean negation without qualification, but negation with the connotation of aptitude in a subject. Therefore from the lack of this connoted feature a subject can exist, to which neither of the opposites belongs. For example, a stone is neither blind nor does it see, and yet it is necessarily either seeing or non-seeing." *DM* LIV, 5, n. 13, vol. 26, pp. 1034–35; tr. Doyle, *On Beings of Reason* ..., p. 106.

38 That is: "in relation to the being of actual existence."

39 See note 33, above.

itself and essentially such is in act according to all its perfection, this [first being] necessarily also lacks all passive potency, with the result that it is pure act.

In the opposite direction, by a similar reasoning one may conclude, in the opinion of many, that every being which is potential in relation to existence is also potential in a way which involves passive potency. But this requires much discussion and clarification, which we will give below when we discuss the being and essence of creatures.[40] At present we are content that the argument that was made proceeds in a proportionately unequal way, because it is necessary that an active potency correspond to one which is passive, inasmuch as it is necessary that this latter receive act from something. However, simply speaking, to an active potency it is not necessary that a passive potency correspond. For it is not necessary that an agent act upon something or from something, since it is possible for it to produce something and do it from nothing.

Accordingly, it does not seem necessary, by virtue of the terms, that every being which is potential in its existence contains passive potency. Nevertheless, in reality it is true that every being of this kind is potential by reason of passive potency, whether this is because it entails a relation to that, or because by reason of that it can be actually composed with another, or because it itself is composed of such potency and act. But in what way any of these necessarily follows from a prior potentiality for existing cannot be explained in this place briefly and as it were in passing. However, we will speak of it below[41] when we explain the proper character and imperfection of created being. Therefore, within our concern here, the first sense of the division, given in the words expressed above, is sufficient and clear.

The First Division Is Compared with the Others and from Them It Is Better Clarified.

17. Finally, from all that has been said, we may conclude that the same judgment should be passed about this division under these terms in which it has been proposed: in reality it is equivalent with those that have preceded. For that being is infinite which is first and of itself by its own essence; but the rest, which are beings by participation, are finite. In this way, without doubt it is the best division, and in reality there is no doubt that these two grades or orders of beings exist, and most of all differ between themselves. And perhaps, therefore, this division is given by many under these terms because through them it is more openly indicated that these two members are most of all different and utterly

40 See *DM* XXXI, vol. 26, pp. 224–312. Translated by Norman J. Wells as *Francis Suárez, On the Essence of Finite Being as Such, On the Existence of that Essence and their Distinction* (Milwaukee: Marquette University Press, 1983).

41 Cf. *DM* XXXI, s. 2, vol. 26, pp. 229–32.

diverse, and thus before all others should be separated and distinguished. But, on the other hand, it is more difficult as far as we are concerned to prove and demonstrate it, because indeed it is not immediately by the terms themselves so evident that there is among beings one which is infinite (for about a finite being there is no difficulty) as it is evident that there is some being which is independent of another. Neither, again, is it self-evident that a being which is such by its essence is consequently infinite. Hence, about this we will treat ex professo below[42] when we demonstrate the attributes of God insofar as they can be inferred by the light of nature.

18. *The Concepts of 'Finite' and 'Infinite' are Explained by Analogy to Quantity*.– Now we are simply clarifying the division by explaining its terms, which, taken from the quantity of a mass, we transfer to signify a quantity or a degree of perfection, in the way that Augustine, in Book 6, Chapter 8 of his work *On the Trinity*, said: "In things which are not great in mass, that is greater which is better."[43] For, because we conceive things only through the senses, we apprehend and explain everything else in the manner of bodies and by proportion with bodies. But we understand a body to be finite in quantity insofar as reaches a certain limit and is not extended beyond that. And among finite quantities we understand one to be greater than another because it reaches a farther limit. And in order to define a certain size for something, we use some definite measure, through the multiplication of which we know the thing to be of so much lesser or greater quantity. Thus, we use something analogous in order to specify the entitative perfection and the active power of things. For we apprehend in things a certain, as it were, range of entitative perfection, in which there are various degrees and quasi-parts of the perfection. And we understand each being to be finite or limited by a certain proper degree of perfection, which is limited thus within its own perfection in such way that it is separate from other things and in no way, neither formally nor virtually,[44] includes them in itself. And in this way we call all created beings limited and finite. And among them we conceive one to be greater than another inasmuch as we understand that one to possess many of

---

42 See *DM* XXX, s. 2, vol. 26, pp. 64–72.

43 Cf. *De Trinitate* VI, c. 8, in *PL*, vol. 42, col. 929.

44 That is to say in the same way or by its power. On the use of the terms, "formally, virtually, and eminently" (cf. immediately below), consider the following from a seventeenth-century Jesuit, who was in main a follower of Suárez: "*Formally*, *Virtually*, and *Eminently* are words expressing ways in which effects are contained in causes and as such they are applied to causes in relation to effects. For example, fire is said to be *formally* hot, because in itself it *formally* contains heat. Pepper and wine are said to be *virtually* hot, because even though in themselves they do not *formally* possess heat, nevertheless, they have the power to cause it in a stomach and to heat that stomach. God in turn is said to have heat *eminently*, although not *formally*, because

these perfections or, as it were, a certain greater share of perfection from the whole range of being.

But since all these beings receive their perfection from some superior being, we understand that there must be a certain being in which there is somehow contained, either formally or eminently,[45] every possible perfection in the range of being. And we call this being infinite without any qualification, not in quantity of mass, but in excellence of perfection. Hence, this infinity does not consist in some unlimited extension, but in such perfection of being, which, although it is in itself one and indivisible, does not prescind from other beings in such way that it does not somehow contain in itself the perfections of them all. And thus it includes in itself not a part of the perfection of being, but in some way all of it. Therefore, although in the range of being more and more perfect finite beings can be multiplied to infinity, that being ever surpasses them all and can be infinitely superior to all. Therefore, this excellence of perfection in being and entity is expressed through this infinity. Hence, just as Augustine, in Book 6, Chapter 8 [*sic*] of his work, *On the Trinity*, says: "It is not one thing for God to be and another to be great, but for Him to be is the same as to be great,"[46] so we can say it is nothing else for God to be infinite than to be being itself, or being by essence, embracing in Himself whatever perfection can be possessed by any being.

And in this way the stated division contains the first, the greatest, and the most essential distinction of beings; and, as is clear enough from what has been said, it coincides in reality with the preceding divisions. However, that there is some being, to which the stated infinity belongs, will be, as I have said, explicitly demonstrated in what follows.[47] For now, let this suffice, which is well enough inferred from what has been said, and which Augustine touches upon in the men-

in his perfection and eminent power he has the capacity to produce heat, as well as to produce all things – which is why God contains all things *eminently*." ("*Formaliter, Virtualiter, Eminenter* sunt voces explicantes modos, quibus effectus continentur in causis, et sic applicantur causis respectu effectuum: quare dicitur ignis *formaliter* calidus, quia *formaliter* habet in se calorem; piper, et vinum dicuntur calida *virtualiter*; quia licet in se *formaliter* non habeant calorem; habent tamen virtutem ad causandum illum in stomacho, et ad hunc calefaciendum. Deus etiam dicitur habere calorem *eminenter*, licet non *formaliter*; quia in sua perfectione, et eminenti virtute habet potentiam ad calorem producendum, et ad producendum omnia: quare Deus omnia continet *eminenter*." Miguel Viñas, S.J. (1642–1718), *Philosophia Scholastica*, Praefatio, ANTELOQUIUM XXI n. 35 (Genuae: Typis Antonii Casamarae, 1709), vol. 1, p. 72.

45 That is: in the same or in a higher degree.

46 Cf. *De Trinitate* VI, c. 7, n. 8, in *PL,* vol. 42, col. 929.

47 That is to say in the following Disputation. Here Suárez himself indicates the dividing line between Disputations 28 and 29.

tioned book, *On the Knowledge of True Life*, chapter 7:[48] that there is necessarily some being, from which as from a fountain all others flow forth, and therefore all must be contained in it and in such a way that it has not just this or that perfection but all without limit. Hence also there is the saying of Augustine in Book 8, Chapter 3 of *On the Trinity*: "This is good and that is good; take away this and that, and see, if you can, good itself; then you will see God, not good by some other good, but the good of every good."[49]

A Response to the Arguments Proposed at the Beginning.

19. *Infinity in God is a Negation, not a Privation.*[50] – In response to the first reason for doubting,[51] I say: these terms, *finite* and *infinite*, are in the present context not to be taken as they properly belong to the quantity of a mass, but by a certain analogy (*proportio*) to that. And, therefore, being should not be called finite or infinite on account of an intrinsic extension, limited or unlimited, but because of a perfection completely prescinding from others, or rather not prescinding but indeed containing those others.

Hence, in answer to the confirmation,[52] I say: *infinite* is there said not in a properly privative way, but rather negatively in regard to that being to which it is attributed, in which it expresses an unlimited perfection apart from any aptitude that it be limited insofar as it is such. Nor does it follow from this that every indivisible perfection is infinite, because, even though it is indivisible, it can be limited and have an endpoint, not such as is found usually in the quantity of a mass, but such as can be designated in a quantity of perfection. Moreover, [this endpoint] can be assigned either as intrinsic, which is nothing else than the thing's nature itself, constituted by a certain difference, which of itself has to prescind entirely from all other [natures]; or [this endpoint can be assigned] as extrinsic, and in this case it is any second perfection, especially one which appears to be most related and proximate, to which the first does not reach, as when we say the degree of rational is a limit to which the sensitive degree does not reach.

20. In response to the second difficulty, I say: this division is not stipulated to be *more known to us*, but as *first in itself*, that is, as positing the greatest distance of one being from another, as well as the first and last degrees of being.

---

48 Cf. note 12, this Section.

49 Cf. St. Augustine, *De Trinitate* VIII, c. 3, in *PL*, vol. 42, col. 949.

50 On negation and privation, cf. *DM* LIV, s. 5; vol. 26, pp. 1031–39; tr. Doyle, pp. 98–11; also see note 37, this Section.

51 Cf. § 1, above.

52 *Ibid.*

Therefore, even though it contains some difficulty, it was necessary to put it before other divisions and to explain it in various ways.

SECTION TWO

Whether Being Is Sufficiently and Adequately Divided by Finite and Infinite, and Other Equivalent Members.

1. *The first reason to doubt.–* The second.– This question is usually raised most of all because of relative beings, which as such seem to be neither finite nor infinite. Not infinite is self-evident. Nor finite, because they have no quantity either of mass or of perfection. This difficulty is especially and normally pressed in the case of Divine relations,[53] because, if they entail no perfection, there is already in them a medium between these two members [finite and infinite]. But if they entail some perfection, necessarily it is not finite, because it is in God. But also it is not infinite, because otherwise it could not be multiplied.

2. *The second [reason to doubt].–* Secondly, the division of being into created and uncreated is not adequate. Therefore, neither is the division we are treating now, since these [two divisions] are equivalent to one another. The antecedent is clear, first in the case of those Divine relations, which evidently are not created beings and cannot, according to their proper character, be called uncreated beings, since under that precise character they are not God and do not include the Divine essence. Second, the same antecedent is clear in the case of Christ, who cannot be called an uncreated being, since he was produced in time, and also not a created being, since he was not made from nothing. Third, an argument for the same conclusion can be taken from those beings which neither have being of themselves, and therefore cannot be called uncreated, nor have being by creation so that they may be called created. This can be especially pressed in the case of certain beings or modes of beings,[54] which cannot be produced by a creation, such as, for example, motion, inherence, and the like.

3. *The third [reason to doubt].–* Thirdly, the division of being into necessary and non-necessary does not seem adequate, especially in view of the free acts of the Divine will. For those acts are not simply necessary, because that would contradict [God's] freedom, nor can they be called non-necessary or contingent, because in such an event they would be something created and would be accidental to God. This argument can also be made with respect to the other divisions of being touched on above. For such an act [of the Divine will] cannot be called an uncreated being, because it is not entirely independent, since absolutely it could not be. But neither also is it created, for it is in God. And, by the same rea-

53 That is, the Divine Persons.

54 For Suárez's teaching on "modes of being," cf. José Ignacio Alcorta, *La teoría de los modos en Suárez* (Madrid: Consejo Superior de Investigaciones Cientificos, 1949).

soning, it is not a being by participation, because without doubt it is within God; but neither can it be called a being by essence, because, inasmuch as it is able not to be, it is not essentially God.

An Opinion of Scotus Is Explained.

4. As can easily be understood from the difficulties proposed, this question is in large part theological. But, nevertheless, it should not be omitted in this place, both because it is necessary in order to complete the teaching [of metaphysics] as well as to cover, let me say, the whole object of metaphysics and also because it is our intention to treat metaphysical things in this science in such a way as to uncover all the foundations which are necessary for theological matters.[55] Therefore, in regard to this question, Scotus, in the last argument of his answer to *Quodlibetal* Question 5, thinks this is not an adequate division of being, but rather a subdivision of being, which should first be divided into quantified and non-quantified being, and then quantified being should be divided into finite and infinite.[56] Hence, a third member could be added to the above division, namely, being which is neither finite nor infinite.

---

55 Compare Suárez's remarks in the general introduction (the "*Ratio ad lectorem*") of the *Disputationes metaphysicae*, vol. 25: "Inasmuch as no one can become a finished theologian unless he first lays the firm foundations of metaphysics, so I have always understood that it would be worthwhile, before I would write theological commentaries ... that I would put forward this carefully elaborated work, which I am now offering you, Christian reader. .... in order to give, or better to restore, to this metaphysical doctrine its place and basic position. .... In this matter, I am acting as a philosopher, however in such a way that I am always aware that our philosophy should be Christian and it should be the servant of divine theology. I have prefixed this goal for myself, not only in treating questions, but much more in selecting views or opinions, leaning toward those which would seem to me more to serve piety and revealed doctrine. For that reason, halting in the philosophical progression, I do turn sometimes to certain theological matters, not so much to spend time examining or more accurately explaining them (which would be outside the task upon which I am now embarked) as to sort of point a finger for the reader at the way in which principles of metaphysics are to be accommodated for and related to the confirmation of theological truths."

56 Cf. Joannis Duns Scoti, *Quaestiones quodlibetales*, q. V, a. 3, n. 58, in *Obras del Doctor Sutil Juan Duns Escoto, Cuestiones cuodlibetales*, edicion bilingüe, introducción, resúmenes y versión de Felix Alluntis, O.F.M. (Madrid: Biblioteca de Autores Cristianos, 1968), p. 200. For an English translation, see John Duns Scotus, *God and Creatures: The Quodlibetal Questions*, translated with an introduction, notes, and glossary by Felix Alluntis, O.F.M. and Allan B. Wolter, O.F.M. (Washington, D.C.: The Catholic University of America Press, 1975), p. 129.

Lychetus also defends the same opinion in that place[57] and in [his *Commentary on Duns Scotus*] at Book 2 of the *Sentences*,[58] Distinction 1, Questions 4 and 5, where he even suggests a fourth member.[59] For, he says, a certain being includes perfection and no imperfection, and this is infinite being. A second being, however, includes perfection together with imperfection, and this is quantified finite being. There is a third being which includes neither perfection nor imperfection, and this being properly is non-quantified, neither finite nor infinite being. Finally, there is a fourth being which includes no perfection, but does not exclude any imperfection (and he considers a created relation to be a being of this kind), which he thinks also is comprehended under quantified being, even if it includes no perfection but rather only imperfection.

This clearly involves a contradiction in terms, as Scotus himself states in the mentioned *Quodlibetal* question. For in that place he states that a quantified being is that which has some quantity of perfection.[60] Therefore, that which does not include any perfection cannot truly be called a quantified being.

5. *The Various Divisions concocted by Lychetus are disproven. – An Objection is Answered.*– From this there is inferred another contradiction in what this author[61] has said: inasmuch as it is contradictory to be non-quantified and to be finite. For according to their[62] doctrine, finite and infinite presuppose quantity. Hence, they conclude that a Divine relation is not an infinite being, because it is not quantified. By an equal argument, therefore, they ought to conclude that a created relation is not finite because it is not quantified.

Again, from the same starting point, it can easily be concluded that a contradiction is involved in that member which is some being that includes no perfection but which does include imperfection. First, because that imperfection is either privative or only negative. We cannot say the former, because a privative

57 Cf. In Ioannis Duns Scoti, O.M., *Quaestiones quodlibetales*, cum commentariis P.F. Francisci Lycheti Brixiensis, Ordinis Minorum Regulatis Observantiae olim Ministri Generalis, qu. 5, *commentarius* nn. 28, 31, and 38, in *I.D. Scoti, Opera omnia* (Lugduni: Sumpt. L. Durand, 1639), vol. 12, pp. 138–41.

58 That is, the *Sentences of Peter the Lombard* (ca. 1095–1160 – a bishop of Paris), which was the standard theological textbook of the Middle Ages on which each medieval master was required to write a commentary before completion of his courses in theology.

59 Cf. Ioannis Duns Scoti, *Quaestiones in lib. II. Sententiarum*, d. 1, q. 4, *Commentarius [Lycheti]*, n. 2, in *Opera* (Lugduni, 1639), vol. 6, p. 68.

60 See Scotus, *Quaestiones quodlibetales*, q. V, a. 3, n. 58, in *Obras*, ed. Alluntis, p. 200; *God and Creatures* ..., p. 129.

61 That is, Lychetus.

62 That is, Lychetus and Scotus.

imperfection is the absence of an expected perfection. But in such a being there cannot be the absence of an expected perfection, because in it no perfection is required, since it is said of itself to include no perfection. However, no greater negative imperfection can be conceived than the absence of all perfection, which [absence] every thing includes which in its own entity includes no perfection. Hence, speaking of negative imperfection, no being can be imagined which includes neither perfection nor imperfection. Therefore, a being cannot be understood which, apart from the negation of every perfection, of itself entails some other imperfection.

If this is not so, I further ask of what kind is that imperfection? The same author[63] answers that it is a limitation. But the argument already made weighs against this. For a limitation occurs in some quantity of mass or perfection. Therefore, if such a being does not include a quantity of perfection, it does not have that in which it may include a limitation.

Perhaps it will be said to include a limitation not in perfection but in entity? But against this is the fact that in this way a Divine relation will also be called limited in its formal entity, and consequently will be called finite in entity. And so in the end, every being will be finite or infinite in entity, whatever it is with respect to perfection.

The first consequence[64] is proven (for the others are clear) *ad hominem*: for in the doctrine of Scotus[65] a Divine relation, according to its formal and precise entity, does not, either eminently or formally, include the entity of the [Divine] essence. Therefore, it is limited in its formal entity. Nor is it enough that it "identically" includes the entity of the Essence. For, as Scotus at length argues, this is not enough that it be called infinite in perfection, even though it identically includes the infinite perfection of the Essence. Therefore, neither will it be enough in order to be called unlimited in entity that it identically include the infinite entity of the Essence.

6. Perhaps someone will say that relation itself by virtue of its formal entity is apt to be identified with essence, and thus of itself it is neither unlimited nor limited. But a created relation of itself is incompatible with an infinite entity and it cannot include that entity even "identically," with the result that of itself it is

---

63 Lychetus.

64 That is: "a Divine relation will be called finite in entity."

65 For this precise instance of the famous Scotistic "formal distinction *a parte rei*," see Duns Scotus, *Ordinatio* I, d. 2, p. 2, q. 4, in *Joannis Duns Scoti Opera omnia*, vol. 2 (Civitas Vaticana: Typis Polyglottis Vaticanis, 1950), 349–61. Cf. *ibid.* in *Obras del Doctor Sutil Juan Duns Escoto*, edicion bilingüe, *Dios uno y trino*, versión de los Padres Bernardo Aperribay, O.F.M., et al. (Madrid: Biblioteca de Autores Cristianos, 1960), pp. 563–74, esp. n. 403, pp. 570–71.

not only not unlimited, but even of itself it is limited and finite. And this is an imperfection which it includes and in which it is distinguished from a Divine relation.

But, first of all, that aptitude, which is said to be in a Divine relation, to be identified with the Divine essence, does not absolutely exclude that relation being limited with respect to its own formal entity. For it does not formally include infinite entity and absolutely it is less apt to be identified with infinite entity than formally to be an infinite entity. Moreover, if in a created relation that limitation of entity, by reason of which it cannot, either formally or identically, be infinite, is an imperfection, certainly in a Divine relation that aptitude to be able to be completely identified with the Divine essence is a kind of great perfection. Therefore, that relation, however much it is formally prescinded, inasmuch as it is understood to be such that it can be identified with the Divine essence, is understood to be of some perfection and of much greater [perfection] than every created entity. Hence also, conversely, in the case of a created relation, by the fact that its limitation to a created entity is a certain imperfection in the genus of being,[66] it is necessary that it not be a mere negation of perfection but that there be some perfection which has that negation joined to it, as we were discussing [just] above.[67] Thus, finally we conclude that it is not necessary to imagine some entity lacking all perfection, which could properly be a medium between finite and infinite being. We have dealt with this more at length above when in *Disputation* 10 we treated of *goodness*.[68]

The Resolution of the Question.

7. *This division, which is adequate to being, is expressed by whatever terms were used in the preceding section.*– It must be said, therefore, that the aforesaid division is sufficient and adequate to being insofar as it is being.[69] This assertion can easily be proven from what was treated in the preceding Section, especially

66 Here Suárez is speaking broadly. For his denial of the generic character of being; cf., e.g: *DM* II, s. 5, n. 10, vol. 25, p. 96; *ibid.*, s. 6, nn. 10, 12, pp. 101–2; *DM* XXXII, s. 2, n. 15, vol. 26, p. 323; and *DM* XXXIX, s. 3, n. 18, vol. 26, p. 529.

67 Cf. § 5, just above.

68 For a translation of Disputation 10, cf. *The Metaphysics of Good and Evil according to Suárez: Metaphysical Disputations X and XI and Selected Passages from Disputation XXII and Other Works*, Translation with Introduction, Notes, and Glossary, by Jorge J.E. Gracia and Douglas Davis (München: Philosophia Verlag, 1989).

69 That is to say, "being insofar as it is *real* being," the object of metaphysics; cf. note 1, above in Section 1.

if this division is taken under these terms, namely, being by itself and being by another. For, since these terms include an immediate contradiction, this disjunction must fit any being at all. Therefore, it is an adequate and sufficient division, since there is nothing contained under the divided [concept] which cannot be placed under one or other of the dividing members.

The same thing is evident with respect to those two members, *absolutely necessary* or *non-necessary* being, and of these: *created* or *uncreated* being. However, we have shown that under all these modes the division is really the same, even though they [i.e. the modes] may be rationally distinguished by our concepts – which distinguishing cannot be enough to make the division adequate in one way and not in another. Then, it is in a particular way proven under the terms *finite* and *infinite*. For quantified being is adequately divided into finite and infinite. But every real being, by the very fact that it is real, is quantified with a quantity of essential or formal perfection, as was touched on in the arguments which were made a little before and was shown more at length in the mentioned *Disputation* [i.e. *Disputation* 10] about transcendental goodness. And this opinion will be confirmed more evidently by responding to the difficulties raised at the beginning [of the present Section].

The Difficulty of the First Argument Is Treated.

8. *A created relation is included under finite being.*– Therefore, in answer to the first reason for doubting, we must deny that relative beings lack all perfection in terms of which they could be either finite or infinite. And in this there is plainly no difficulty as regards created relations. Indeed, from those relations we can take an argument: for no one will deny (I think) that a created relation, in the way in which it is a real being, is a finite being. Hence, as we see, even the Scotists concede that. For who would deny that it is a limited being and consequently one that is finite, therefore one having a finite perfection, and therefore one having some perfection?

But if some obstinate person argues that it is called a finite being in its entity but not in its perfection, an *ad hominem* argument can be effectively turned back against him. For it follows from this that finite and infinite are not immediately said of a quantified being by reason of perfection, but rather by reason of entity. From this it further follows that even the Divine relations by reason of entity as such are finite or infinite. And thus, at least by this conception the division will be immediate and adequate, and against Scotus and others the arguments will proceed by which they [themselves] are trying to prove that Divine relations are neither finite nor infinite, as we shall now see.

9. *An Uncreated Relation, as it includes the Essence, is simply infinite.*– With regard to Divine relations, therefore, we have already answered above that

they are indeed simply infinite and in the genus of being,[70] by reason of the Essence which they include. Therefore, under this aspect they are not multiplied, but they are one Being. For it is true that a being which is infinite in this way cannot be multiplied. However, with respect to their proper natures, in which they are opposed, they are infinite only in such a genus under as it were a species of relation, in which way it is not contradictory that several infinites be multiplied, because under that aspect they are opposed. Therefore they can be distinguished and multiplied.

But perhaps someone will object, let us say: if under that latter aspect, those relations are beings, they will be either simply finite or infinite. For if we admit neither of these, we are then admitting a middle term in that division. However, we could not say that they are simply infinite beings, since under that aspect they are multiplied and do not include the Essence. But that they would be finite beings seems to contradict Divine perfection. For, as Scotus argued above,[71] every finite being is like a part of being, because only an absolutely infinite being is, as it were, all being, inasmuch as it includes the whole perfection of being. Therefore, a finite being, by comparison with that, is like a part of being. But it is incompatible with a Divine relation to be a part of being, both because, were that the case, it would be a being by participation and also because what is a part is exceeded by what is a whole. But a Divine relation cannot be in this way exceeded by Divinity [i.e. the Divine Essence], since they are in every way really the same.

10. *In its objective concept,*[72] *a Divine relation necessarily includes the [Divine] essence.*– But if this argument were to have any value, it would prove not only that a Divine relation formally entails no perfection, but also that it formally entails no entity. Otherwise, my question will be, whether that entity is a whole or a part of being. One cannot say the first, because that entity of relation *as such* is said not to include the entity of the Essence, and consequently not to contain in itself formally or eminently the whole [Divine] being. But against the second [alternative] the argument just made proceeds in the same way. Therefore, in every opinion, this argument must be answered.

One can reply, therefore, that a Divine relation, for example, Paternity, however much precisely and formally we conceive it, is an absolutely infinite being, for the reason that it can never be prescinded or abstracted without including essentially in its objective concept the whole perfection of the Essence. For

70 See note 66, just above.

71 Cf. § 4, this Section.

72 On Suárez's distinction between the formal concept (the act of the mind) and the objective concept (that which is represented by that act), cf. esp. *DM* II, s. 1, n. 1, vol. 25, pp. 64–65.

although our mind is said to prescind, from the side of a formal concept or an explicit consideration, Paternity in the abstract from the Essence, because through that act the mind does not indeed consider Paternity as including the Essence nor the Essence as included in the relation, nevertheless, on the side of the objective concept the Essence still cannot be prescinded or excluded from Paternity, but is rather essentially included in it, in such way that if the mind reflects and considers what is included in that conceived Paternity, it necessarily discovers the whole Divinity and Infinity of God, because Divinity is of the essence of all things which are in God.[73] From this it results that, even though Paternity conceived according to our way of conceiving is like a part, in reality, however, the thing conceived is a whole being, not less than the Father, just as Divinity also is conceived like a part, but it is the whole being, equal to God.

11. *The three Divine relations, as they include the [Divine] essence, are simply one infinite thing.*– To the argument, therefore, the reply in form, according to this opinion, is that the [Divine] relations are beings which are simply infinite, but they are not several infinite things, because they possess this infinity only as they include the Essence, in which they are one. Nor is it a problem, that, as Scotus objects, they include the Essence only by identity. For they do not include it by a kind of material identity,[74] but actually by one which is formal and essential, because indeed Divinity is of the essence of a [Divine] relation, according to the thing conceived, in whatever way it is conceived. And this is enough in order that there not be a medium between finite and infinite being, since there is no being which according to its own essential entity is neither finite nor infinite.

You will say, granted that the Essence cannot be excluded from a relation in the sense mentioned, nevertheless, what the Divine Paternity has can be considered precisely by us, according to that only which it is understood to add beyond the absolute perfection of the Essence, whether it is finite or infinite. I answer that it is infinite in a certain genus, namely of relation or Paternity, but not infinite without qualification in the genus of being. For this infinity cannot be added, even according to reason, beyond absolute perfection, but rather it is formally possessed through that.

However, neither does it seem that it should be said without qualification that what the relation as such adds is finite. For this denotes imperfection, namely, a limitation and a contraction to an entity which is simply finite. And this does not weigh against the sufficiency of the given division, because its sense is that every being, by reason of its own entity, is simply finite or infinite, but not that the entity of each thing has it, from any degree or mode whatever conceived in

73 Note this extremely long and complicated sentence for commentary on the respective roles of formal and objective concepts.

74 That is: a kind of sameness in a single subject.

it, that it be finite or infinite. But it is enough that it has something which works to constitute its entity as either finite or infinite.

And, for the sake of greater clarity, we can distinguish the term "finite." For it can be taken either positively or negatively. Positively, it signifies being so limited in entity and perfection as to be incapable of infinite perfection. Negatively, however, it signifies that which of itself does not bring infinite perfection, even though it is not impossible that it have it from something else. That, therefore, which a [Divine] relation as a relation adds cannot be called "finite" in a positive way, as the argument made above proves – because this involves imperfection and because that [relation] itself, though not of itself, still of its essence can be infinite. But negatively, it can be said, of its precise nature, merely not to provide infinity – and this is no problem, because it involves no imperfection. For it is not necessary, nor does it pertain to the perfection of a thing, that from any prescinded concept it have a total infinity without qualification in the genus of being. But it is enough that it have this from its own adequate entity, and that from some precisely conceived character it have infinity in that genus. In this way it is best understood that there is no medium between finite and infinite being, if they are taken with proportion.

12. Accordingly, those who think that Divine relations can simply prescind from the Essence, in such way that they are neither formally included in it, nor essentially include it, are necessarily forced to confess that the relative entity, thus precisely and formally conceived, is not simply infinite, as the argument made above proves. But when they may be further asked whether [those relations] should simply be called finite beings, they should reply that they are finite negatively, not positively – according to the sense we explained, which is more fully explained in the following way. For, although the word "infinite" is negative, by that negation we are circumscribing a certain supreme entity or excellence. Then, with respect to this positive [reality], that [relation] can be said to be negatively finite, because of itself it does not convey that whole excellence, although it does not exclude it and is not adverse to it. Hence, in this way they should say it is not wrong to admit something in God that is finite as precisely conceived by us. Indeed, those who think they are avoiding this difficulty by denying Divine relations all perfection, must for even more reason say that these are negatively finite, for if they impart no perfection, they do not of themselves bring infinity. If, then, they do not think it disturbing that these bring neither perfection nor infinity, why do they think it disturbing, and not rather necessary, that they bring a perfection in its own way infinite but they have infinity not simply from themselves, but from the Essence?

The Difficulty of the Second Argument[75] *Is Resolved.*

13. *In whatever way it is conceived a Divine relation is truly an uncreated*

75 Cf. this Section, § 2, above.

being.– In reply to the second difficulty: we deny that being is not adequately divided as created and uncreated, which is almost obvious if those terms are taken in proportion [to each other], since they entail an immediate [mutual] contradiction.

And with respect to the first argument [for the antecedent],[76] we deny that a Divine relation is not an uncreated being, even if it is conceived under any precise concept whatever. Neither, in our view, does the opposite argument have any weight; for we think that a [Divine] relation can never be so prescinded, unless it essentially includes the Essence and therefore is God. Indeed, it can be added here, a relation, even according to what it is understood to add to the Essence, of itself is something uncreated, because it is that kind of being for which it is altogether contradictory to be made by a proper creation or making.

But either it is entirely unproduced, like Paternity, or, if it is produced – or (in our way of speaking) "coproduced," like Sonship – that production is not a creation, nor a proper making, but rather a generation or a procession, of a far superior kind. Nor is such a relation producible in any other way. And this is enough that, under any precision or reduplicatiom[77] whatever, as such it is in fact an uncreated being.

14. *Whether Christ should be called an uncreated or indeed a created being*.– In reply to the second argument [in support of the antecedent]: Christ is without qualification an uncreated being; for he is God. But we add the limitation or the determination, "as man," designating a nature or the whole composite of nature and Person, in this way he is a created being. For under that reduplication, he cannot be called God, but rather man and a creature, since as such he is in fact made and procreated in time.

But in reply to the objection suggested, because even as man he was not made from nothing, since, although his humanity is from nothing, nevertheless the whole composite is not, inasmuch as one member of the composite is uncreated, we should answer that created being can be spoken of in two ways. In one way, because according to its whole being it has been produced, or is producible, from nothing. And in this way, we concede, that, as the argument proves, Christ even as man is not a created being. In a second way, a being is called created, because it was truly made anew, and because it consists of some created being. And in this way, that composite is called created, and Christ insofar as he is man is a created being, and created being [here] is taken in all its fullness inasmuch as it is adequately distinguished from uncreated being. For, if it is taken in the first and strict way, there can be given a composite being, in some way a mean

---

76 *Ibid.*

77 Relation conceived precisely is "relation as such." Relation conceived reduplicatively is "relation as relation."

between and as it were mixed of created and uncreated [being], about which mean, however, philosophy knows nothing but Christian faith alone teaches.

15. In reply to the third argument [in support of the antecedent],[78] we must say that all beings, and all modes of being, outside God are something created, not because they all are made immediately and first directly from nothing, but because they are either created or concreated with those beings which are produced from nothing, as for instance, the potencies with the soul, or certainly because they can be concreated, even though perhaps in fact they may not be concreated, or finally (and it comes to the same thing), because they are made from those things which have been created from nothing.

The Third [Principal] Argument Is Answered.

16. In the third [principal] argument,[79] we touch upon a most serious theological difficulty with respect to God's free activity, to which we cannot now explicitly turn, but later, treating of the naturally known attributes of God, we will pursue it insofar as it pertains to metaphysics.[80] Briefly now I say that the arguments suggested in that difficulty conclude for me that a free act as free, or as freely terminated at some object, does not add to God anything that is not in God and could not be in him. Otherwise, I do not see how that could be called a necessary being, or a being by essence, since it could simply not be, and the same is true with respect to infinity in perfection and other similar attributes, as is proposed in that place. Therefore, even though God freely wills things other than himself, he still wills them only by an act of will that is necessary and connatural with himself. For the perfection of that act is so great that through it God could will or nill a creature without any addition being made in that act.

When therefore we are talking about a free act of God, there are two things involved, by our way of conceiving and speaking. One is the act itself by which God wills; the other is a relation of reason[81] to the object willed. The first is a necessary, uncreated, and by essence being; hence in no way can it not be in God. The second is not something real which could be or not be, but rather something of reason only, and therefore it is neither created nor uncreated nor should it be included under that division, since it is not a real being.

---

78 Cf. § 2, this Section.

79 Cf. this Section, § 3, above.

80 For this, cf. *DM* XXX, s. 16, vol. 26, pp. 184–206.

81 For Suárez on relations of reason, cf. *DM* LIV, s. 6, vol. 26, pp. 1039–41; tr. John P. Doyle, in *Francisco Suárez, On Beings of Reason (De Entibus Rationis): Metaphysical Disputation LIV* (Milwaukee: Marquette University Press, 1995), pp. 116–22.

SECTION THREE

Whether the Aforesaid Division Is Univocal or Analogous. The First Opinion: The Division Is Equivocal.

1. This question is ordinarily treated in other terms: whether being is said analogously of God and creatures. There are three opinions on this: two extremes and one in the middle. The first is that being is said of God and creatures neither univocally nor analogically, but merely equivocally. This opinion is usually attributed to Aureoli, in [his commentary on the *Sentences*] Book I, Distinction 2, Question 1.[82] But he did not maintain this, but only that being does not express one concept or a nature common to God and creatures, which could very well stand with analogy, as is self evident. Indeed, many think that is of the nature of every analogous [term], as we shall in short order see.

St. Thomas then relates, in Question 7, Article 7 of [his work] *On the Power [of God]*, that Rabbi Moses [Maimonides] held that opinion, because inasmuch as finite being is infinitely distant from God, there could be no proportion between them which would be a basis for analogy.[83] However, in the same place, St. Thomas rightly refutes this opinion with many arguments. For otherwise, if only a name were common between them, nothing could be demonstrated about God from creatures. That is, we could not use names common to God and creatures in order to demonstrate anything about God, because [in such demonstration] the middle term would be equivocal.[84] But the consequent[85] is rather absurd. Again, [St. Thomas refutes it] because there is some likeness between God and a creature inasmuch as they are related as caused and cause; therefore [this likeness is] especially in the concept of being, which is first of all. Therefore, whether we look to the imposition and signification of a name, or to the concept signified by that name, it is evident that this is not a division of a name only, nor is "being" said merely by chance and fortuitously of God and creatures, but rather because of some likeness, proportion, or agreement of these between themselves. Finally, it is clear even from experience itself that not only the name, but also the concept is in some way common in this division.

---

82 For the basis of this attribution, cf. Peter Aureoli, *Scriptum super primum sententiarum*, d. 2, s. 9, 2, ed. Eligius M. Buytaert, O.F.M., II Distinctions 2–8 (St. Bonaventure, NY: The Franciscan Institute, 1956), pp. 491–505.

83 S. Thomae Aquinatis, *De Potentia*, q. 7, a. 7, in *Quaestiones disputatae*, vol. 2, ed. VIII, P. Bazzi, et al., p. 204.

84 This reasoning is central to Suárez for a metaphysical demonstration of the existence of God as well as anything else about God; cf. e.g. *DM* II, s. 2, n. 14, vol. 25, p. 74; *DM* XXVIII, s. 3, n. 15, below; and *DM* XXXII, s. 2, n. 17, vol. 26, p. 324.

85 That is, that we can demonstrate nothing of God.

The Second Opinion: The Division Is Univocal.

2. *The Bases of the Second Opinion.*– The second opinion is that being is univocally said of God and creatures. This opinion Duns Scotus held in [his commentary on the *Sentences*] Book I, distinction 3, questions 1 et 3,[86] and in Book III [*sic*], distinction 8, question 2 [*sic*],[87] and the Scotists follow and defend him in those places. The proof is that being immediately signifies one concept, common to God and creatures; therefore, it is said of them not analogically but rather univocally. The antecedent was proven by us in the first *Disputation* of this work. But the consequence is proven in various ways. First, from the definition of univocals that Aristotle gives in the *Antepredicaments*:[88] Univocals are those whose name is common and the concept (*ratio*) of the substance fitted to the name is the same.[89] But in the present case, not only the name is common but also the concept of substance. For this corresponds to the objective concept adequately signified by such a name. Hence, if this concept is one and the same, also the concept of the substance fitted to the name will be the same.

3. *Second.*– Secondly, [the consequence is proven] from the common concept of an analogous term, which agrees with an equivocal term in this that it is crafted (*positum*) not with one, but with many, impositions [of meaning] in order to signify many things. The difference is that in equivocals it happens by chance that one term is imposed in order to signify other things; but in analogicals an imposition is first made in order to signify one thing and then by a likeness or proportion it is extended to another. However, in the present case, this is not so. But by a single imposition the term *being* signifies that which is, and by virtue of this it applies to God and creatures, because that common significate is found in both. Therefore, no concept of analogy can be imagined [here].

4. *Third.*– In the third place, this is more fully explained from a distinction with respect to analogy. For analogy is commonly distinguished in two ways: one is called by many "analogy of proportionality" and the other "[analogy] of proportion." Others, however, call the first, "analogy of proportion," and the second, "analogy of attribution."[90] I note this only because of the equivocation of the

86 Cf. Duns Scotus, *Ordinatio* I, d. 3, p. 1, q. 1, in *Joannis Duns Scoti Opera omnia*, III (Civitas Vaticana: Typis Polyglottis Vaticanis, 1954), pp. 18–19, nn. 26–29; *ibid.*, q. 3, pp. 81–85, nn. 131–36.

87 Cf. D. Scotus, *Ordinatio* I, d. 8, p. 1, q. 3, in *Opera*, vol. IV, p. 195, nn. 88–89.

88 The *Antepredicaments* are Chapters 1–4 of Aristotle's *Categories*.

89 Cf. *Categories* 1.1a6–7.

90 In what follows, I have for the most part translated "*attributio*" by the English cognate "attribution." However, on occasion, I have in brackets suggested "reference" as

terms, because the reality is the same. Aristotle has clearly taught this in Book I, chapter 6 [*sic*], of his *Ethics*, where he calls an analogy of attribution "from one" or "to one," while he calls the other "a comparison of proportions (*rationum*)."[91]

Therefore, the first analogy is taken from a proportion of several things in relation to some terms, and consists in this that the principal analogate is denominated such from its own form considered absolutely, whereas the second, although it receives a similar denomination from its own form, nevertheless, [does not receive it from that form] as absolutely considered, but because in relation to that [form] it has a certain proportion with the relation of the first analogate to its form. For example, a man is said to smile from his own act of smiling taken absolutely; but a meadow is said to smile from its verdure, not taken absolutely, but insofar as a verdant meadow has a certain proportion to a smiling man. And, because this is a proportion between two relations, it is therefore ordinarily called a proportion of proportions, or a proportionality.

The second analogy is taken from a relation to one form, which is in one thing properly and intrinsically, but in another improperly and extrinsically, in the way that "healthy" is said of an animal, and of medicine, and of urine. This analogy is properly considered between the principal (*proprium*) analogate and any of the rest, as between an animal and medicine, or between an animal and urine. But it can also be considered among those secondary significates themselves, for example, between urine and medicine. For both are called "healthy" not merely in an equivocal way, as is clear; nor again in a univocal way, since they do not have an entirely unitary character or a common concept. Therefore, [they are called such] by some analogy, which could indeed in some way be reduced to what is prior. For, just as medicine is related to health inasmuch as it causes health, so urine [is related to health] as signifying it. But in fact neither of them receives this denomination from this proportion to one another, but both [receive it] from a reference to a healthy animal, with which they have an immediate analogy in the character of "healthy," and from that there results a kind of mediated analogy of attribution [or reference] of them between themselves.

From all of this, therefore, an argument is made[92] that neither of these analogies is found in being with respect to God and a creature. As regards the first [kind of analogy], this is clear, since a creature is denominated being simply from its own being and not from any proportion which it has to the being of God. As regards the second, it is proven, because a creature is not called being by an

---

a better translation for "*attributio*." The reader may keep this mind even for those contexts in which I have simply used the English cognate without further comment.

91 Cf. *Nichomachean Ethics* 1.5.1096b25–30.

92 That is, by the Scotists.

extrinsic denomination[93] from God's entity. But in these analogates of attribution the second is extrinsically denominated from a form that is in the first. For this reason, in these analogates the second is defined through the first; but a creature is not defined in the character of being through God.

Finally, [the argument in] both [cases] can be confirmed because the character of being is conceived in a creature in an entirely absolute, intrinsic, and proper way. Indeed, if we speak of ourselves, it is first conceived by human beings in finite rather than in infinite being. Therefore, this term is in no way used by analogy from God to creatures.

The Third Opinion: The Division Is Analogous.[94]

5. The third opinion denies that being is equivocal or univocal, and consequently affirms that it is analogous and says that the term "being" is said primarily of God and secondarily of creatures. This is the opinion of St. Thomas, in the First Part [of his *Summa Theologiae*], Question 13, Article 5,[95] and in the aforementioned[96] Question 7 of *On the Power [of God]*, Article 7, and in Book I, Chapter 32, and following, of *Contra Gentiles*,[97] and Cajetan[98] as well as Ferrara[99] defend it in these places. [Also see] Cajetan, [in his Commentary on] *De Ente et essentia*, chapter 1, question 2 [*sic*];[100] Capreolus, in [his *Defensiones*] Book 1, distinction 2, question 1;[101] and Soto in [commentary on] chapter 4, of the *Antepredicaments* [i.e. chapters 1–4 of Aristotle's *Categories*].[102]

93 For Suárez's doctrine of extrinsic denomination, or naming things from outside themselves, cf. John P. Doyle, "*Prolegomena* to a Study of Extrinsic Denomination in the Work of Francis Suarez, S.J.," *Vivarium*, XXII (1984), 2, pp. 121–60.

94 For an extended study of Suárez's doctrine of analogy, cf. John P. Doyle, "Suarez on the Analogy of Being," *The Modern Schoolman*, XLVI (1969), pp. 219–49 and 323–41.

95 Cf. *Summa Theologiae* I, q. 13, a. 5, in *Opera*, vol. 4, pp. 146–47.

96 Cf. § 1, this Section.

97 Cf. *Summa contra Gentiles* I, cc. 32–34, in *Opera*, vol. 13 (Romae: Typis Riccardi Garroni, 1918), pp. 97–98, 102–4.

98 Cf. *Commentaria Cardinalis Caietani* [*In Summam Theologiae* I, q. 13, a. 5], in Sancti Thomae Opera, vol. 4, pp. 147–50.

99 *Commentaria Ferrariensis* [*In Summam contra Gentiles* I, 32–34], in *Sancti Thomae Aquinatis Opera*, vol. 13, pp. 98–101, 102–3, and 104–9.

100 Cf. Thomae de Vio, Caietani, *In De Ente et Essentia D. Thomae Aquinatis commentaria*, c. 2, q. 3, n. 20, ed. P.M.H. Laurent (Taurini: Marietti, 1934), p. 38.

101 Cf. Johannis Capreoli, O.P., *Defensiones theologiae Divi Thomae Aquinatis* I, d. 2, q. 1, a. 1, concl. 9, de novo editae cura et studio RR. PP. Ceslai Paban et Thomae Pègues, eiusdem Ordinis, tomus I (Turonibus: Sumptibus Alfred Cattier, 1890), p. 124.

102 See: R.P. Dominici Soto, *Summularum aeditio secunda* ..., I, c. 4, nn. 2–3 (Salmanti-

The whole force of this opinion is in its second negative part, namely, that this division is not univocal. For the first part, namely, that it is not equivocal is presumed to be evident from what has been said. Hence, necessarily, we conclude to the last part: that [the division] amounts to an analogy. Therefore, in order to confirm that part, various arguments are advanced.

Certain ones are general, by which it is proven universally that "being" cannot be univocal with respect to any beings at all. I do not think these [arguments] can be convincing, since nothing prevents "being" from being univocal with respect to some things, about which I will speak below in Disputation 32, treating the analogy of being with respect to substance and accident,[103] in which place we will examine these arguments.

Other arguments are proper and distinctive with regard to being as compared to God and creatures. Among these, the principal and fundamental one seems to be the one St. Thomas mentioned above.[104] For when an effect does not equate to the power of its cause, a name common to both is not said of them univocally, but rather analogically. But creatures are effects of God that do not equate to his power. Therefore, they are beings not univocally but analogically with God. The major is proven: for when an effect does not equate with the power of its cause, it does not receive a likeness of that cause according to the same character (*ratio*). Therefore, neither can it have a common name according to the same concept (*ratio*). Therefore, neither can it have a univocal name, since that is a name of the kind which is said according to the same concept (*ratio*).

6. But this argument seems weak and ineffective. For when it is said that an effect which is not adequate to the power of its cause is not similar to that cause according to the same character, that is true with respect to a specific or ultimate character, but not with respect to a common, generic, or transcendental character. This is clear in all equivocal causes with regard to which it is true that effects are not adequate to the power of the causes, for they do not receive a likeness which is specific with them, and nevertheless they can have a univocal likeness in some common predicate. In this way fire, gold, and similar bodies do not measure up to the power of the sun whose effects they are and, nevertheless, they univocally agree with that sun in the concepts of body, substance, and other things. And the immediate reason is that in order for an effect not to equate to the power of its cause it is enough that it not come up to the specific perfection of that cause. Therefore, by virtue of such causality it is not directly necessary that there be a univocal agreement in other predicates.

---

cae: Excudebat Andreas a Portonariis, 1554; reprint: Hildesheim: Georg Olms, 1980), fol. 7r–v.

103 For this, cf. *DM* XXXII, s. 2, vol. 26, pp. 319–29.

104 Cf. § 1, this Section.

7. *An effect that does not equate to the power of its cause on that level on which it depends upon that cause, does not agree in a univocal way with that cause.*– The answer is that this proposition is not to be understood about a specific, a generic, or a transcendental feature, but precisely and formally about that feature in virtue of which the effect proceeds from the cause. And in this way [the proposition] is evident from its terms. For if an effect proceeds from a cause not only in virtue of an ultimate feature but also in virtue of a common feature, and in neither feature the effect equates with the power of the cause, there cannot be a univocal term [between them] whether [that term] signifies the ultimate or the common feature, for the argument is the same for both. But a creature is the effect of God not only insofar as it is a certain kind of being but also insofar as it is being [as such] because a created being depends upon God for all its features and under no feature does a creature equal the power or the essence of God. Therefore, under no feature can any term be said univocally of God and creatures.

Moreover, the objections brought forth have no place here. For example, fire and gold are not equivocal effects of the sun, except in accord with their proper characteristics. But according to their common features, in which they agree univocally with the sun, either they are univocal effects, or better, as such they are not effects. For, as Aristotle has said elsewhere, a thing is not produced essentially, but rather only accidentally, with respect to that character according to which it is presupposed precisely as it is an effect or a subject. Rather it is produced essentially with respect only to that character which is not presupposed. For example, when water is produced from air, it does not as such become an element or a simple body, but rather [it becomes] water, and the other features follow accidentally. So therefore when the sun generates fire or gold it always presupposes the characters of being, of substance, and of body, and therefore it does not as such cause its effect according to those features. Hence, there is no barrier to them [i.e. the sun, fire, and gold] agreeing univocally in those features. A creature, however, is essentially the effect of God not only according to some determinate kind of being, but also according the very character of being itself as such, inasmuch as it is found in that creature. For in no way is being presupposed in a creature prior to the action of God, but rather in every way it flows from and depends upon God.

8. *It is demonstrated that no creature equals the power of God.* The second argument is taken also from St. Thomas and it confirms the preceding one. It especially shows that a creature in no feature by which it proceeds from God equates with the power of God, whether that be the feature of being or of substance or anything else. For the character of being in God is such that it essentially includes every perfection of being; but in a creature it is not found in this way, but rather as definite and limited to some kind of perfection. Therefore, a creature does not equate with God even in the common feature of being.

Therefore, being is not said of God and a creature according to the same adequate character. Therefore, it is not said [of them] univocally.

The antecedent[105] is explained: because God, by the fact that He is by essence a most simple and infinite being, includes essentially and in a unified way every perfection of being. Hence, the very character of being itself, insofar as it is in God, essentially includes the characters of substance, of wisdom, and of justice. And therefore (what is the main point) it essentially includes existence itself (*ipsum esse*), completely independent and of itself (*a se*). Contrariwise, in a creature the character of being as such is completely dependent and from another (*ab alio*), and in each being it is limited to a certain kind of perfection. For this reason, the character of being is said to be in God by essence, but in creatures by participation. Likewise, it is said to be in God as it were totally, that is, as if gathering together all being, but in other things as if divided into parts. Therefore, the character of being is found in a far more inferior and inadequate way in creatures than in God; and consequently it is not said of them [both] univocally nor according to a concept that is completely the same. For if God and a creature were defined or in any way described, God would be found to be a being in a far different way than would the creature.

9. *The Problem with the Preceding Arguments.–* These arguments and similar ones are indeed serious and astute. However, there remains in them always the problem that either they prove too much or they are not effective. For they would doubtless prove not only that being is not univocal, but also that it does not have one objective concept common to God and creatures, which we have above shown to be false.[106] And many Thomists who employ these arguments do not admit that, nor does St. Thomas himself, I think, as I have shown above.[107] The consequence is proven because if the character of being insofar as it is in God includes something essentially other than it does in a creature, that character then cannot be one in such a way that it is represented by one formal concept and that it constitutes one objective concept. For it cannot be understood that in one concept as such there is an essential variety.

This is explained as follows. For when God is said to include in his essential nature the whole perfection of being while a creature [includes] as it were a part [of being] (and therefore they are not equal), either we are talking about God and the creature as they are beings or as they are such beings. This latter cannot be said because it is in no way relevant to the present case, first, because now we are not treating of such being, nor of a community which it has as it is such, but of

---

105 That is: "the character of being in God is such that it essentially includes every perfection of being."

106 Cf. § 1, this Section.

107 Cf. *DM* II, s. 2, n. 8, vol. 25, p. 72.

being simply and its community; and, second, because that also is not enough to block univocity. For in the same way we can say that animal includes something different in a man than it does in a horse, by reason of which a horse does not equate to the perfection of animal as it is in a man, that is, considering each as it is such an animal and not precisely under the concept of animal [simply].[108] But if we are talking about God and a creature precisely as being, in this way it is false that something is included in the concept of one and not of the other, because by the very fact that something of this kind may be included they are not then being considered precisely as they are beings but as they are *such* beings. Or indeed, if also as they are beings they have that distinction and variety, it is impossible that they have one [common] objective concept.

What Sort of Analogy Can Exist Here?

10. Therefore, in order that the truth of this position and the probability of the aforesaid arguments, which I think is great, may be better understood, I think we should begin from the other position[109] affirming that being is analogous to God and creatures. For, even though, if it is neither equivocal nor univocal, from a sufficient enumeration of parts it follows that it would be analogous, nevertheless, it is necessary to directly show and explain this, so that from that the second position which denies it to be univocal will be more evident. But in order to prove this, we must ask what kind of analogy can be present here. Thus, some persons think that there exists here an analogy of proportionality. St. Thomas thinks this way in [his work] *On Truth*, Question 2, Article 11, where he also seems to admit only that and to exclude every analogy of attribution from the aforesaid division,[110] as Cajetan too thinks in his little work, [on] *De Ente et essentia*, Question 3.[111] But others teach that indeed there is here an analogy of proportionality, however not that alone but together with an analogy of attribution. Ferrara indicates this in [his commentary on] *Contra Gentiles*, Book One, Chapter 34,[112] and Fonseca [says it] more clearly in Question 1, Section 7 [of his commentary on] *Metaphysics*, Book 4, Chapter 4 [*sic*].[113] The basis can be that

---

108 For some background here, cf. Armand Maurer, "St. Thomas and the Analogy of Genus," *The New Scholasticism*, 19 (1955), pp. 127–44.

109 That is, another position from the one which Suárez himself will eventually espouse.

110 Cf. St. Thomas, *Quaestiones disputatae de veritate*, q. 2, a. 11, in *Opera*, vol. 22/1, pp. 78–80, esp. 79.

111 Cf. *In De Ente et Essentia D. Thomae Aquinatis commentaria*, c. 2, q. 3, n. 20, ed. Laurent, p. 38.

112 *Commentaria Ferrariensis* [*In Summam contra Gentiles* I, 34], in *Opera*, vol. 13, pp. 104–9.

113 Cf. Petri Fonsecae, S.J., *Commentariorum in libros Metaphysicorum Aristotelis*

in the character of being [as it is found] between God and a creature there truly exists a certain proportion of two relations. For just as God is related to his being so in its own way a creature is related to its being. But I think it should be noted that not every proportionality is enough to constitute an analogy of proportionality. For this proportion of relations can be found between univocal things or things which are completely similar. For just as four is related to two, so eight is related to four, and just as a man is related to his senses, or to the source of his sensation, so a horse is related to its, and nevertheless that proportion does not constitute an analogy, nor any kind of common name. For the univocal name of "animal" is not taken from that comparison but from the unity of a character which is found in the individual members.

11. *There is no proper analogy of proportionality between God and creatures.*– Accordingly, for this [kind of] analogy it is necessary that one member be absolutely such through its own form, while the other be such not absolutely but rather as it is subject to some proportion or comparison with the first. But in the present case this is not so, whether we consider the reality itself or the imposition of the name. For a creature is a being by reason of its own being in an absolute way and considered without any such proportionality, because, without doubt, by that being it is outside nothing and has some actuality. Also the name "being" is applied to a creature not from the fact that it has some proportion or proportionality with God, but simply because it is something in itself and not absolutely nothing. Indeed, as we will say below, that name can be understood first to be applied to created rather than uncreated being. Finally, every genuine analogy of proportionality includes something metaphorical and improper,[114] just as "to smile" is said of a meadow by a metaphorical transference. But in this analogy of being there is no metaphor or impropriety. For a creature truly, prop-

---

Stagiritae, Tomi quatuor, IV, Cap. 2, q. 1, sect. 7 (Coloniae: Sumptibus Lazari Zetzneri, 1615; reprinted Hildesheim: Georg Olms, 1964), Tomus I, cols. 704–10. On Fonseca, cf. John P. Doyle, "Fonseca, Pedro da (1528–99)," in *Routledge Encyclopedia of Philosophy* (London and New York: Routledge, 1998), vol. 3, pp. 688–90.

114 For other places where Suárez has explicitly mentioned the extrinsic and improper character of metaphor, cf. *DM* VIII, s. 7, nn. 21 and 22, vol. 25, pp. 302–3; *DM* XXXII, 2, n. 13, vol. 26, p. 323; *DM* XXXIX, 3, n. 1, p. 523. In the tradition before Suárez, for St. Augustine referring to metaphor as the transfer of a word from its proper use to one which is improper, see *Contra mendacium*, c. 10; versión del P. Ramiro Flórez, O.S.A., in *Obras de San Augustín*, Tomo XII, Madrid: Biblioteca de Autores Cristianos, 1954. For places where St. Thomas has contrasted "metaphorical" with "proper," cf. *De fallaciis*, c. 5, in *Opera*, vol. XLIII, p. 406; *In Sent.* I, d. 45, q. 1, a. 4 c., ed. Mandonnet, tom. I, p. 1039; *In Sent.* II, d. 13, q. 1, a. 2 c, tom. II, p. 329; *Summa Theologiae* I, q. 13, a. 3, ad 1, in *Opera*, vol. IV, p. 143.

erly, and simply is being. This therefore is not an analogy of proportionality, either alone or in conjunction with an analogy of attribution.

The result, therefore, is that if there is some analogy [here of being], it is one of attribution. And this in the end is what St. Thomas taught in [*Summa Theologiae*] I, Question 13, Articles 5 and 6;[115] in *Contra Gentiles* I, Chapter 34;[116] in [his work] *On the Power [of God]*, Question 7, Article 7;[117] and in [his commentary on the *Sentences*], Book I, the Prologue, Question 1, Article 2, In Reply to Objection 2.[118]

12. *God and a Creature do not entail an Analogy of Attribution to a Third Thing.–* It remains to ask of what sort this attribution can be? In this, it is first of all certain that this attribution is not of several things to one thing, that is, of God and creatures to one third thing, which attribution we have above called "mediated."[119] For nothing can be imagined prior to God and a creature in such way that by relation to it both God and the creature will be called "beings."

It is therefore an attribution of one to another. About this it is again certain that it cannot be an attribution [i.e. a referring] of God to a creature, but rather, the opposite, of a creature to God, because God does not depend upon a creature but a creature upon God. Neither is "being" said more principally about a creature rather than about God, but just the opposite.

In this we should look at what St. Thomas remarked above:[120] both this name and others which are properly said of God and creatures, even though, with regard to us, they have first indicated creatures, or they have been imposed in order to signify creatures, with regard to the thing signified, they first and more principally belong to God. For men, who philosophize by the natural light [of reason], have first known the being, the wisdom, or other perfections, of creatures, and from that they have first named them. Therefore, if we look to the purpose or intention of those who applied these names in order to signify, these names first signify these perfections in creatures. However, because the names themselves by virtue of their absolute application do not include created imperfections in their signification, therefore by virtue of the things themselves which are signified, first and more principally they signify the same perfections as they

115 Cf. *Summa Theologiae* I, q. 13, aa. 5–6, in *Opera*, vol. 4, pp. 146–47 and 150.

116 Cf. *Summa contra Gentiles* I, c. 34, in *Opera*, vol. 13, pp. 103–4.

117 S. Thomae Aquinatis, *De Potentia*, q. 7, a. 7, in *Quaestiones disputatae*, vol. 2, ed. VIII, P. Bazzi, et al., p. 204.

118 Cf. S. Thomae Aquinatis, *Scriptum super libros Sententiarum Magistri Petri Lombardi*, Prol. q. 1, a. 2, ad 2, editio nova, cura R.P. Mandonnet, O.P., vol. 1 (Parisiis: Sumptibus P. Lethielleux, 1929), p. 10.

119 Cf. § 4, this Section.

120 Cf. § 5, this Section.

exist in God. For the perfections of this kind signified by those terms in creatures flow from another perfection that is most properly and most perfectly in God.

13. *In What Way do the Platonists Say that God is Not Being, but rather Above Being*? – Similarly, an absolute and common signification must be distinguished from a mode of signifying. For, since we speak as we conceive, and we conceive simple things in the manner of composite things, therefore, we also name them in this way. And in this way we distinguish a concrete name from one which is abstract (which [both], properly speaking, with respect to this mode of signifying have no place in God), and so we sometimes say that God is "being itself" (*ipsum esse*) rather than "*a* being" (*ens*). For a concrete being both is and signifies "something which has being" (*habens esse*), as if in some way the one having it would be distinguished from being itself and would be a being by a certain participation of that [being itself]. And in this way, the signification and the designation of "a being" belongs more properly to a creature than to God. Because of this, wise men, sometimes speaking with rigor, say that God is not being (*ens*) but "above being" (*supra ens*), as Pico della Mirandola, in Chapters 3 and 4 of his little work, *On Being and the One*, has very well explained from many Platonists,[121] as well as [Pseudo] Dionysius in Chapter 5 of his *On Divine Names*,[122] and also Chapter 5 of his *Mystical Theology*.[123] In part, Augustine imitates him in Book 5 of [his work] *On the Trinity*, at the end of Chapter 10 [*sic*];[124] [and also St.] Basil, in Book 5, Chapter 13 [*sic*] of his [work] *Against Eunomius*;[125] [St. John] Damascene, Book 1, Chapter 4 of his work *On Faith*;[126] and Boethius, in Book 1 [of his *Theological Works*], *On the Trinity*, toward the beginning.[127]

---

121 For this, see Pico della Mirandola, *On the Dignity of Man* (tr. Charles G. Wallis); *On Being and the One* (tr. Paul J.W. Miller); *Heptaplus* (tr. Douglas Carmichael), with an Introduction by Paul J.W. Miller (Indianapolis/New York: The Bobbs-Merrill Company, 1965), pp. 41–46; Giovanni Pico della Mirandola, *De hominis dignitate, Heptaplus, De ente et uno, e scritti vari*, ed. E. Garin (Firenze: Vallechi, 1942), pp. 396–406.

122 Cf. S. Dionysii Areopagitae, *De divinis nominibus*, c. 5, in *Patrologiae cursus completus, series Graeca*, ed. J.-P. Migne (Paris: Garnier, 1857–91), [hereafter: *PG*], vol. 3, cols. 815–25.

123 Cf. *De mystica theologia*, c. 5, in *PG*, vol. 3, cols. 1046–47.

124 Cf. *De Trinitate* V, c. 1, n. 2, in *PL*, vol. 42, cols. 911–12, and V, c. 7, n. 8, cols. 915–16.

125 Possibly: S. Basilii, *Adversus Eunomium*, IV, in *PG*, vol. 29, cols. 683–84, or V, cols. 749–50.

126 Cf. Saint John Damascene, *De fide orthodoxa*, versions of Burgundio and Cerbanus, ed. E.M. Buytaert, O.F.M. (St. Bonaventure: Franciscan Institute, 1955), c. 4, nn. 4–5, pp. 20–21.

127 For this, cf. An. Manlii Severini Boetii, *Opera theologica: Quomodo Trinitas unus Deus ac non tres dii*, Prooemium, in *PL*, vol. 64, cols. 1247–49.

However, because that mode of signifying does not in fact flow back upon the reality signified and does not attribute any imperfection to it, therefore being (*ens*) simply signifies "that which is" and in this way is said most properly and principally of God, without any relation to a creature. In this way, in *Exodus*, Chapter 3, God says "I am who am," in which place the *Septuagint* has: ἐγώ εἴμι ὁ ὤν, that is, "I am being itself," because indeed, (as Dionysius said above) "God exists not in any particular way, but absolutely and freely without any limitation, comprehending and holding in himself all that is being."[128]

14. *Two ways of attribution of one thing to another.*– Next we should observe that something can be designated by attribution [i.e. reference] to something else in two ways. One is when the designating form is intrinsically in only one extreme, while it is in others by only an extrinsic relation. In this way, "healthy" is said absolutely of an animal and of medicine by reference to an animal. The second way is when the designating form is intrinsically in both members, even though it is in one absolutely but in the other by a relationship to that one, for example, as "being" is said of a substance and an accident. For an accident is not designated as being extrinsically from the entity of a substance, but from its own proper and intrinsic entity, which is such that it consists entirely in a certain relation to a substance.

Among these two there are many differences. *One* is that in the first attribution the name is attributed to the thing secondarily signified only improperly and by metaphor or by another figure [of speech]. In the second [attribution], however, the designation is most proper and can even be essential, because it is taken from an intrinsic form or from the proper nature [of the thing which is signified]. *Two* is that in the first attribution the secondary analogate as it is such or as it is signified by such a name is defined through the prime analogate, in such way that it is necessary that this be put into its definition. For if you want to explain what it is for a medicine to be healthy, you will say that it is causative or conservative of the health of an animal. For, since it is designated such only in an extrinsic way from that form, it can be defined only through that form, as St. Thomas has noted [in *Summa Theologiae*] I, Question 13, Article 6.[129] But in the second attribution it is not necessary that a second analogate be defined through the principal one, as Cajetan has remarked, in the same Article 6 [i.e. commenting on *Summa Theologiae* I, q. 13],[130] from St. Thomas in [the work] *On Truth*,

128 Cf. *De divinis nominibus*, c. 5, in *PG*, vol. 3, col. 816.

129 Cf. *Summa Theologiae* I, q. 13, a. 6, in *Opera*, vol. 4, p. 150.

130 *Ibid.., Commentaria Cardinalis Caietani*, pp. 151–52.

Question 2, Article 11.[131] And this is proven by induction. For, even though *wisdom* is said analogically of created and uncreated [wisdom], created wisdom is not however defined through uncreated [wisdom]. And an accident, even though insofar as it is an accident it is defined through a substance, is not [so defined] insofar as it is being. The reason is that the form from which that designation is taken is not extrinsic but rather intrinsic, which as it is signified by that name, since it is abstractly and precisely signified, does not include in its concept the proper mode by which the said form is in any of the analogates.

The *third* difference is that in the first attribution there does not exist one concept common to all the analogates. For the form from which it is taken is intrinsically and properly only in one and in the others by metaphor and an extrinsic denomination. But in the second attribution there exists one common formal and objective concept, because the analogates properly and intrinsically are such and they truly agree in a certain character which the mind can conceive abstractly and precisely in one concept common to all.

A *last* difference can be added inasmuch as a name which is analogous with the first attribution cannot be the middle term of a demonstration,[132] because a middle term is not such by reason of a name but by reason of a concept. Therefore, since the name [in the first attribution] is subordinated to several concepts, it is not one middle term, but rather many with different meanings (*multiplex et aequivocum*). But the case is otherwise in analogies of the second kind, for the opposite reason.

15. *In the case of creatures the attribution [or reference] to God is not like that of something not having a form intrinsically to something that does have it so.–* From what has been said, therefore, it is clear that the attribution which is found between God and a creature cannot be of the first kind, namely, that in which the form with respect to which the attribution is made is intrinsically and properly only in one thing and in others extrinsically and by transference. For it is evident that a creature is not designated a being in an extrinsic way from the entity or the being that is in God, but rather from its own intrinsic being. And therefore it is called a being not by metaphor but truly and properly. Likewise, it is clear that a creature is not defined as a being through the Creator or through the being of God, but rather by being as such and because it is outside nothing. For if there is added a relation to God, for example, that a creature is a being

131 Cf. *Quaestiones disputatae de veritate*, q. 2, a. 11, in *Opera omnia*, vol. 22/1, p. 79.

132 Once again, this is a most important difference related to the basic Suarezian proof for the existence of God. Because the common concept of being can serve as a middle term in demonstration it is possible to pass from the being of creatures to the being of God. Cf. § 15, immediately following.

because it is a participation of the Divine being, in this way a creature is not defined as it is a being but as it is a certain kind of being, that is, one that is created.

Finally, it was shown above[133] that being is said with one concept of all things contained under it, and therefore it can be a medium of demonstration, and the character of being in creatures can be the starting point for finding a similar character existing in a higher way in the Creator. Nor is it an objection against this that the name "being" is sometimes attributed to God as singular and proper to Him, as is manifest from the cited words of *Exodus*, Chapter 3. In this way also, creatures are sometimes said "not to be" in the sight of God, or in comparison with God; cf. *Isaiah*, Chapter 40 [v. 17]: "All the nations are before him as if they had no being at all and are counted to him as nothing and vanity." Plato also sometimes used this way of speaking, as Augustine relates in Book 8, Chapter 1, of his work *On the City of God*.[134] And he [i.e. Plato] suggests it in the *Sophist* when he says that what exists in an absolute way contains all perfections and lacks nothing.[135] This and similar things, I say, are no objection because in them it is not indicated that creatures are not truly and properly beings, but rather that they are infinitely distant from God and that God in a certain singular and excellent way is that which He is and the source of all being, from which other things are beings and are named, as Dionysius has indicated, in the place cited,[136] and [St.] Jerome elegantly [has said in commentary on] *Ephesians*, Chapter 3, [v. 15] when he treats the words: "From whom all paternity in heaven and on earth is named."[137] In that place, he has explained in the same way those passages of Scripture in which God alone is said to be good, wise, or immortal, [e.g.,] *Mark*, Chapter 10 [v. 18]; *Luke*, Chapter 18 [v. 19]; the last Chapter of *Romans* [v. 27]; and *First Timothy*, Chapter 5 [*sic*].[138] And Augustine has indicated the same thing in [his work] *On the Trinity* Book 1,

133 Cf. § 14, immediately preceding. Also see: Suárez, *Index locupletissimus* IV, 2, vol. 25, p. xv; *DM* I, 1, n. 29, p. 12; *DM* II, 2, n. 14, p. 74; *ibid.*, n. 25, p. 78; and *DM* XXXII, 2, n. 18, vol. 26, p. 324.

134 Cf. *De civitate Dei* VIII, c. 1, in *PL*, vol. 41, col. 225.

135 Possibly, this is not a direct reference to Plato but rather to someone like Marsilio Ficino: cf. *In omnia opera Platonis, commentaria et argumenta in Platonis Sophistam*, c. 26, in Marsilii Ficini, *Opera Omnia*, Tomus Secundus (Basileae: Ex Officina Henricpetrina, 1576; reproduced by P. Kristeller, Torino: Bottega d'Erasmo, 1962), p. 1188.

136 Cf. *De divinis nominibus*, c. 5, in *PG*, vol. 3, esp. cols. 819–23.

137 Cf. S. Eusebii Hieryonymi, *Comm. in Ephesios*, L. II, c. 3, v. 14 [*sic*], *PL*, vol. 26, cols. 486b–90a.

138 Cf. *I Timothy*, 1.17

Chapter 1,[139] and Book 5, Chapter 2;[140] the *Confessions*, Book 7, Chapter 11,[141] and *On the City of God*, Book 12, Chapter 2;[142] as well as Hilary, *On the Trinity*, Book 7, a little after the beginning.[143]

The Resolution of the Question.

16. *Of what kind is the analogy of a creature to God*? – It remains, therefore, that this analogy or attribution which a creature can have to God under the concept of being is of the second kind, that is, founded on a proper and intrinsic being which has an essential relationship to or dependence on God. About this attribution two things must be shown: first, that such an attribution does truly exist between a creature and God; and second, that it is enough to constitute an analogy.

The first is very well proven by the reasons drawn above from St. Thomas,[144] of which the principal one is that a creature is a being essentially by its participation in the being which is in God by essence and as in the first and universal source from which some participation of it is derived to all other things. Therefore, every creature is a being by some relationship (*habitudo*) to God insofar, that is, as it participates or in some way imitates the being of God. And insofar as it has being, it essentially depends upon God much more than an accident depends upon a substance. Therefore, in this way, being is said of a creature by relation or attribution[145] to God.

This must not be understood in such a way that a creature, conceived under the most abstract and most confused concept of being as such, is thought to express a relationship to God. For that is plainly impossible, as the arguments made above[146] correctly prove, since under that concept a creature is not conceived as a finite being and as it is limited, but rather it is completely abstracted and is conceived only confusedly under the character of existing outside nothing.

---

139 Cf. *De Trinitate* I, c. 1, in *PL*, vol. 42, col. 821.

140 Cf. *ibid.*, V, c. 2, in *PL*, vol. 42, col. 911.

141 Cf. Sancti Augustini Hipponensis, *Confessionum libri tredecim* VII, c. 11, in *PL* 32, col. 742.

142 Cf. *De civitate Dei* XII, c. 2, in *PL*, vol. 41, col. 350.

143 See Sancti Hilarii Pictavensis, *De Trinitate, libri duodecim*, VII, n. 11, in *PL*, vol. 10, col. 207b.

144 Cf. §§ 1, 7, 8, this Section.

145 Note here the equivalence that was indicated above between attribution and reference.

146 Cf. this Section, §§ 11 and 15; also see *DM* II, 2, n. 8, vol. 25, p. 72, and *ibid.* n. 15, p. 75.

Therefore, it is to be understood so that in reality that creature participates in the character of being only with a certain essential subordination to God, which is most self-evident, since it is essentially a being from another, as was also explained above.[147]

17. *A true analogy of attribution is found in members which possess a form in an intrinsic way.*– But the second part, namely, that this relation and subordination constitutes some mode of analogy, is proven from Aristotle, in Book 5, Chapter 6, of the *Metaphysics*, where he says that those things are one by analogy "which are related as to another."[148] For this is the way [Cardinal] Bessarion translates it. But the Greek literally has "as other to other."[149] Hence, almost all the commentators (*expositores*) think that Aristotle is speaking about an analogy of proportionality, in which this is related to that as other to other. However, the words can correctly be understood in a more general way. For both St. Thomas[150] and Alexander of Hales,[151] as well as [Duns] Scotus,[152] understand these words to be about those analogies which are said with respect to a third thing, for example, as urine and medicine are called "healthy" with respect to the health of an animal. And by the same reasoning, those words can be understood about those things of which one is said to be in relation to another. For about these it is also true to say that they are so related as other to other. But a creature is related to God in this way in the character of being. Hence, Aristotle again, in the *Metaphysics*, Book 4, Chapter 2, says "being is said in many ways, but in relation to one."[153] And he repeats the same thing in Book 7, Chapter 4, where in a general sense he says that all things that are said in relation to one are analo-

---

147 Cf. Section 1, § 13; Section 2, § 8, and this Section, §§ 13, 15, and 16.

148 Cf. *Metaphysics* 5.6.1016b34–5.

149 ὡς ἄλλο πρὸς ἄλλο. *ibid.* This is worth noting for a number of reasons. First, is Suárez's use of Bessarion's translation. Second, is his ability and his willingness to check the Greek text. Third, by this time he had Fonseca's edition and translation.

150 Cf. S. Thomae Aquinatis, *In duodecim libros Metaphysicorum Aristotelis expositio* V, c. 6, lect. 8, ed. M.-R. Cathala, O.P. et R. Spiazzi, O.P. (Taurini: Marietti, 1950), n. 879, p. 236. Note in passing that William of Moerbeke, O.P., whose translation, which St. Thomas is following, is reproduced in this Marietti volume, has rendered Aristotle's Greek literally "as other to other" (*aliud ad aliud*); *ibid.*, p. 234.

151 Cf. Alexandri de Ales, O.M. [actually, Alessandro Bonini], *In duodecim Aristotelis Metaphysicae libros dilucidissima expositio* V, t. 12 (Venetiis: Apud Simonem Galignanum de Karera, 1572), fol. 118r.

152 Cf. Joannis Duns Scoti, *In XII. libros Metaphysicorum Aristotelis* V, c. 5, n. 59 (Lugduni: Sumptibus Laurentii Durand, 1639), vol. 4, p. 173. Actually, this is a spurious work of Duns Scotus.

153 *Metaphysics* 4.2.1003a33.

gous.[154] And in these places he includes the analogy of attribution of accidents to substance, which clearly is such that the character of being properly and intrinsically belongs to both; but because accidents do not participate in that character except through a relation to substance, that is enough to constitute an analogy of attribution. Therefore, for the same or greater reason it will be enough in the present instance.

Finally, [the point] is explained by reason.[155] For being itself, however much abstractly and confusedly conceived, by virtue of itself demands this order, that first, and essentially (*per se*), and as though completely, it belongs to God and through that it descends to the rest of things, in which it is only with a relation to and dependence upon God. Therefore, in this it falls short of the nature of a univocal [term], for what is univocal is of itself so indifferent that it descends to its inferiors equally and without any order or relation of one thing to another. Therefore, being with respect to God and creatures is rightly reckoned to be analogous. And this will become more evident from solutions of the arguments [against it]. However, to tell the truth, among those who admit one confused concept of being there can scarcely be in this question any dissent about the fact but [only] about the way of speaking. For, without doubt, being has a great similarity with univocal terms, since by means of one concept it is predicated simply and without addition of God and a creature, which similarity alone is considered by those who call it univocal.[156]

This way of speaking is sometimes used by Aristotle, as is clear from *Metaphysics*, Book 2, Chapter 1, at the end, where the Greek literally has: "But each thing most of all such before others is that according to which there is a univocity in the others."[157] Hence he concludes that that is most of all true or most of all being which is for others the cause that they are such. However, if the mentioned difference be carefully considered, as well as the manner in which the character of being is found in God and in other things, it is easily understood that it falls far short of a true univocity and that it constitutes as it were a first order of analogates.

Response to the Arguments.

18. *The response made by some is rejected.–* Accordingly, with regard to the

---

154 Cf. *Metaphysics* 7.4.1030a35–b3.

155 That is, by arguments as opposed to citations of authorities.

156 For example, Duns Scotus, *Ordinatio* I, d. 3 (ed. Vat. vol. 3, p. 18, n. 26. For comparison of Scotus and Suárez here, cf. W. Hoeres, "Francis Suarez and the Teaching of John Duns Scotus on the *Univocatio Entis,*" in *John Duns Scotus, 1265–1965,* "*Studies in Philosophy and the History of Philosophy,*" ed. J. K. Ryan and B. M. Bonansea (Washington, D.C.: Catholic University of America Press, 1965), pp. 263–90.

157 Aristotle's Greek here is: ἕκαστον δὲ μάλιστα αὐτὸ τῶν ἄλλων καθ' ὅ καὶ τοῖς ἄλλοις ὑπάρχει τό συνώνυμον ..." *Metaphysics* 2.1.993b24–5. Suárez's Latin is:

basis of the second opinion,[158] this consequence is denied: Being expresses one concept common to God and creatures; therefore, it is said univocally of both.

In reply to the first proof[159] some[160] distinguish with respect to the concept of being: for either it is taken as it includes the proper features of its inferiors or insofar as it excludes them or does not include them. In the first way, they say, being is analogous, because it includes many things which have an order among themselves, and for this reason they deny that the character of being is the same in a creature and in the Creator. Indeed, they also deny that there is one concept of being, because those members, according to their proper features, cannot be included in one concept.

"Unumquodque vero illud prae caeteris maxime tale est, secundum quod aliis univocatio inest." Fonseca's slightly free translation (cf. *In Metaphy. Aristotelis* II, cap. 1, t. 4, vol. 1, col. 384) is: "Unumquodque autem maxime tale est prae caeteris, cuius causa caeteris et nomine et ratione idem convenit" (i.e. "But each thing most of all such is before others [that] because of which the same both in name and concept belongs to the others"). Earlier, William of Moerbeke (cf. S. Thomae Aquinatis, *In duodecim libros Metaphysicorum Aristotelis expositio*, ed. Cathala-Spiazzi, p. 84, n. 151) translated: "Unumquodque vero maxime id ipsum aliorum dicitur, secundum quod et in aliis inest univocatio" ("But each thing is said to be most of all that among others according to which there is also in the others a univocity"; or, as John P. Rowan [in *St. Thomas Aquinas, Commentary on the Metaphysics of Aristotle* (Chicago: Regnery, 1961), vol. 1, p. 120] has rendered William's text: "Now anything which is the basis of a univocal predication about other things has that attribute to the highest degree.") St. Thomas's paraphrase (*In duodecim libros Metaphy. ...*, ed. Cathala-Spiazzi, p. 85, n. 292) is: "Unumquodque inter alia maxime dicitur ex quo causatur in aliis aliquid univoce praedicatum de eis" ("Anything is said to be most of all among others from which there is caused in the others something univocally predicated of them"; or as Rowan freely translates: "When a universal predicate is applied to several things, in each case that which constitutes the reason for the predication about other things has that attribute in the fullest sense.") W.D. Ross (cf. *The Basic Works of Aristotle*, ed. R. McKeon [New York: Random House, 1941], p. 712) translates Aristotle: "And a thing has a quality in a higher degree than other things if in virtue of it the similar quality belongs to the other things as well." Rábade's Spanish version of Suárez (in: Sergio Rábade Romeo *et al.*, *Disputaciones metafísicas* [Madrid: Editorial Gredos, 1960–1966], vol. 4 [1962], p. 235) reads: "una cosa es sobre las demás maximamente tal, en cuanto las otras guardan univocación con ella" ("One thing is above others maximally such insofar as the others show univocity with it"). From all of this the reader may glimpse something of Suárez's virtuosity in handling the text and thought of Aristotle.

158 Cf. §§ 2, 3, and 4, this Section.

159 Cf. § 2, this Section.

160 The Vivès edition gives a note to Javellus, IV *Metaph.*, q. 1; cf. Chrysostomi Iavelli Canapicii, *In omnibus Metaphysicae libris: quaesita testualia metaphysicali modo*

However, in the second way they concede that being is one in name, in concept, and in nature, but they deny that it is univocal, for the reason that under that concept it does not express an order to its inferiors. But something is said to be univocal or analogous only through an order to inferiors.[161]

But this response supposes a distinction which we rejected above[162] as useless for explaining the signification of this word "being" and the unity of its concept. For being, as including the proper features of its inferiors, is not signified by this word "being" nor can it be conceived by a proper and adequate concept corresponding to that. For being, insofar as it includes its inferiors according to their proper features, is not being alone, but it is finite and infinite being, substance and accident, etc., which, just as they cannot be conceived by us according to their proper features in one concept, so also they cannot be signified by one name. Therefore, that distinction about being including or not including inferiors profits nothing toward explaining its analogy.

This is confirmed and clarified: for either we are speaking about being as actually and distinctly including its inferiors, and the argument which was made proceeds against this, because a concept of this kind neither corresponds to this word "being" nor pertains to being insofar as it is being but insofar as it is substance or accident, etc.; or we are speaking about being only confusedly and as it were including its inferiors in potency, and in this way it is false that there does not correspond to it one common concept, but rather proper concepts of God and creature, of substance and accident, because there is an obvious incongruity that in a confused concept there be included a distinct conception of particular kinds of being.

Finally, for the same reason it could be said that animal, insofar as it includes its inferiors, is not univocal, that is, insofar as it is sub-ordered to the proper and distinct concepts of its inferiors, for as such it does not have one concept. But that would be a useless and trivial response. For those concepts do not correspond to the word "animal" as such nor is that [animal] only animal, but it is man, or horse, etc.

19. Again, from another angle, what is said in this response seems false: that being, as not including its inferiors, is neither univocal nor analogous since as such it is not compared to its inferiors. For either we are talking about an actual comparative knowledge from the side of the intellect, and this is not necessary for univocity, for the concept of man is univocal even though it is not actually

---

determinata... (Venetiis: Apud Haeredes Ioannis Mariae Bonelli, 1576), IV, q. 1, pp. 46v–52r.

161 Javelli, pp. 47–49.

162 Cf. § 9, this Section. On the relation of the concept of being to its inferiors, cf. *DM* II, vol. 25, pp. 64–102.

compared to inferiors through a reflex knowledge; or we are talking about an aptitudinal comparison from the side of the objective concept itself of being as not actually including its inferiors, and in this way it is false that it is not compared or is not comparable to them, because it is evidently predicable of them. For when we say that a creature, or a substance, or an accident, is being, we are not predicating being insofar as it actually includes its inferiors, but only according to the confused concept of being. Therefore, it is necessary that according to that concept it is either univocal or analogous.

20. *Another response to the argument.– The earlier mentioned response is explained* (*expeditur*).– Therefore, in another way it can be replied that Aristotle in his logic never distinguished analogous from univocal or equivocal [terms]. Accordingly, since analogous [terms] are mid-way between those two extremes, they are to be reduced to that extreme with which they most agree. Hence, Aristotle, in the mentioned Chapter [1] of the *Antepredicaments*, has placed an analogous [term] which signifies inferiors, together with several concepts (such as "animal" when it is said of a living [animal] and of one in a painting) under equivocal [terms].[163]

In this way, therefore, it can be said that, in line with such definitions, being is reduced to univocal rather than equivocal [terms], and therefore, in relation to logical practice it can be called univocal, because it can both be a medium of demonstration and also simply and without addition it is said of created and uncreated being, and it is common according to name and concept. However, metaphysically it is analogous, because it is in its inferiors in an unequal relation and order, as has been explained.

But if you say that according to this response being is as much univocal as any genus, since a genus, although it is logically univocal, can be physically or metaphysically analogous because inequality hides within it or because it descends to its inferiors with some of their inequality[164] – as is taken from Aristotle, *Physics*, Book 7, Text 31,[165] and *Metaphysics*, Book 10, Text 26,[166] and more clearly from St. Thomas, in Book 1 [of his *Sentences* commentary], Distinction 19, Question 5, Article 2, In Reply to Objection 1[167] – the answer is that the argument is not the same. For in the case of a genus there is between its

163 Cf. *Categories* 1.1a1–5.

164 On the whole issue here, cf. Sven K. Knebel, *In genere latent aequivocationes: zur Tradition der Universalienkritik aus dem Geist der Dihärese*, (Hildesheim: Georg Olms Verlag, 1989). Also see Maurer, as cited in note 108, above.

165 Cf. *Physics* 7.1

166 Cf. *Metaphysics* 10.9

167 Cf. *Scriptum super libros Sententiarum Magistri Petri Lombardi* I, d. 19, q. 5, a. 2, ad 1, ed. Mandonnet, tom. I, p. 492

species merely an inequality of perfection that results only from their differences. But there is not an inequality that results from the common generic concept itself, which of itself demands to be first and absolutely in one species and then in the others by a relation to that first, which could be called an inequality of essential dependence, which is required in the community of being. Therefore, although physically and according to the being which the species of a genus have in reality, a genus is said to be in a certain way analogical or equivocal, it is not however [said to be such] metaphysically according to its objective and common concept. But being is analogous also metaphysically according to its common objective concept, even though in line with those logical definitions it may seem to be included under univocal [terms]. Accordingly, this response is probable – however, it does too much favor the univocity of being.

21. *The third and true response.–* Therefore, a third response may be [made] by denying that the concept of being is entirely the same in a finite and an infinite being. For the latter is being because it is from itself, while the former is being because it is from another. But if you say that by these words there is not explained the concept which is proportioned to being as such, but rather the proper concepts of such and such a being, the answer is that first of all the concept of being is transcendent and intimately included in all proper and determinate concepts of beings and in the modes themselves which determine being itself. Therefore even though the common concept as abstracted is in itself one, nevertheless, the features which constitute individual beings are diverse, and through them as such each thing is constituted in an absolute way in the reality of being (*in esse entis*). Then (something very relevant to this matter), the common concept itself of itself demands such a determination with an order and relation to one, and, thus, although as a confused concept it is the same, just as it is one, nevertheless, it is not entirely the same, because it is not of itself entirely uniform – which uniformity and sameness univocals require in their concept, and the definition of univocals must be explained in this way.

22. *The solution of the second argument.*[168] – To the second argument the answer is that by that argument it is correctly proven that being is not one of those analogous [terms] that are said by metaphor or by transference, but from this it does not result that it is in no way analogous. For that property of an analogous term, namely, that it is not common to many by virtue of one application, is not of the essence of all analogous [terms], but only of those which are said by metaphor or transference. Hence, we must carefully consider that a transferred or metaphorical analogy, even though it may have some foundation in things [themselves], does not however arise entirely from those things, but from human application and usage. But the present analogy of being is entirely founded in and aris-

---

168 Cf. § 3, this Section.

es from things themselves, which things are subordinated in such a way that, insofar as they are beings, they are necessarily referred to one. And, therefore, the name of being could not be imposed to confusedly signify that which has being, without consequently having to signify many things with a relation to one. And in this way it will be analogous not by transference but by a true and proper signification.

And from this the third argument[169] is also dissolved, since in that argument there is an incomplete enumeration of [terms which are] analogous by attribution. For besides those which are said by extrinsic denomination of things secondarily signified, there are others which are said intrinsically and properly of all that is signified. And these have their own rules and properties which are diverse from other analogous [terms], as has been sufficiently explained.

169 Cf. § 4, this Section.

DISPUTATION 29

About God, the First Being and Uncreated Substance, Insofar as He Can by Natural Reason Be Known to Exist.

1. *Why this Disputation is located in this place.* – Those who treat metaphysical doctrine usually leave this Disputation about God for almost the last place – imitating Aristotle, who treats it in Book 12 of his *Metaphysics* where he discusses God and other Intelligences[1] together and almost without distinction. Other [philosophers] then have followed him in this. And the reason seems to have been that although God is of himself most of all knowable, nevertheless, as far as we are concerned, he is less known than the material effects through which he is known by us. This reason, with due proportion, will be common also with regard to the other Intelligences.

But, since in these *Disputations* we intend as much as possible to follow the order of teaching (*ordo doctrinae*), we are discussing the uncreated being before [discussing] other beings in detail,[2] because that [being] is the principal object of this science and is of itself most excellent, and knowledge of it brings great light so that we can know other beings not only in an *a posteriori* way, but also, as our ability permits, in an *a priori* way.[3] And albeit by natural reason we know, as we

---

1 These are the Aristotelian "separate substances" which are responsible for heavenly motion.

2 Suárez has in mind *Metaphysical Disputations* XXXI–LIII (*Opera*, vol. 26, pp. 224–1014), in which he discusses the essence, the existence, and the categories of created being.

3 Note the contrast here between our natural order of discovery and "the order of teaching." Also, look again at *DM* XXVIII, s. 1, n. 5, above, where Suárez has distin-

are now saying, God not in Himself but from his effects, nevertheless, in order to compose this *Disputation* about God I think it is enough to have premised it with what we have said in general about being and the first division of being and about causes and effects.[4] This is especially since this doctrine, as we are giving it, presupposes from philosophy[5] both some principles which help in order to know God and also sufficient knowledge of the terms which we can use in order to explain Divine perfection, at least, as regards their signification or their meaning as words (*quid nominis*).[6]

2. Therefore, this *Disputation* comes appropriately in this place and in it we are briefly gathering all that natural theology teaches about God, leaving aside those things which are possessed or can be possessed only by Revelation. We will mention those things only insofar as will be necessary to pre-fix the boundary to which natural reason can come. And even though in God existence (*esse*), what he is (*quid est*), and such as he is (*qualis est*) are the same, nevertheless, following our way of conceiving, we will discuss them separately and in order.

SECTION ONE

Whether It Can Be Demonstrated – either by a Physical or a Metaphysical Argument – that an Uncreated Being Exists.

1. Two things are suggested in this title: first, whether this can be demonstrated; and second, by what means, physical or metaphysical? These two questions can also be asked about God – and in reality it is the same thing to ask about an uncreated being and to ask about God. However, for greater clarity and in

---

guished the order of teaching from the order in which things are more known to us. The idea seems to be that while we naturally proceed from the universal, the confused, and the imperfect to what is particular, distinct and perfect, we can only teach from principles which we have already discovered or known. On this, cf. John of St. Thomas, *Naturalis philosophiae*, I. pars, q. 1, a. 3, vol. 2, p. 20–22, as mentioned in the present translator's note 10, *DM* XXVIII, s. 1. On the kind of secondary *a priori* knowledge which is involved here, see note 225, below.

4 The thought is that while we know God from his effects, we do not have to enumerate all of those effects individually, but it is enough to approach God out of the general background of being and its divisions such as these have been already treated.

5 That is, natural philosophy or Aristotelian physics.

6 For a fuller explanation of this, see the present Disputation, Section 2, §§ 4–5, below. On the role of the name of God as taken from his effects in the Thomistic demonstration of his existence, cf. St. Thomas, *Summa Theologiae*, I, q. 2, a. 2, ad 2, in *Opera*, vol. 4, p. 30; also: E. Gilson, *The Elements of Christian Philosophy* (New York: New American Library, 1963), pp. 61–62; and Joseph Owens, C.SS.R., *An Elementary Christian Metaphysics* (Milwaukee: Bruce Publishing, 1963), p. 338, note 18.

order to better perfect the argument, we are distinguishing these, as we will explain in the next Section.

With regard then to the first question, Aliacus [i.e. Peter d'Ailly], who will be cited below,[7] has denied that this can be demonstrated. However, about this matter almost enough has been said in the last *Disputation* [i.e. 28]. For by showing in various manners and under different terms the first division of being – that is, into infinite or finite, created or uncreated – in numerous ways we have shown that it is necessary that there be in the totality [of being] some being which has being of itself, in such way that other things which have received being could emanate from it. Therefore, let the answer to the first question briefly be: by natural reason it can be demonstrated that there is in the totality [of being] some being which is uncreated or not produced. This is proven by the arguments which were made in that place [i.e. *Disputation* 28], which arguments will be more fully explained and confirmed by inquiring about and by examining the medium of this demonstration.

2. With regard to the second question there are various opinions which are either extremely opposite to one another or somewhere in between. The first [opinion] is that the fact that there is a first and of itself necessary being of this kind can be demonstrated only by a physical medium. The Commentator [i.e. Averroes] holds this [opinion], in [commenting on] *Metaphysics* Book 12, Text 5,[8] and *Physics*, Book 1, the last Text[9] – who is speaking in general of all substances abstracted from matter, because he perhaps thought that all immaterial substances are of themselves necessary beings. But the basis of his [opinion] is that only from the eternal motion of the heavens can it be inferred that there is some eternal substance which is separate from matter. And he adds this argument: that no science demonstrates the existence of its own subject,[10] but rather it supposes that as self-evident or as demonstrated in another science. But God, or immaterial substances, belong to the object[11] of metaphysics; therefore, they are not proven to exist by a metaphysician. Since, then, their existence is not self-evident, it is assumed to be demonstrated by a philosopher [of nature].

---

7 Cf. Section 2, §§ 2 and 6.

8 Cf. Averroes, *In Metaphys.* XII, t. 5, in *Aristotelis Metaphysicorum libri XIIII. cum Averrois Cordubensis in eosdem commentariis* (ed. Venetiis: apud Junctas, 1574), VIII, fol. 293r1.

9 Cf. *In Physic.* I, t. 83 (Venetiis: Apud Junctas, 1562), fol. 47r2–v1; and *In Physic.* VII, t. 3, fol. 349r 2.

10 For this, cf. Aristotle, *Posterior Analytics* 1.10.76b4–8. Aristotle seems to restrict this principle to particular sciences and not to apply it to metaphysics; cf. *Metaphysics* 6.1.1025b1–16; for Suárez's recognition of this, see *DM* I, s. 4, n. 4, vol. 25, p. 29.

11 Note for all intents here the equivalence of "subject" and "object."

3. The second opinion, directly contrary to the last, is that the task here belongs to a metaphysician and not to a natural philosopher. This is what Avicenna holds, in Book 1, Chapter 1, of his *Metaphysics*, where, on the other side, from the fact that this science proves that God exists he concludes that God does not belong to the object of metaphysics.[12] He holds the same in his *Metaphysics*, Book 8, Chapters 1 and 3.[13] Alexander of Aphrodisias, [commenting on] *Metaphysics*, Book 12, text 6;[14] Albert [the Great, commenting on] *Physics*, Book 1, the last chapter;[15] and [Duns] Scotus, in [his commentary on the *Sentences*], Question 2 of the Prologue to Book 1,[16] have also held the same. Their basis is that otherwise [natural] philosophy would be more noble than metaphysics, and metaphysics would in the greatest way depend upon that [natural philosophy], if it took from it the knowledge of God and the separate substances, even as regards their existence.

4. *Third.* – A possible third opinion is that this task can belong to both physics and metaphysics separately or to each of them in full (*in solidum*). I do not find this opinion explicitly in any author, but it can be based upon Aristotle. For he, in Book 8 of the *Physics* and in Book 12 of the *Metaphysics*, has proven that there exists in things some principle which is immobile and separate from matter.[17] Therefore, he thought that [principle] pertained to both sciences and without dependence of one on the other. For since metaphysics is more excellent

---

12 Cf. Avicenna, *Liber de philosophia prima ... I–V*, ed. Van Riet (Louvain/Leiden, 1977), Tractatus I, c. 1, p. 4.

13 Cf. *ibid.*, Tr. VIII, cc. 1 and 3, ed. Van Riet (1980), pp. 376–81, 393–97. While in these places, within his *Metaphysics*, Avicenna is dealing with proof for the existence of God, I have not found him here treating the question of which science proves that existence.

14 Cf. Alexander of Aphrodisias, *In Aristotelis Metaphysica Commentaria*, 12, 1, ed. M. Hayduck, in *Commentaria in Aristotelem Graeca* I (Berolini: Typis et Impensis Georgii Reimeri, 1891), p. 671. [This portion of Alexander's commentary was most likely the work of Michael of Ephesius (11th and 12th cent.); cf. Hayduck, *ibid.*, Praefatio, p. v.].

15 Cf. Beati Alberti Magni Ratisbonensis Episcopi, O.P., *In libros Physicorum* I, Tr. 3, c. 18, in *Opera omnia* (Lugduni: Sumptibus Claudii Prost, et al, 1651), vol. 2, p. 55.

16 Cf. Duns Scotus, *Ordinatio* prol., pars. 3, q. 1–3, ad arg. 2, in *Joannis Duns Scoti Opera omnia* I (Civitas Vaticana: Typis Polyglottis Vaticanis, 1950), pp. 130–31, n. 194.

17 On Aristotle's different doctrines in his *Physics* and his *Metaphysics*, cf. Joseph Owens, "The Reality of the Aristotelian Separate Movers," *Review of Metaphysics*, 3 (1950), 319–37.

it cannot depend in this upon physics. But since physics is first, at least for us, in the order of generation,[18] it also cannot in this depend upon metaphysics. For it completes its own demonstration before metaphysics is acquired.

5. A possible fourth opinion is that this task belongs to both sciences not separately but together, in such way that neither can complete the demonstration without the help of the other. For physics begins it while metaphysics perfects it. Soncinas [Paulus Barbus Soncinas] seems to think almost in this way in his [commentary on] *Metaphysics*, Book 12, Question 1, where, although in the first conclusion he asserts that properly it belongs to metaphysics to demonstrate the existence of separate substances, immediately in the second conclusion he adds that every medium by which this is demonstrated is either natural [i.e. physical] or concludes only in virtue of some natural medium.[19] Javellus [Chrysostomus Javelli], in the same Book [of the *Metaphysics*], Question 3,[20] makes another distinction, saying that to demonstrate the existence of separate substances as such or in general belongs to natural philosophy, but to show that among these there is one First, which is God, is the task of the metaphysician. [To support this] he offers St. Thomas, in *Contra Gentiles*, Book 1, Chapter 13, saying that Aristotle, in Book 8 of the *Physics*, arrived only at this that he proved with respect to the motion of heaven the need to distinguish a mover from a *mobile* and that the same mover was separate from the heaven; but then in *Metaphysics*, Book 12, from this mover he progressed farther to demonstrate that God exists.[21]

6. *A judgment about the opinions presented.* – Of these opinions, I think the second is without qualification true and the fourth can be understood in an acceptable sense. For, as it is stated by its authors, it cannot be proven absolutely. However, there is no more appropriate or efficacious argument confirming our own opinion than the employment and, as it were, the experience of the physical and the metaphysical means by which this is usually proven, examining the efficacy of both.

---

18 Since we naturally know through sensation, we naturally come to know physics, which deals with sensible things, before we come to know metaphysics which abstracts from sensible things.

19 Pauli Soncinatis, O.P., *Quaestiones metaphysicales acutissimae* XII, q. 1 (Venetiis, 1588; reprinted: Frankfurt: Minerva, 1967), p. 298.

20 Cf. Chrysostomi Iavelli Canapicii, *In omnibus Metaphysicae libris quaesita testualia metaphysicali modo determinata. In quibus clarissime resolvuntur dubia Aristotelis, et Commentatoris, eaque ut plurimum decisa habentur iuxta Thomisticum dogma.* XII, q. 3 (Venetiis, Apud Haeredes Ioannis Mariae Bonelli, 1576), fols. 320v–22v.

21 Cf. St. Thomas, *Summa contra Gentiles* I, c. 13, in *Opera*, vol. 13, pp. 30–34.

Accordingly, there are just two physical means which we can use to demonstrate separate substance either in general or in the particular case of a first uncreated being.[22]

An Examination of the Physical Arguments by which God Is Proven to Exist.

7. *The first [argument], taken from local motion, is treated at length.* – The first means is taken from the motion of heaven, which Aristotle used, in Book 8 of the *Physics*, and again used in Book 12, Text 26 [*sic*][23] of the *Metaphysics*, where from the eternal motion of the heavens he came to demonstrate a first immobile mover. But this means, if it is taken essentially and precisely, appears in many ways to be ineffective for demonstrating that there is in reality some immaterial substance, let alone for demonstrating a first and uncreated substance.

And first of all I am laying aside (*omitto*) that principle on which this whole proof is based: "Every thing which is moved is moved by another,"[24] as up to now not sufficiently demonstrated in every kind of motion or action.[25] For there are many things which seem to move themselves by virtual act and to reduce themselves to formal act,[26] as may be seen in an appetite or a will, and in water reducing itself to its original coolness.[27] Therefore, the same thing can happen in the case of local motion. And in this way heaven can be said to be moved by nothing else than itself through its own form or some innate power from which such motion results, just as motion downwards results in a stone from its intrinsic heaviness (*gravitas*). From this it follows that it is a question still to be decided whether heaven is or is not moved by an Intelligence. In what way, therefore, from principles so uncertain can a true demonstration be fashioned by which it will be proven that God exists?

22 In what follows it will be clear that the two physical means are (1) the motion of the heavens [cf. §§ 7–17], and (2) the human soul [§§ 18–19].

23 Probably: Text 36, i.e. *Metaphysics* 12.7.1072a24–27.

24 On this, cf. James A. Weisheipl, O.P., "The Principle *Omne quod movetur ab alio movetur* in Medieval Physics," *Isis*, 56 (1965), pp. 26–45; Reprinted in *Nature and Motion in the Middle Ages*, ed. W.E. Carroll (Washington, DC: Catholic University of America Press, 1985), pp. 75–97.

25 In an earlier Disputation, Suárez has remarked that Aristotle himself came to this principle through an induction whose instances were all material changes with the obvious result that the principle itself would apply only to bodily change; cf. *DM* XVIII, 7, n. 11, vol. 25, p. 633; *ibid.*, n. 43, p. 644.

26 That is, things which in virtue of some intrinsic power pass to an actualization of that same power. For discussion of virtual act as it is found here, cf. J. Owens, C.SS.R, "The Conclusion of the Prima Via," *The Modern Schoolman*, 30 (1952), esp. pp. 208–11.

27 On this, cf. *DM* XVIII, s. 3, n. 4, vol. 25, p. 616.

8. But then, let us stipulate the truth of that principle, "Every thing which is moved is moved by another" (for rightly understood it is indeed probable enough)[28] and following that let us stipulate that heaven is moved by another. By what necessary or evident consequence, I ask, can it be concluded from this principle and from the motion of heaven that there is some immaterial substance? For either that is inferred from eternal motion or from motion alone. If the first, the inference is immediately made from a false principle and thus there is in fact no demonstration, whatever Aristotle may have thought.[29]

9. It is possible to answer from Scotus and others that the motion of heaven as a matter of fact is not eternal, but that of itself it can be so. For, since it is circular, of itself it has neither a beginning nor an end; and therefore the mover of heaven of itself is apt to move with an eternal motion, and from that it is very well concluded that such a mover is a spiritual substance.

But this reply supposes something not only uncertain, but even less probable, namely, that the motion of heaven could be from eternity. For, even though from its own specific nature it does not demand a definite beginning or an end, and therefore it could have begun before any particular instant, nevertheless, from the generic nature of motion and of a successive being, an eternal duration without a beginning is incompatible with it.

This is so because otherwise [that motion] could never have been completed (*pertransiri*). And it is most of all so because every creature existing from eternity must necessarily endure through an eternity in that condition in which it has been created – not because it will endure in that way for eternity ever after (*a parte post*), for clearly that is not necessary, but because it would have necessarily remained in that condition through an infinite duration and without a beginning from ever before (*a parte ante*) – whether that is a condition of substance or existence, or of quality, or of position, or of any other of this kind.

For if a thing is created from eternity in some condition, that condition also has been created from eternity. Therefore, that condition also has a duration without beginning. Moreover, such a duration necessarily is infinite from the side of one extreme. For if it is finite in such way that it is bounded by two extremes, already it has a beginning and an end, and consequently it is not eternal. But if that condition is said to have endured through only one indivisible instant of our time, this is much more incompatible with eternity, because such a duration is by far more brief (if it can be said so) than any finite time. Indeed, that as such is not a genuine duration but the beginning of a duration. Hence, that instant is rather inferred to be the extrinsic beginning of the motion which is immediately

28 For further discussion of this principle as Suárez understands it, cf. *DM* XVIII, s. 7, vol. 25, pp. 631–50.

29 For Aristotle's thought, cf. *Metaphysics* 12.6.1071b20–22.

following, and therefore that motion is not eternal but rather temporal. Because, therefore, a thing cannot be created even from eternity except in a definite and determinate condition and in that condition it necessarily remains through some infinite duration, therefore it is contradictory that motion be eternal. For through motion a thing begins to be deprived of that condition in which it was created.

This is easily illustrated by an example in the matter itself of which we are treating. Let us suppose that the heaven of the sun[30] was created from eternity: it was [then] necessary that the star of the sun be created in a definite and determinate place. Therefore, let us suppose that it was created in our hemisphere.[31] It would have been necessary [then], for the reason given, that it would have endured through a certain eternity in that place and in our hemisphere. Therefore, from eternity that heaven could not be moved; otherwise, neither through a whole day or a [whole] hour, nor through any duration which could have coexisted with a day or an hour, would the sun have endured in that place in which it was created. Therefore, for this reason, to omit others, I think that eternity is incompatible with motion and motion includes an incompatibility with a kind of immutability which eternity includes, and therefore, not only is motion not eternal in fact, but neither can it be so. Therefore, from "eternal motion" an eternal or immaterial mover cannot be inferred.

10. You will say: granted that it is incompatible with motion on its part to have been eternal, nevertheless, a mover can be understood to be of itself apt to move eternally if this would not be contradictory from the side of the *mobile* or of motion, and this would be enough for the force of the reasoning that was made. But this aptitude on the part of the mover can be inferred from the motion of heaven, because it can endure for eternity, since it does not have a contrary and it does not of itself demand a certain time. Therefore, the mover, insofar as it exists in itself, has the power to move eternally. Therefore, in like manner, insofar as it is of itself, it can do that, from ever before (*a parte ante*) just as for ever

30 That is, the solid sphere around the earth which was thought to be carrying the body of the sun. In the astronomy found in the Sphere of Sacrobosco, the universe is geocentric and the earth is enclosed within nine spheres ordered up from it as follows: that of the moon, followed by those of Mercury, Venus, the Sun, Mars, Jupiter, Saturn, the "Sphere of the Fixed Stars," and the *Primum Mobile*. Each of the spheres below that of the Fixed Stars carries a planet (with the moon and sun counted as such), which then has its proper zodiacal motion even as it is carried within the sphere which encloses it. For this, cf. Lynn Thorndike, *The Sphere of Sacrobosco ...*, *Tractatus de spera Magistri Iohannis de Sacrobosco*, cap. 1, p. 79. For glimpses of Suárez's views in this regard, cf.: *De opere sex dierum* I, c. 10, n. 10, vol. 3, p. 57; *ibid.*, c. 8, n. 16, vol. 3, p. 153.

31 For Suárez on the place in which the sun was created, cf. *De opere sex dierum* II, c. 3, nn. 10–12, vol. 3, pp. 109–10.

after (*a parte post*) – if it is not otherwise impossible from the side of the effect. Likewise, the duration of that motion, so prolonged and invariable or uniform, plainly shows that its mover moves without weariness or fatigue. Consequently, insofar as it is of itself, it can always and perpetually move, and thus it is immaterial.

But, first of all, the inference from eternity after (*a parte post*) to eternity before (*a parte ante*) is not correctly drawn. For a motion begun in time can endure to eternity because a motion which is supposed to be in reality itself is always finite, and the whole infinity which is understood in a future motion will never exist in reality itself in such way that at some time it may be true to say that the whole infinity exists or has existed – which will not be so if the motion is supposed to have been produced from eternity, for in that case its whole infinity would have existed in reality. Hence, to have power to move forever in the future is only to have power to cause a motion to infinity; but to have power to move from eternity is to have power to cause an infinite motion, which is very different and more inconceivable (*repugnans*). Therefore, from the capacity to cause the first, it is not right to infer a potency on the part of the mover also to cause the second, especially because there is no potency to that which involves a contradiction in itself.

11. But wait: let us grant, because the conjecture is probable, that the mover of heaven has the power to cause an eternal motion, or even let us imagine that it has moved the heaven from eternity in the same way and invariably – how from this is it rightly inferred that that mover is an immaterial substance?

You will say: [it is such] because it does not grow tired in its moving. But what if someone imagines that it is not one and the same mover but several movers who move in turns (and therefore in this way never grow tired) without resting before it is necessary either to interrupt or to slow down the motion? For although this is a figment, nevertheless from the motion alone of the heaven it cannot be shown to be false, except by weakening the intended inference and argument, as I am now explaining. For although it is true that the mover of the heaven does not grow tired in its moving, it does not from that follow that it is immaterial, but it follows only that the "moveable" (*mobile*) does not resist or react when it is being moved and that the mover is eternal. But both can be true apart from the immateriality of the mover, just as the sun, if it would exist from eternity, would not become tired from perpetually illuminating, because it illumines the medium without resistance or itself being acted upon (*repassio*).

However, as Soncinas says above,[32] from Aristotle, *Metaphysics*, Book 12, Text 30,[33] from eternal motion it is immediately inferred that the mover is not in

32 *Quaestiones* ..., XII, q. 1 (ed. Venetiis, 1588), p. 298.

33 Cf. *Metaphysics* 12.6.1071b20–22.

potency, because it is always actually moving. But a being which is in act and in no way in potency is immaterial.

But, whatever the mind of Aristotle, about which we will see in what follows, that argument is extremely ineffective. For it only concludes that one who is always actually moving is not in potency to moving, but not that it is, like a pure act, in no way in potency – otherwise, an angel perpetually moving the heaven would also be a pure act. But if it is not correctly inferred to be a pure act, it also cannot be inferred to be an immaterial substance. For if, notwithstanding the action of moving, it can be perpetually in potency to other actions or receptions, by the same argument someone could say it is in potency to material motions or qualities, and it could not be shown from eternal motion alone that this is more contradictory (*repugnans*) than that. But if we are speaking about being in potency only with respect to substantial being, it is true that an eternal mover is not in potency in this way; however, from this it is not inferred to be immaterial. For a moveable (*mobile*) which is such with respect to eternal local motion also is not in potency in this way, and still it does not from that become immaterial or incorporeal, as is evident in the case of heaven [itself]. Therefore, from eternity of motion or from the perpetual power of moving it cannot be correctly deduced that there is an immaterial substance that moves.

12. And from this reasoning, *a fortiori* it seems much less possible to deduce that this is inferred from the motion of heaven taken either absolutely or as temporal, because eternal motion is something greater than motion simply. But let us argue further in more detail (*ex propriis*); for the heaven can be supposed to be moved by another in two ways. In one way, as by someone impressing an internal impetus which would be immediately causative of the motion,[34] as a heavy [body] is said to be moved by the generator [of that body]. In another way, as by a proximate separate mover, the way a wheel is moved by a hand. And indeed I think that up to now it has not been demonstrated which of these ways is more true, although the second is more probable, reasoning by conjecture and because the first motion does not seem necessary for the heaven because of the heaven's peculiar nature. For since it is inanimate and it always remains in its connatural place, there is no reason why because of itself it requires motion; and, therefore,

34 Suárez was very much aware of, and to some extent influenced by, the impetus theory of the later Scholastics. For other passages which display this, cf.: *DM* XVIII, s. 3, n. 20, vol. 25, pp 621–22; *ibid.*, s. 4, n. 3, p. 624; *ibid.*, s. 7, n. 26, p. 638; *ibid.*, s. 8, n. 5, p. 652; *ibid.*, n. 22, p. 659; *DM* XXI, s. 2, n. 27, p. 801; *DM* XXII, s. 2, nn. 5–6, p. 811; *DM* XXXV, s. 6, nn. 24–25, vol. 26, pp. 475–76; *DM* XLIII, s. 3, n. 1, p. 637. On the general issue of the doctrine of impetus against its ancient and Scholastic background as well as its comparison with the modern doctrine of momentum, see: James A. Weisheipl, O.P., "Natural and Compulsory Movement," *The New Scholasticism*, 29 (1955), pp. 50–81.

there is no internal active impetus needed for such motion. Hence, that motion is necessary because of the conservation, the governance and the perfection of this world; and therefore it is more probable that it comes from an extrinsic mover. However, because this is not certain, it is necessary to speak about both members [i.e. both ways of motion].

13. If, therefore, we suppose the heaven to be moved by another in the first way, nothing can be proven from that. For, even though from that it be correctly inferred that there is another substance prior to the heaven, nevertheless, this is not in this way so much proven as it is presupposed. For that mover of heaven is not said to move the heaven in any other way except because it impresses an internal, intrinsic, and connatural impetus on it, which impetus is impressed only by the generator or the author of the nature. Therefore, that argument presupposes that the heaven has an author by which it has been created. But this is not demonstrated by that reasoning nor can it be demonstrated from physical motion alone, but only by the metaphysical means which we will afterwards see. This is because for the local motion of the heaven it matters nothing that the heaven is created or that it is of itself a necessary being.

Therefore, precisely from that motion it cannot be demonstrated that the heaven has been created by another, but at most it can immediately be inferred that it is a being which is of itself imperfect inasmuch as it is capable of motion, and from this it can be further gathered that it is not a being which is of itself necessary because so great an imperfection does not exist together with such perfection. However, this now pertains to the metaphysician, as is evident from the terms themselves. Therefore, from this motion by another it cannot be demonstrated, but rather it must be supposed, that there is another substance superior to the heaven. And much less can it be proven that that substance is immaterial. For if someone imagines that the heaven was created by a certain superior corporeal and material cause and that it received from the same cause an intrinsic impetus by which it is continuously moved, how, by means of local and physical motion alone, could he be convinced of his error?

14. And this argument is valid, even if we suppose the heaven to be moved by another extrinsic and immediate proper mover. For what does the motion of heaven possess which would require that the mover be immaterial?

For either it is the perpetuity of the motion or its long span, which of itself can last perpetually. But this is not it – because for that it is enough that there be a similar duration and perpetuity in the mover and in its power, which it could have even if it were corporeal, just as the heaven itself or the sun has it.[35]

Or it would be the invariability of the motion, which indicates an indefatigible power in the mover. But, omitting other things which have been mentioned

35 On this, cf. *DM* XXX, s. 2, n. 2, vol. 26, p. 64.

above,[36] this at most shows the mover to be incorruptible. However, it could be incorruptible even if it were corporeal, just like the heaven itself.

Or it would be the harmony[37] or the order of the celestial motions, with a wonderful proportion and uniform diversity (*difformitas*),[38] apt and fitted for the conservation and governance of this sublunar world.[39] And this indeed does show plainly enough that the author of the universe is intellectual and that he has created and governs all things with supreme wisdom. But [it does not show] that the immediate mover of each [sphere of] heaven is intellectual. For someone could imagine that to each [sphere of] heaven there has been given a proportionate

---

36 Cf. § 11, this Section.

37 Here I am, with Rábade Romeo *et al.* (*Disputaciones metafísicas*, vol. 4, p. 253), reading "concentus" instead of the Vivès edition's "conceptus." The Mainz (1605) edition also has "concentus;" cf. R. Patris Francisci Suarez e Societate Jeus, *Metaphysicarum disputationum*, tomus posterior (Moguntiae: Excudebat Balthasarus Lippius, Sumptib. Arnoldi Mylii, 1605), p. 20.

38 On this, cf. a later Jesuit who was broadly a follower of Suárez: "A created agent commonly operates within its own sphere of activity in a uniformly diverse way: that is, [it operates] more intensely in closer regions and more weakly in more remote regions. This is clear from experience itself. For fire produces a more intense heat in a neighboring body than it does in one which is distant. ... I say 'commonly' (1) because when the subject [of the agent's activity] is equally disposed, the agent can operate more effectively in a remote subject than [it does] in one which is less remote – as is seen in a mirror, in which the sun produces a more intense light than it does in an opaque body, for example, in lead, even though this last is closer. And (2) because if an agent and a patient were intimately [com]penetrated, the agent could produce an equally intense effect throughout the patient." (*Agens creatum intra suam sphaeram communiter operatur uniformiter difformiter: idest, intensius in partibus propinquis; remissius in partibus remotioribus. Hoc liquet experientia ipsa. Nam ignis intensiorem calorem producit in corpore vicino, quam in distanti: ... Dixi communiter 1. Quia quando subiectum non est aeque dispositum, potest agens efficacius operari in subiecto remotiori, quam in minus remoto, ut videtur in speculo, in quo Sol intensiorem lucem producit, quam in corpore opaco, v.g. plumbo, licet istud sit vicinius. 2. Quia si agens, et passum essent intime penetrata, possent agens in passum effectum aeque intensum producere.*) Miguel Viñas, S.J., *Philosophia Scholastica*, Laurea II, Pars I. Lib. III (*De Actionibus Corporis Naturalis*), Controv. VIII (*De Alteratione*), Exam. VI, Punct. I: p. 326. Interpreting Suárez then in the present context, my best guess is that he is speaking of the diversity in the uniform motions of the heavenly spheres, as they are nearer to or farther from the earth and as they proceed at different angles and with different speeds relative to one another around the earth.

39 That is, the world of our immediate experience which lies beneath the last situated heavenly sphere, which is that of the moon.

mover which acts by way of nature and that this order arises from several movers with diverse powers. Then, even if we grant that in some way from that it be inferred that the movers of the heavens are intellectual, it would not, however, be inferred that they are incorporeal. For even if the angels were ethereal, as many have stated, they could move the heaven and by virtue of the motion of heaven alone one could not be convinced that this is an error.

15. Some say that from the very fact that heaven has a separate mover the immediate conclusion is that this is incorporeal, because heaven is the first body – otherwise [a series of bodies] would proceed to infinity. However, this proves nothing, for [in this hypothesis] heaven is without proof supposed to be the first body. But while it can be said to be the first visible [body], there could be other prior invisible [bodies], or it could be the first among simple inanimate [bodies], while there are other absolutely more prior and more excellent [bodies] animated by intellectual forms, which can be supposed to be finite in number, and therefore it would not be necessary to proceed to infinity.

But the argument can be pressed: for from the motion of heaven it is proven on one hand that the mover is incorruptible and on the other hand that it is intellectual. Finally, from this it can be concluded to be immaterial, because an incorruptible body can be of no use for an intellectual act, and therefore there cannot be an intellectual principle that by its nature is united to an incorruptible body. Thus if the mover of the heaven is a complete, intellectual, and incorruptible substance, it must necessarily be separate from matter.

The answer is that this argument, which we will take up again more at length below[40] when we treat of created intelligences, is somewhat probable. However, the argument is not based now on physical and local motion alone, but it is partly supported from the science of the soul (*doctrina de anima*)[41] and partly and chiefly it is based on this principle: that an intellectual form is not united to matter unless it be helped by that for its intellectual operations, which is a metaphysical principle, and thus this demonstration, however it is pursued, is metaphysical, even though the way is prepared for it in some manner by physical arguments, which indeed, as has been stated, are not evident but at most probable.

16. All of this is generally valid with respect to substances moving the heavens – from which *a fortiori* it is evident that by virtue of heavenly motion alone we cannot conclude that there is some first immaterial and uncreated being. For the motion of heaven of itself leads only to some proximate mover of heaven, in which [that motion] of itself does not require and consequently does not demon-

---

40 Cf. *DM* XXXV, s. 6, nn. 15–30, vol. 26, pp. 472–77.

41 This would be the philosophical psychology based upon Aristotle's work "On the Soul." For this, cf. Suárez, *Tractatus de Anima*, vol. 3, pp. 401–816.

strate, as we have explained, those perfections. Therefore, neither from that motion nor from any physical effect is it possible to ascertain whether that mover is one for all the heavens or many. And if there are many, are they all reduced to one first, from which they depend or by which they are in some way moved and by what kind of motion? Therefore, much less could it be proven from the motion of heaven that there is some first being in which those perfections come together. But it will always be necessary to add some metaphysical means by which that may be concluded.

17. What therefore some say – that although simply from heavenly motion those properties may not be concluded to be in any [or every] mover whatsoever of heaven, still they are concluded to be in that which of itself and by its own power moves heaven; for what moves of itself and by a power which is completely its own, also exists of itself and therefore is uncreated and consequently immaterial – this, I say, is not relevant. For this proof, however it is formulated, is not physical but rather metaphysical. For the whole force of the argument consists in this middle [term] "moving of itself" – which is not acquired from motion alone. For motion indeed shows in the mover a power to move, but whether it has that power of itself or from another, and whether it operates through that power with dependence or without dependence upon another, is not shown from motion alone.

Again, in what way from that property of moving of itself other properties may be inferred can be much less shown from motion or a physical means, but rather it is necessary to use metaphysical means. A clear sign of this is that from all efficient causality the same consequence can be followed up to a cause that is efficient of itself, which of itself abstracts from physical motion and from efficiency with or without matter. Therefore, from heavenly motion alone there is no way that is sufficient for constructing a demonstration of this kind.

18. *The second means, taken from the operations of the rational soul and its essence.* – Another means or another way can be taken from the operations of the rational soul and the knowledge of its substance that is derived from those operations. For in things which involve matter, there is none either more like God or more immediately depending on Him in its being and its operation than the rational soul. Therefore, in no physical means does it seem that God can be more known than in the contemplation of the rational soul and its operations. But it is evident that this means is physical; for although the rational soul is immaterial, it is however a form of matter. Similarly, its operation, although it is in itself spiritual, in some way depends upon a body, and therefore the consideration of the soul joined to the body and of its operations pertains to the physicist (*physicus*).[42]

42 That is, the philosopher of nature. On this, cf. *DM* I, s. 2, n. 19, vol. 25, pp. 18–19. On later seventeenth and eighteenth century thinkers who, influenced by Suárez, also

19. However, this way also cannot serve to demonstrate anything about God, except by supposing something demonstrated in metaphysics and by always using metaphysical means and principles in order to ultimately conclude to the thing [in question]. For unless we suppose that the rational soul has a Supreme Author by which it was first created, from the perfections of the soul similar and better perfections in God could not be demonstrated. However, that the soul has a cause of this kind cannot be demonstrated by a [natural] philosopher from the operations of the soul alone, but it is necessary to use some principle common to other agents and created effects, about which we will presently see. Therefore, from this physical means, [precisely] as it is physical, it cannot be demonstrated that there is one uncreated being.

However, if we suppose that the soul has a superior cause of its being, which [cause] we call the first being or God, indeed it is very well demonstrated that if the soul is intellectual, free, immaterial, immortal, and the like (which simply express perfection) much more are all of these to be found in God.[43] However, this demonstration is based upon a metaphysical means and a general principle that the perfections of an effect exist in a more noble way in a principal cause and especially in a first cause. But a demonstration properly belongs to that science to which the means of demonstration belongs.

Add, with respect to the attribute of immateriality, that from this precise means God cannot be proven to be completely immaterial but at most [immaterial] in the manner of the rational soul.

We conclude, therefore, that all physical means are of themselves insufficient for demonstrating that there is some first uncreated being. Indeed, it has been shown indirectly that of themselves they do not suffice in order to demonstrate what or of what kind that being is by the way in which it can be demonstrated through effects, but this is always the task of the metaphysician. At the same time, however, it has been in some way explained how [natural] philosophy to some extent may prepare the way, offer an occasion, and also present effects, by which it may help to construct a demonstration of this kind – which will be more explained in what follows.

---

treated the rational soul in physics, cf. Martin Grabmann, "Die '*Disputationes Metaphysicae*' des Franz Suarez in ihrer methodischen Eigenwart und Fortwirkung," in *Mittelalterisches Geistesleben*, vol. 1 (München: Hueber, 1926), p. 545.

43 After Suárez has metaphysically proven the existence of God as being from Himself (*ens a se*) he will use the rational nature of man to argue to God's intelligence; cf. *DM* XXIX, s. 2, n. 21, below. Also, in at least one place, he has affirmed that any created intelligence can come to the existence of God from itself as His effect; cf. *DM* XXXV, s. 4, n. 4, vol. 26, p. 460. Evidently, the way in this would be through its own being as an effect to the being of God as its cause.

Metaphysical Arguments and Means Are Examined.

20. In the second place, it now remains to show how metaphysics can demonstrate that there is some uncreated being. This we will now briefly sketch, because already in Section 1 of the preceding *Disputation* [i.e. 28], almost all things which could be said here have been mentioned.

First, therefore, in place of that physical principle, "Everything which is moved, is moved by another," we must take another metaphysical one which is far more evident: "Everything which is made, is made by another," whether it is made in the sense of being created, being generated,[44] or in any other sense. This principle is demonstrated from this – that nothing can effect itself. For a thing which comes to be by being effected acquires being; but a thing which makes or produces [anything], is supposed to have being. Therefore, it is clearly repugnant that one same thing make itself; for before a thing is, it cannot be in either formal or virtual act to make itself. And for this reason, this principle: "Everything which is produced is produced by another," is far more evident than that: "Everything which is moved is moved by another." For what is moved is presupposed to be, in which being there can be understood some virtual act to move itself. However, what is made is not presupposed to be, but rather it is supposed not to be before it is made. But in that non-being there cannot be a power to make itself. And therefore that principle, properly understood, is evident with regard to a first and true making – so as to now abstain from the theological question of whether the same thing could exist twice and as first existing it could concur in the making of itself as existing secondly and in another place. For even if such a miracle were accepted, it would not weaken the stated principle – both because here we are treating of natural and proper causation or production and also because that second making in the case described would not so much deserve the name of production as of conservation, since it presupposes an existing thing.

21. Therefore, this principle having been stated, the demonstration is concluded as follows. Every being is either made or not made, that is uncreated. But all beings in the totality [of being] cannot be made. Therefore, it is necessary that there be some being which is not made, or which is uncreated. The major [premise] is evident, because: of two contradictories one must be found in something or other.[45] The minor [premise] is proven: because every being which is made is made by another. Therefore, either that other by which it is made is itself made or not. If it is not made, then there is given some uncreated being, which is what we are looking for. But if it also is made, it will be necessary that it be made by another, about which the same question will have to be then asked. Thus, in the end, either we will have to stop with a Being that is not made, or we will have to

44 Cf. Aristotle, *Metaphysics* 7.7.1032a13–14; *ibid.* 8.1033a24.

45 On this, cf. *DM* III, s. 3, n. 5, vol. 25, pp. 112–13.

proceed to infinity, or we will have to reason in a circle. But we cannot reason in a circle, nor can we proceed to infinity; therefore we must necessarily stop with some Being that is not made.

22. The first part of the minor [premise] is explained and proven; for I say [reasoning in] a circle is committed if someone says that one thing is produced by another and this in turn is produced by that which it itself had produced, either immediately or mediately and after many generations. For in this way someone could imagine that everything is produced by some other thing distinct from itself and that no thing is unproduced. Therefore, we say that this circle is impossible and equally incompatible with that principle: "Everything which is produced is produced by another," as that the same thing produce itself. For if one thing is made by another which has been made by itself, mediately at least, and as it were virtually, it is causing itself. Likewise, because existence is supposed in a thing which makes another, if it has existence by causation, it is therefore also supposed that it has [already] been made. Therefore, it cannot be made by its own effect.

23. You will say this argument proves that a thing which makes another thing, as it is existing while it is causing that thing, is not made by the same thing which it is causing insofar as it receives being from that thing. Yet, nevertheless, that thing which has caused another can be understood to lose that being which it then had and still afterwards [it can be understood] to be reproduced either by the same thing which it itself had made or by some effect of that thing – for example, among men that a dead father be generated by a son, or a grandfather by a grandson or by a great grandson, or after the hundredth generation. To be sure, the Pythagoreans, who thought that the same souls returned to bodies,[46] were easily able to philosophize in this way.

24. However, this evasion has no place, unless there is joined with it a process to infinity. For, in fact in those circles or changes of generations we stop at some first ungenerated producer, and about that producer in no way can it be said that it was made by any of its effects, because it is supposed to exist before every one of its effects. And in that case an argument is fashioned: because either that first author of the generations is absolutely not made, and then we conclude to what we intend: namely, that there is some Being which is absolutely not made; or it also has been made by another, and about that other the same question returns, which will never stop until we come to an uncreated being. But if in those circles and changes of generations we never stop at any first generator,

46 Cf. Suárez, *Tractatus de Anima*, I, c. 5, n. 2, vol. 3, p. 499. On the Pythagorean doctrine of transmigration of souls, cf. G.S. Kirk and J.E. Raven, *The Presocratic Philosophers: A Critical History with a Selection of Texts* (Cambridge: The University Press, 1960), nn. 268–70, pp. 222–23.

there is already added besides the said circle a process to infinity and moreover there are multiplied problems, namely, that the same individuals are reproduced through natural generations, and the like, without which that process to infinity would suffice, if it could exist.[47]

There Cannot Be a Process to Infinity in Efficient Causes and Their Effects.

25. It remains, therefore, that we prove the second part of the minor [premise] stated above,[48] which is that it is impossible to proceed to infinity in the emanation of one being from another, which Aristotle, in Book 2, Chapter 2, of his *Metaphysics*, demonstrated in every kind of cause.[49] The principal argument seems to be that from a process to infinity it follows that all causality is destroyed. For in essentially ordered causes the latter depend upon the former and all the latter upon some first. But if we posit a process to infinity, there is no first. Therefore, there will be no causality.

Others[50] explain this as follows: if we proceeded to infinity, we would never arrive at the effect, for the reason that something infinite cannot be crossed. To explain this, let us suppose that this process can occur in two ways, that is, either by ascending from lower to higher causes, or opposite-wise by descending from universal to proximate causes. In this second way, it is evident that we must necessarily stop at some cause that is last or proximate to the effect, because otherwise we would never reach the effect. For it cannot be understood that an effect be produced in being and that it not be produced proximately and immediately from some cause.

Therefore, it is the first process, turned upward, which contains difficulty and which pertains to the present question. In this process, therefore, the argument made does not seem effective. For that progression to infinity can be understood either [1] between proximate causes and those more and more remote, which are said to be subordinated by accident, and it is not necessary that these all concur simultaneously, nor indeed that they exist together at once when the effect is produced, but in a certain succession, as a son is [caused] by a father, and a father by a grandfather, etc. Or [2] [it can be understood to be] between essentially (*per se*) subordinated causes, which simultaneously and each in its own order immediately have influence on the effect, as a first and a second cause.[51]

47 That is, such a process, if it were possible, does not need these added difficulties.

48 See § 21, this Section.

49 Cf. *Metaphysics* 2.2.994a1–b20.

50 See, e.g.: Dominicus Bañez, O.P., *Scholastica commentaria in primam partem Summae Theologiae* I, q. 2, a. 3, ed. P. Luis Urbano (Madrid: Editorial FEDA, 1934), pp. 115–16. Bañez's commentary dates from 1584, thirteen years before the appearance of Suárez's *Disputationes metaphysicae*.

51 On the broader background here of simultaneity and grades of causes, cf. Jacob

Therefore, in the first way it does not seem contradictory (*repugnare*), especially according to Aristotle's opinion, to progress to infinity. For if the world had existed from eternity, a process like this would have been necessary. But this process to infinity is enough to avoid the argument that was made, because each thing will be said to be made by another thing and never will an end be reached in a thing not made.

But in the second way, even if a process to infinity were granted, we could arrive at an effect, because causes subordinated essentially in this way do not operate successively one after another, but rather simultaneously.[52] However, it is not contradictory that infinite causes, if they exist, operate simultaneously in this way. For what is said: "that something infinite cannot be crossed," is true insofar as this signifies a succession. For, if one thing is numbered after or acts after another, [the succession] will never be exhausted on the side on which it is infinite. But that a simultaneous whole, or a whole multitude of causes existing simultaneously, also simultaneously act and exert influence on the same effect is not against the nature of the infinite.

Finally, he who will suppose this infinite subordination of causes, will deny that they all depend upon some first cause. Hence, Aristotle, when he supposes the contrary, seems to beg the question.

26. Nevertheless, evidently (I think) it can be shown that we must necessarily stop at some first unproduced cause beginning also from causes essentially subordinated, of which one essentially and actually depends upon another either in being or in acting.

First, it is possible to bring forward here all the arguments by which is proven the impossibility of an actually infinite multitude in things, without which multitude that process to infinity in subordinated causes cannot be understood. But I am omitting these [arguments], both because they are general and remote [from the present concern] and because they are not so evident.

Therefore, I argue in this way, as Aristotle argued, from the proper nature and subordination of causes. For it is impossible that the whole collection of beings or of efficient causes be dependent in its being and in its operation. Therefore, it is necessary that among them there is something independent. Therefore, we cannot go on in that progression to infinity, but we must stop at an

---

Schmutz, "La doctrine médiévale des causes et la théologie de la nature pure," *Revue Thomiste*, 101 (2001), pp. 217–64.

52 For the distinction between essentially (*per se*) and accidentally (*per accidens*) subordinated causes, cf. Aristotle: *Physics* 2.3.195a27–b3; *ibid.* 5.198b24; *Metaphysics* 5.2.1013b29–1014a5. See also St. Thomas: *In Librum de Causis expositio*, Pr. I, lect. 1, ed. C. Pera O.P. (Taurini: Marietti, 1955), n. 41, p. 7; *Summa Theologiae* I, q. 7, a. 4, in *Opera*, vol. 4, p. 79; *ibid.* q. 46, a. 2, ad 7, p. 482.

unproduced being which is also independent in its causing. The first antecedent is evident from the mentioned principle: "Everything which is produced is produced by another." For this is the same as to say: "Everything which depends depends upon another." If, therefore, the whole collection of things were dependent, it would necessarily depend upon another. But that is impossible, since outside the collection there is nothing else. But if the whole collection were to depend on some being within that collection, that being would also depend upon itself, which is impossible. In this way, therefore, it is impossible that the whole collection of beings be made or that the whole collection of causes be dependent in acting with the proper dependence by which a later cause depends on one that is prior.

27. *The answer to an objection.* – You will say: does not a whole composite depend on a part, for example, on a form, and still on that account the form does not depend upon itself? The answer is: first of all, it is one thing to speak about formal or material dependence and another about the effective [dependence] of which we are now speaking. For that a whole depends upon its parts is nothing more than its being composed from them. And therefore it is not necessary in the case of a form, for example, that it compose itself, but only that it confer its own proper and intrinsic being on the composite. But to depend efficiently (*efficienter*) is to receive from another one's own being distinct from that which is in the cause.

Therefore, if some total multitude as such depends efficiently (*effective*), it is necessary that it depend upon something not included in that multitude. For if it depended upon something included in that, either that something would depend upon itself or indeed the whole multitude, [taken] adequately and according to its whole self, would not be dependent. But those words "adequately and according to its whole self" are used deliberately, in order to exclude dependence to a certain extent or in part, such as is, for example, the dependence of an effect on a second cause, for example, of fire on a generated fire. For the whole generated fire is said is to depend upon a generator, because without the action of that [generator], in fact that whole [fire] would not have existed. However, that dependence is only by reason of a form and its union with matter, but it is not adequate, as well as direct and primary (*per se primo*) or according to its whole self, because the entity of the matter as such does not depend upon the action of the fire.

When, therefore, we say that the whole collection of beings cannot be dependent, we understand it in this way, namely, "adequately and according to its whole self." For according to a part it can be called dependent, since, with one part taken away, that collection, formally speaking, would not exist. And in this way also, by reason of one part, the collection can depend upon another that is included in it, as is self-evident. However, this will not prevent there being in that collection some being absolutely independent and not made, which we intend to prove. But speaking of the collection of beings depending according to its whole self and adequately, that is, according to all the beings which as it were compose it, in this way it is impossible that a whole collection which is so dependent depend upon something included in it, but [that something] must be outside this collection. Hence, conversely, considering the whole collection of beings outside of which there is nothing, it is impossible that the whole be dependent, which was the proposal taken up.

28. Next, the first consequence[53] is proven, because if every being taken separately or distributively would be dependent and made, the whole collection also would be dependent and made, not indeed by one single dependence or making (*actio*), but by a collection of all dependences or makings by which all beings depend or are made. For by no other reason can the whole collection of beings be dependent except because there is in it no being which does not depend. Therefore, if, as was shown,[54] the whole collection cannot be dependent, it is necessary that there be in that collection some Being which is completely independent and not made.

And the argument is the same for the whole order of causes, of which one depends upon another in being or in making. For the whole collection of causes cannot be dependent, because outside that collection there is no cause on which it may depend, as has been stated. Also, as was extensively proven in the discussion above,[55] it is impossible to imagine a kind of mutual dependence such that there would be a circle in that [dependence]. For we are treating of a genuine dependence by which a lower cause depends upon one that is higher, in such a way that the whole being, the power, and the acting of the first be based upon the second. Therefore, it is necessary that in a whole collection of essentially subordinated causes (of whatever kind they are) there be conceded some [cause] completely independent of any higher [cause]. For otherwise the whole collection would be dependent, which has been shown to be impossible.[56]

29. Finally, from this the second consequence[57] has been proven. For the possibility of a process to infinity in essentially subordinated causes can be understood in two ways. First, by going up from a proximate and particular cause to ones higher which are more and more perfect and universal, in such way that

---

53 That is, it is necessary that within the whole collection of beings there be something independent; cf. § 26, just above.

54 Cf. § 26, this Section.

55 Cf. § 22, this Section.

56 Cf. § 27, this Section.

57 That is, that we cannot proceed to infinity in produced beings; cf. § 26, above.

there is never a stopping at any one which does not depend upon one higher. And in this sense, this process is evidently impossible, as the reasoning just made proves. That is, because otherwise the whole series and collection of causes would be dependent. Hence, in order to prove what we intend, it is enough that in this sense there cannot be a process to infinity in causes of this kind. And this is the way Aristotle's argument proceeds: that all causes, apart from the last which is immediately joined to the effect, would be middle [causes] and no one would be first – which is impossible. For it is the same thing to be middle causes as to be dependent. And it is just as much repugnant that they all be dependent distributively as that the whole collection be dependent (as Scotus rightly noted there[58]). For the whole collection cannot be dependent except by reason of all and each contained within it.

In the same sense, there can easily be explained the argument that otherwise never could we come to that making (*actio*) nor could those infinite dependents be crossed. For the making (*actio*) must primarily and principally begin from the higher cause on which a lower depends. Hence, it is impossible that a lower [cause] begin to act unless a higher, in an order at least of independence and primacy,[59] first influences it. But if every cause whatever has one superior to it and we never arrive at one that is supreme, there is no cause from which, first and through itself, the making (*actio*) will begin. Therefore, every making (*effectio*) will be impossible. Or in another way, if we proceed to infinity in that manner, the result is that the whole series and collection of causes is dependent. Therefore, it depends upon some higher [cause]. Therefore, the making (*actio*) will have to be principally begun by that [cause]. If therefore there is no such cause, neither could any making (*actio*) begin. Therefore, this sense is both true and sufficient for us to demonstrate what was intended.

30. Yet a process to infinity in essentially subordinated intermediate causes could be imagined in another manner, in such way, however, that they all are contained under some first or entirely independent [cause]. For, it is probable that between the proximate cause and the First [Cause] there exist some universal middle causes that are essentially subordinated – at least it is not contradictory that this occur. Again, the number of causes that can exist between the Supreme and the proximate [causes] is not completely fixed and determined, especially in relation to the absolute power of God.[60] For God can bring it about that the middle causes are three, or four, or more in any number at all, even though it would

58 Cf. § 3, this Section.

59 That is, not necessarily in a temporal order.

60 On the absolute versus the ordinary power of God, cf. *DM* XXX, s. 17, nn. 32–36, vol. 26, pp. 216–18.

proceed to infinity. From this, therefore, someone could go farther and could say that God can create infinite middle causes that are also essentially subordinated, from which the effect of the proximate cause may depend, as for example, infinite heavens or angels; and in this way it is not impossible that there be a process to infinity in causes that are essentially subordinated under one first [cause]. And in this sense it is indeed difficult to prove that this process is impossible, especially from the argument that an infinite cannot be crossed, or that the making (*actio*) could not begin.

Against this it seems the argument made above[61] correctly proceeds: that without succession, through a simultaneous concurrence [of causes] the making (*actio*) could simultaneously proceed from all those causes, especially with the first [cause] beginning the making (*actio*), which [first cause] could help or move all the others to operation, even if they were infinite.

Neither is this[62] sufficiently shown to be impossible from the fact that between the two extreme termini (which are the first and the proximate cause) a progression to infinity or an infinite multitude of causes does not seem to be possible for the reason that it is finite inasmuch as it is enclosed by the terms or the extremes. For this is true in a continuous magnitude, but not in a multitude, especially when the extremes are of diverse natures, and especially if one of them is infinite. For in this way it is certain that between the lowest angel and God the species of intellectual substances can be multiplied to infinity. Hence, if the whole collection of those species is imagined as being in reality, there would be an infinite multitude contained between those two extremes; "contained" (I say) not in number, but in perfection. Therefore, in this way an infinite multitude of essentially subordinated causes can be imagined.

31. Still, whatever about the possibility of this fiction, it is not an obstacle to the intended demonstration. For already that [fiction] presupposes some first cause or some independent being. Moreover, even if that infinite concurrence of causes were possible, it would be outside all reason to imagine that it is in fact given in the case of essentially subordinated causes. For neither can it be shown to be necessary nor can there be found in things any sign or vestige of such a multitude or of infinite influencing. This is especially since it is very probable, as I said above,[63] that there are no causes which are essentially subordinated in a proper way, that is, total in their own order and immediately exercising influence upon individual makings (*actiones*) apart from the proper or proximate cause and the first or supreme [cause].

---

61 Cf. § 25, this Section.

62 That is, an infinity of essentially subordinated intermediate causes.

63 Cf. § 28, this Section.

Finally, even though that actually infinite multitude of causes cannot perhaps, precisely from the nature of their causing, be demonstrated to be impossible, from the concept itself of an actually infinite multitude it more probably is impossible. This is also most difficult to understand, because in that case no created cause can be designated to be proximately subordinated to God, that is, [that it be one] between which and God no more perfect [created cause] intervene. Consequently, also no [cause] can be designated which would depend in its acting upon God alone.

These and similar things (as I see it) can be objected in the case of possible things or causes. However, the argument is not the same, because just as possible things are in potency only, so they can be, as they say, "syncategorematically" infinite or indeterminate.[64] But things which have actually been made must be determinate, and therefore it is impossible to understand causes that are actually subordinated under the first cause, without there being given among them some one which proximately proceeds from or depends upon the first alone, and thus there could not be infinite [causes] between the first and the last [cause]. However, these things are plunging us into the subject matter of the infinite, which [subject matter] is infinite, and therefore I am putting them aside, lest we be diverted from our purpose.

32. Further from all of this it can easily become evident what must be said in the case of accidentally subordinated causes.[65] For the answer must be given with the same distinction. Thus if we think of an infinite process that is not contained under one superior cause which is independent of such a series, that process to infinity is plainly impossible.

This can be shown by the same argument proportionately applied. For if

---

64 Syncategorematically is the opposite of categorematically. Something is said to be such "categorematically" which is actually and absolutely such. Thus, God is said to be categorematically infinite. Oppositewise, something is "syncategorematically" such which is such in potency. For example, a mathematical quantity, which can be understood as never ending, is called "syncategorematically" infinite. Accordingly, something that is infinite syncategorematically, or infinite in potency, is actually finite but other parts can always be added to it. On this, cf. e.g. N. Signoriello, *Lexicon peripateticum philosophico-theologicum in quo Scholasticorum distinctiones et effata praecipua explicantur*, editio novissima (Neapoli: Apud Officinam Bibliothecae Catholicae Scriptorum, 1906), p. 58.

65 These would be a series of efficient causes whose being and/or causality does not now depend upon a prior cause in the series. For example, although a man may have been conceived by his parents and thus in past time be somehow caused to exist by his parents, he does not now need his parents in order to exist or to act. This contrasts with a series of essentially subordinated causes each of which in its being and/or acting requires the simultaneous action of a cause that is prior in nature to it.

there is no man who does not depend or has not been made, then the whole collection of men or the whole human species is dependent and has been made. Therefore, it is necessary that it depend upon and has been made by another superior cause that is not contained within the human species. Therefore, even if it is imagined that the series of men proceeding one from another is infinite within their own species, nevertheless, taking the whole species, it is necessary to have some superior cause. And proceeding in this way, either from one individual to another or from one species to another that has been made, it will be in the end necessary to stop at a thing that is completely not made.

33. This argument is even more evident when this progression in accidental causes is among individuals of the same species. For if one individual is such that of itself it does not have being unless it receive that being from an agent cause, it cannot be the case that another individual of the same species of itself have being which is completely independent and not communicated by any agent cause. For to have being either from oneself or only from another are differences or modes of being which are more than generically diverse. For if corruptible and incorruptible being differ essentially and generically, as Aristotle says in Book 10 of the *Metaphysics*,[66] much more do made and non-made, dependent and independent being. For the latter [being] is absolutely necessary while the former is not at all so, as was explained in the preceding Disputation.[67] Therefore, since individuals of the same species are of the same essence, it cannot happen that one have being which is received and the other not. Therefore, it is necessary that the whole species and the whole collection of individuals [of that species] have a received being; therefore, [received] from another which is not contained in that species. Therefore, among those individuals we cannot proceed to infinity in dependence or emanation of one from another, but we must necessarily stop at some thing which does not depend nor emanate from any individual of that species, and consequently neither from the whole species, because a species acts only through individuals. Then we will have to proceed further with respect to that superior cause, asking whether it is absolutely independent. For, if it is such, it is that uncreated being for which we are looking. But if it is dependent, we will have to ask further about the cause upon which it depends, until we stop at a cause that is completely independent. For we cannot proceed to infinity, on account of the reason given, because the whole collection of causes or things cannot be dependent.

About Accidentally Subordinated Causes.

34. However, a process to infinity in accidentally subordinated causes which

---

66 Cf. *Metaphysics* 10.10.1058b27–28.

67 Cf. *DM* XXVIII, s. 1, n. 12, above.

flow from and are dependent upon one superior is, according to Aristotle's opinion, not only acceptable, but it is even necessary for the perpetual succession and duration of generations.[68] And according to the opinion of many Catholic [authors], even though it is not necessary nor given as a matter of fact, it is however possible. But even if we admit this, it is no obstacle to our demonstration, because in this process there is presupposed a superior cause either absolutely not made or at least not made in such a way, nor contained within such a series of generations, from which it is easy to come to a cause which is absolutely not-made, with the same form of argument as has been often said and done.

35. But I (to say here incidentally what will be treated at greater length elsewhere) think that also in this way it is impossible to proceed to infinity, even in causes which are accidentally subordinated and flowing from another [cause]. I [will] explain this briefly in the case of the human species, and the argument is the same for the rest. For if the human species is such that it could not exist in actual reality (*in rerum natura*) unless it had received that [existence] from a higher cause, for example, from God, then it is necessary that it would have received it in some particular and determinate individual, which individual would have proceeded from that higher cause alone and not from another individual of that species.

The reason for the first part of this consequent is that actions are directed to singular things, and therefore a species cannot be made except in some particular and determinate individual. For a "vague individual" (*individuum vagum*)[69] is not perfectly singular, but in some part it is something common and confused. But the reason for the second part [of the consequent] is that, when an individual proceeds from another individual of the same species, that is not the first making (*effectio*) of that species in actual reality. For it is presupposed to have already been made in the other individual from which the second proceeds. Therefore, in that emanation in which such a species is first made in actual reality, it is necessary that the individual in which it is made not proceed from another individual of the same species, but only from that superior cause on which the whole species depends. Again, in order to grant such a process to infinity, it would be necessary that that species be produced from eternity, at least in that individual which proximately and immediately flows from God or that superior cause alone. For the succession of generations cannot be infinite from ever before (*a parte ante*) unless it be from eternity, as is self-evident.

---

68 Suárez is referring here to the infinite series of causes required by Aristotle to account for the perpetuity of specific types in the sublunar world.

69 By a "vague individual" Scholastic writers meant simply "something" without specifying a particular individual thing.

36. But from these principles the impossibility of proceeding to infinity in accidentally subordinated causes is evidently inferred. First, indeed, because when there is a procession to infinity in this way, in that order there can never be assigned a first cause from which the rest will have emanated. But in this series of accidentally subordinated causes it is necessary to come, for example, to a first man from whom the generation of men began – to a man, that is, who was produced (*procreatus*) not by a man but by a higher cause.

37. Second, because from that man whom we imagine as produced by God from all eternity another man could not be generated from eternity. Therefore, [that other man] would have to be generated in time, and, consequently, the succession of men cannot be infinite, since it would have begun to be multiplied in time.

The consequence is evident and the antecedent is proven: because a man produced from eternity could not in the instant in which he was created generate another man, since human generation requires a succession.[70] But he himself would have been created at once and without succession, and he could not have been produced from eternity otherwise. Hence, it is necessary that a man generated by another man, even by a man existing from eternity, be later than that man in duration. Therefore, he is later either with a finite or an infinite duration. The first cannot be said, for otherwise neither would exist from eternity (which contradicts the hypothesis), or between eternity and time there would be only a finite distance, or both would be eternal and nevertheless one would be before the other by a finite duration, all of which involve clear and open contradiction. For if the duration of one man surpasses that of another man in only a finite way, and that [duration] which is less is finite, then also the other which surpasses it is necessarily finite, and consequently not eternal. For if something finite is added to something finite, the result is not something infinite, but what remains is finite and enclosed within limits. But if both are infinite, it is impossible that one exceed the other in that way in which it is infinite. For, if both are infinite, both are eternal, and both are without beginning. How, therefore, is one before the other and by a finite excess? Therefore, in all these [suppositions] there is clear contradiction, and hence it is impossible that a man created from eternity not precede by an infinite duration a man whom he generates. Consequently, the series of generations proceeding from that man can never be infinite. Conversely, ascending from any particular man generated in time through all his progenitors, who are accidentally subordinated causes, it is impossible to progress to infinity.

---

70 According to Suárez, generation itself, as the extrinsic term of the changes (*alteratio*) leading to it, is instantaneous while the changes leading to it involve succession; cf. *DM* XVIII, s. 2, nn. 16–17, vol. 25, pp. 603–4. For a fuller account of the succession which leads up to the instant of generation, cf. Suárez, *Tractatus de Anima*, II, c. 8, in *Opera*, vol. 3, pp. 595–98.

38. I am omitting another argument that was mentioned above:[71] that a successive thing cannot be eternal. I am also omitting other [arguments] that are usually made on the subject of the eternity of the world,[72] which are probable but not equally demonstrative. Finally, I am omitting the response of some who think to avoid the argument that has been made by denying that in the case in which the generations of men would be eternal it would be necessary that some definite man be created by God from eternity or at least some men (which would be the same) from whom or from which the others who have been procreated by human generation may draw their origin. For this response both cannot be conceived in the mind and has also been sufficiently refuted by what was said above.[73] Hence, it is impossible to understand an infinite procession in human generations, never coming to some man who would be a kind of first parent for the rest, except by supposing a human species not produced by a higher principle. For if it has been produced, it must have indeed been necessarily produced in some definite individual. But that consequent not only is erroneous by Faith, but it is also evidently false, as has been proven. Thus, therefore, it is left proven (in whatever way we proceed from effects to causes and from proximate to remote causes, essentially or accidentally subordinated) that we must necessarily stop at some cause which is not made, either in a certain way, if the progression is effected only in a particular order, or absolutely unproduced and which is absolutely an uncreated being, if the ascent is realized absolutely in the whole order of causes, or in the whole universe [of being].

39. But I conclude further from the demonstration that has been made that an uncreated being of this kind must necessarily be some substance. For substance is of itself prior to accident and an accident is always based upon a substance. Hence, it cannot happen that an accident be the first being which is uncreated and not made, because whatever such [accident] is imagined to be it must necessarily be in some substance. Therefore, much more will that substance be uncreated and not made. Thus it is evidently proven by the argument that was made that the being which has being of itself without a making by (*effectio*) or a dependence upon another must be a substance.

But whether in such a substance there can be understood to be any accident which is consequently also uncreated, we will say afterwards when we inquire

---

71 See this Section, § 9.

72 Cf., e.g. St. Bonaventure, *In libros Sententiarum*, II, d. 18, p. 1, a. 1, q. 2; in, *Opera Theologica Selecta*, editio minor [Quaracchi: Ex Typographia Collegii S. Bonaventurae, 1934], tom. 2, pp. 12–17.

73 Cf. this Section, §§ 36 and 37.

about the Divine attributes.[74] Likewise, we will afterwards see how it can be demonstrated that this uncreated substance is immaterial.[75] For just from the argument made up to now, taken from the connection and the subordination of causes, it does not seem possible immediately to conclude that that uncreated substance is completely immaterial and incorporeal.

40. It could, indeed, very well and easily be inferred from what has been said that this first substance cannot be material as composed from the present matter of generable and corruptible things. For all things which are composed of this matter necessarily require an efficient cause, because this matter does not of itself have any innate form, since it is subject to a change of any form whatever. Hence, it necessarily receives form from some efficient [cause], which is the cause of the whole composite of such matter and form. Since, therefore, every composite of this kind has been made, it is rightly concluded that that being which does not have an efficient cause is not composed of this matter. But whether matter itself is made or not, cannot be decided from the stated argument. Again, whether that uncreated substance can be material, in the sense of consisting of another matter, or even whether it can be corporeal, in the sense of a simple substance subject to quantity, as Averroes thought with regard to the heaven,[76] and finally whether the heaven itself, which is believed to be ungenerable and incorruptible, is a substance which is made or not made, I do not think can be decided from the stated argument alone. But we must go farther, using other principles, as we will afterwards see. Therefore, up to now, it has been demonstrated only that there is some uncreated and immaterial substance in the stated sense.

What Should Be Thought about the Opinions Related Above?

41. Finally, from what has been said, the truth of the second opinion related above[77] is clear; and consequently, it has been shown that the first and third [opinions] are absolutely false with regard to that in which they agree, namely,

---

74 Cf. *DM* XXX, s. 6, vol. 26, pp. 89–95.

75 Cf. *DM* XXX, s. 4, nn. 8–27, vol. 26, pp. 76–83.

76 For this, cf. Averroes: *Sermo de substantia orbis*, cc. 1–2, in *Aristotelis opera cum Averrois commentariis*, vol. IX, (Venetiis: Apud Junctas, 1562), vol. 9, esp. fol. 7rB; *Destructio destructionum philosophiae Algazelis*, Disp. III, *ibid.*, vol. 9, fol. 65rA; and *Destructio destructionis*, Disp. IV, fol. 31va, and Disp. VII, fol. 42ra, *In the Latin Version of Calo Calonymus*, edited by Beatrice H. Zedler (Milwaukee: Marquette University Press, 1961), pp. 231–32 and 305. For some background, see Pierre Duhem, *Le Système du monde: histoire des doctrines cosmologiques de Platon à Copernic*, tome IV (Paris: Librairie Scientifique A. Hermann et Fils, 1916), esp. pp. 545–48.

77 See § 3, this Section.

that through a purely physical means, a substance can be demonstrated which is uncreated and separate from all material things. But with regard to that in which the third opinion agrees with the second, namely, that a metaphysical demonstration is as such sufficient for this, it says what is true. For this is what we demonstrated by the examination and the use itself of both means. But the fourth opinion,[78] if it means that the metaphysical demonstration essentially and intrinsically depends upon some purely physical means or principle, as Soncinas and Javellus think, is also false, because, from what has been said, the argument that was made has no [such] dependence.

Hence, it is also evident that what Javellus says[79] is unacceptable: that it is the task of the physicist to demonstrate that there is a first substance, but it is the task of the metaphysician to show what it is. This is first because the metaphysician does not take his primary subject from the physicist, and then especially because we can only demonstrate that God exists by in some way demonstrating what he is, as will become clear from what will be said. For in demonstrating that certain attributes belong to a certain being which is the source of all others, we demonstrate the existence of God. However, the first and most essential of these attributes is that which we have demonstrated up to now, namely, that he exists by himself and without the causality of another, and all other [attributes] can be demonstrated almost insofar only as they have a connection with this,[80] as we will see. Hence, to demonstrate what God is is especially the task of him to whom it pertains to demonstrate that there is a being by itself or by essence and not by another, and conversely, he properly demonstrates that God exists who demonstrates that there is in actual reality (*in rerum natura*) some uncreated being. For physics and metaphysics cannot divide these tasks between themselves, but the whole enterprise belongs to metaphysics.

However, physics (and in this sense the fourth opinion would be true and would not be discordant with the second) in some manner prepares the way and disposes for constructing the demonstration in question. This is first because from motion and sensible effects we ascend to consider the nature of effect and cause themselves, and from dependence in motion [we ascend] to dependence in

78 Cf. § 5, this Section.

79 *Ibid.*

80 This is the Scholastic doctrine of "the metaphysical essence of God" – our primary understanding of what God is, on the basis of which we may demonstrate his further properties. For a survey of Scholastic doctrines in this regard, cf. Pedro Descoqs, S.J., *Praelectiones theologiae naturalis*, vol. 2 (Paris, 1935), pp. 725ff. A shorter but accurate treatment of the same subject may be found in the article of C. Toussaint, "Attributs Divins," *Dictionnaire de théologie catholique* (3e tirage, Paris, 1930), vol. 1, cols. 2228–30.

being and in origin, through which we come to the first uncreated being. Then second, because if not by a completely evident, at least by a most probable reasoning we come through a physical way to a mover of heaven which is separate from it, from which quite easily a metaphysician reasons to investigate not then the first mover of heaven but the first maker of things, applying proportional principles, which are more evident as they are more abstract, as we have sufficiently explained.

42. To the foundations [of the position] of the Commentator[81] we answer [as follows]. To the first: Aristotle in the *Physics* did not sufficiently demonstrate the existence of God or the proper attributes of God from physical motion alone, which has been partly shown and will be partly demonstrated in what follows, but in that place, he [Aristotle] shows probably enough the existence of a first immobile mover. But in Book 2 of the *Metaphysics* he has correctly taught and proved that there is no process to infinity in efficient causes,[82] from which principle it is evidently concluded that there is some non-made being. To the second: the answer is that metaphysics, since it is the supreme science, can prove its own object to exist, especially since we are talking not about the adequate but about the primary object and about an *a posteriori* demonstration, about which we have spoken above in the first Disputation.[83]

SECTION TWO

Whether It Can Be Demonstrated A Posteriori *that God Exists by Showing that There Is Only One Uncreated Being.*

1. Although by the reasoning given in the preceding Section it has been evidently proven that not all beings can be made, but that there is some being which is not made, nevertheless, that this is one and not many has not yet been concluded from that reasoning. For someone could say that indeed everything which has been made has been made by another, and in this process we must stop in particular orders of things at some principle which is not made, not however in one and the same [principle], but in several [principles] because of the diversity of things and species – in which way some pagans have supposed principles for different things, for example, one god of grain, another of wine, etc. Also, certain heretics, for example the Manichees and the like, posited one principle of spirits and another for bodies, or one for good and another for evil things, which they called supreme good and evil.[84] According to this false error, no being, even

81 That is, Averroes; cf. § 2, this Section.

82 Cf. *Metaphysics* 2.2.994a5–8.

83 Cf. *DM* I, s. 4, n. 14, vol. 25, p. 29.

84 On the Manichees, cf. J. Ries, "Manichaeism," *New Catholic Encyclopedia* (New

if it is uncreated, would be the true God in the way in which we intend to signify that by this word. And perhaps in this sense the fool said in his heart: "There is no God,"[85] which Cicero, in Book 1 [of his work] On the Nature of the Gods, attributed to Diagoras;[86] as well as Augustine, in Book 3, Chapter 21, of [his work] Against the Writing of Petilianus;[87] Lactantius, in his First Book [On False Religion] Chapter 2;[88] and Theodosius [*sic*], in Book 3, of his [work] On Curing the Evils of the Greeks.[89] But if we would show that this uncreated and essentially necessary being can be only one in number because of its nature and essence, the consequent plainly will be that it is the first cause of all other things which exist or can exist, and therefore it is God and consequently the true God. Therefore, the demonstrations which are usually brought forth by philosophers and theologians in order to prove the unity of God from the infinite perfection of the Divine nature, although they are otherwise very good, as we will afterwards see, cannot, however, now be of use to us, because they presuppose as already proven that in actuality there is a God, that is, a certain being of infinite perfection in its essence and nature. This we have not yet proven,[90] but only that there is a being which is essentially necessary inasmuch as it has being from itself.

2. And for this reason perhaps, there have been some Catholics and theologians who said that God cannot be demonstrated to exist, for example: Peter d'Ailly (*Petrus de Aliaco*), in [his *Questions on the books of the Sentences*] Book 1, Question 3, Articles 2 and 3,[91] where he first tries to respond to the demonstration by which it is proven that there is some being which is from itself and uncreated; but he says nothing which is likely or probable to which we need reply.

York/St.Louis/San Francisco/Toronto/London/ Sydney: McGraw-Hill Book Company, 1967) vol. 9, pp. 153–60.

85 Cf. *Psalms* 13, 1 and 52, 1.

86 Cf. M. Tulli Ciceronis, *De Natura deorum,* liber primus, nn. 2, 63, and 117, edited by Arthur Stanley Pease (Cambridge: Harvard University Press, 1955), pp. 122–23, 355, and 512.

87 Cf. S. Aurelii Augustini Hipponensis, *Contra literas Petiliani Donatistae Cirtensis episcopi, libri tres*, III, c. 21, in *PL*, vol. 43, col. 360.

88 Cf. *PL*, vol 6, col. 120a.

89 For this, see Theodoretus of Cyr, *Graecarum affectionum curatio*, Sermones II and III, in *Patrologia Graeca*, vol. 93 (Paris, 1859), cols. 859 and 863.

90 Note this: Suárez will not yet claim to have proven the existence of God.

91 Cf. *Questiones magistri Petri de Alliaco Cardinalis cameracensis super primum tertium et quartum sententiarum*, I, q. 3, aa. 2 and 3 ([Parisiis]: Impressae arte et industria Iohanis Barbier, expensis honesti viri Iohanis Petit, n.d.), fols. 78r–85r.

Then he says that even though it be granted that some being which is from itself is demonstrated [to exist], it is not however demonstrated that it is the only one, and therefore it cannot be demonstrated that God exists. Indeed, he says that even though it be demonstrated or admitted that there is a certain one uncreated being, which is the first cause of all things which have been made, nevertheless, it is not evidently inferred that this is God. For from this it does not follow that there is a first cause of all things which exist, since someone could say that there are several beings which have not been made and that among them there is another superior being, which even though it is not efficiently causing (*efficiens*), is nevertheless the end (*finis*) of other uncreated being. And by the same reasoning there could be imagined several uncreated beings which would have no causal order among themselves, [for example] just as there are two angels, which some have said are essentially necessary beings. And of this opinion, namely, that God cannot be demonstrated to exist, was also Rabbi Moses, Book 6, Chapter 6, of his *Philosophy* [*sic*],[92] as well as some philosophers, as St. Thomas notes in his *Contra Gentiles*, Book 1, Chapters 11 and 12,[93] and in his work *On Truth*, Question 10, Article 12.[94]

3. Indeed, others, on a totally opposite basis, have also said that the existence of God cannot be demonstrated, because it is self-evident. Anselm, in his *Proslogion*, Chapters 2 and 3,[95] and in his *Book Against the Fool*,[96] seems to have been of this opinion. Moreover, [this opinion] is suggested in the *Commentaries*, attributed to Jerome, on *Job*, Chapter 36 [v. 25], with regard to the words: "All men see God,"[97] and on *Psalm* 95, [v. 10], at these words: "He has regulated the

---

92 Cf. Moses Maimonides, *The Guide for the Perplexed*, I, c. 74, translated from the original Arabic text by M. Friedlander, 2nd edition, seventh impression (London: George Routledge and Sons, 1947), pp. 133–38. In this chapter, Maimonides is showing the weakness of the arguments of the *Mutakallimim* (i.e. Muslim theologians) which purport to demonstrate the fact of creation in time. St. Thomas (cf. note 94, following) interpreted this to mean that Maimonides was narrating a position which at once held that (1) the existence of God is not self-evident, (2) it cannot be known by a demonstration, and (3) it must therefore be held by faith.

93 Cf. *Opera*, vol. 13, pp. 24–25 and 28–29.

94 Cf. *Opera*, vol. 22/2 (Romae ad Sanctae Sabinae, 1972), p. 340.

95 See, *Proslogion*, cc. 2–3, in S. Anselmi, *Opera omnia*, ed. F.S. Schmitt, O.S.B. (Edinburgh: Apud Thomas Nelson et Filios, 1946), vol. 1, pp. 101–3.

96 Cf. *Quid ad haec [i.e. Librum pro insipiente] respondeat editor ipsius libelli*, ed. Schmitt, vol. 1, pp. 130–39.

97 Cf. Sancti Eusebii Hieronymi, *Commentarii in librum Job*, c. 36, in *PL*, vol. 26, col. 737b–c.

orb of earth, which will not be moved."[98] Likewise, Damascene favors [this opinion] in his *On Faith*, Book 1, Chapters 1 and 3, where he says that the knowledge of God is infused by nature in men.[99] But this is explained by St. Thomas in the places cited above, and in [*Summa*] I, Question 2, Article 1,[100] in this way: that something has been naturally placed in man by which he can come to the knowledge of God, and Jerome can also be explained in this way. But with regard to Anselm, St. Thomas admits[101] that he was of that opinion, and he [Thomas] was followed by Abulensis,[102] in [his commentary on] *Exodus*, Chapter 6 [*sic*], Question 2.[103] But the fact that this opinion is also false will be clear from the reasoning of this Section, as we will note at its end.

The Resolution of the Question.

4. It must be said, therefore, that it can be evidently demonstrated that the being which is essentially necessary is the source or the efficient cause of all other things and accordingly is only one. And in this way it is evidently demonstrated that God exists.

In order to understand this assertion and the consequence between its parts, it is necessary to presuppose what all men understand by the name of God. For although God, because of his simplicity and infinity, cannot be defined nor even exactly described by us who conceive him imperfectly, nevertheless, in order to be able to reason about him, it is necessary at least to preconceive and presuppose what is signified by this word.

However, in explaining this word, it is necessary to avoid two extremes. One is that in such a description we do not posit all conditions and attributes of God, both [1] because otherwise we could never conclude that God exists unless we would first demonstrate all the attributes of God with respect to some being, which goes against the practice and the conception of all men; and also [2] because there are many properties of God which are much more difficult to know than the fact that God exists.

---

98 Cf. Auctor incertus (Hieronymus Stridonensis?), *Breviarium in Psalmos*, ps. 95, in *PL*, vol. 26, col. 1114c.

99 Cf. *De fide orthodoxa*, ed. Buytaert, cc. 1 and 3, pp. 11–13, and 16.

100 Cf. Sancti Thomae Aquinatis, *Opera*, vol. 4, p. 28.

101 Cf. *ibid.*, p. 27. Actually, this is a free interpretation of St. Thomas, who does not mention St. Anselm by name in this place.

102 That is, Alfonso Tostado de Madrigal, Bishop of Avila (d. 1455).

103 Cf. Alphonsi episcopi Abulensis, *Prima pars super Exodum*, cap. 5, q. 2 (Venetiis: In aedibus Petri Liechtenstein, 1528), fol. 21rv. Abulensis does follow the opinion of St. Thomas. However, he does not refer by name to either Thomas or Anselm.

5. The second extreme [to avoid] is that we do not apply this term to just any property that seems to belong only to God. For example, it is proper to God to be the most excellent among all beings; therefore, some say that by the name of God nothing else is signified but a being that is the most perfect of all. But this is not enough in order to state the concept and the signification of [the term] God. For albeit someone were to imagine that in reality there is only this corporeal world and that in it heaven, or man, is the most noble of all beings, he would not immediately think that heaven or man is the God of this world, unless he were otherwise to believe that the properties of God were in these. Similarly, it can be attributed to God that he is the first mover of the heaven. However, on account of that it will not rightly be said that by the name of God there is signified only the first mover of the heaven, as it is such. For if he were to have nothing else than to be the first mover of heaven, he would not on that account be God.

And I say the same about the attribute which is to be a necessary being, or a being from himself, because even this attribute, taken as such, is not enough for filling out the concept which we intend to signify by the name of God. For, as I was saying a little before, if there were several essentially necessary beings, no one of them would be such as we intend to signify by the name of God.

Therefore, this name signifies a certain most noble being which both surpasses all the rest and from which as from a first author all the rest depend, which accordingly should be worshipped and venerated as the supreme deity. For this is the common and, as it were, the first concept that we all form about God, when we hear the word *God*. And therefore in order to demonstrate that God exists it is not enough to show that there is in reality (*in rerum natura*) some being which is necessary and from itself, unless it is also proven that that [being] is unique and such that it is the source of all being, from whom all things, which participate that being in any way, depend and receive it. But when this has been demonstrated it is sufficiently shown that God exists. For the rest of his attributes which have a necessary connection with a being of this kind have to be demonstrated afterwards.

6. *How great a certitude is in the preceding assertion.* – Therefore, the assertion as so explained has seemed not only true but also so certain to theologians, that they condemn the doctrine of d'Ailly[104] as erroneous. And they are not wrong, because [that doctrine] impugns the teaching of Paul, to the *Romans*, Chapter 1 [v. 19]: "What is known of God is manifest in those things; for God has manifested [Himself] by them." But he calls "known of God" that which can become known about him by natural reason, which at least must be that he exists, for if this is not known, absolutely nothing will be known about God. But explaining this mode of manifestation he adds: "For the invisible things of Him

104 Cf. § 2, this Section.

from the creation of the world are clearly seen, having been understood through those things which have been made; also his eternal power and divinity, so that they are inexcusable, because although they would have known God they did not glorify him as God." [vv. 20–21] From these words it is obviously concluded that such knowledge of God can be derived from creatures, in such way that it makes men inexcusable, if either they do not assent to the existence of God or they neglect to worship him.

But that this knowledge is evident in itself does not appear to be so plainly inferred from these words. For often a knowledge which is less than evident is enough to oblige a man and to render him inexcusable if he does not act in accord with it. But nevertheless, if the words of Paul are carefully pondered they do sufficiently indicate an evident knowledge, as they are: "manifest in those things" and "are clearly seen, having been understood." And there is a similar testimony in Solomon, [the Book of] *Wisdom*, Chapter 13 [v. 1], where those who do not know the true God are blamed: "All men are vain" (he says) "in whom there is not present the knowledge of God, and who from those things which seem good cannot understand Him Who Is, and who looking at the works have not known who is the Worker," and below [v. 5]: "From the greatness of what appears and of the creature their Creator could reasonably be seen." The same thing is indicated by those words of Psalm 18 [v. 2]: "The heavens declare the glory of God," as [St. John] Chrysostom explains them at length in his *Homilies for the People [of Antioch]*, numbers 9[105] and 10.[106] And in the same sense, [St.] Gregory, in his *Moralia*, Book 27, Chapter 2 [*sic*], explains the words of *Job*, Chapter 36 [v. 25]: "All men see him, each one looks from afar."[107] And, finally, the Fathers of the Church think the same thing, whom to cite now seems "strange for someone intent upon being a metaphysician" (*metaphysico instituto alienum*).[108] However, I will suggest some texts, while proving by reason the assertion that was made. This cannot be presented better than by bringing forth demonstrations by which the truth in question may be proven.

The First Demonstration that God Exists.

7. There are, then, two principal ways to prove this. One is completely *a posteriori* and from effects; the other is immediately *a priori*, although remotely it also is *a posteriori*, as I will afterwards explain. The first way is more used by

---

105 Cf. S.P.N. Joannis Chrysostomi, Archiepiscopi Constantinopolitani, *Homiliae XXI de statuis ad populum Antiochenum habitae* IX, in *PG*, vol. 49, cols. 105–6.

106 *Ibid.*, X, col. 116.

107 Sancti Gregorii Romani Pontificis, *Moralium libri, sive expositio in librum B. Job*, XXVII, c. 5, in *PL*, vol. 76, col. 403.

108 Cf. § 2, at the beginning of this *Disputation*.

the Holy Fathers, and it is more consonant with Paul and Solomon in the places cited, and it is most especially indicated in those words of the Wiseman: "From the greatness of what appears and of the creature" [*Wisdom*, Chapter 13, v. 5] that is, "From the greatness and the appearance or the beauty of creatures." From these words we can in this way form an argument: for, although individual effects taken and considered by themselves do not show the maker of all to be one and the same, nevertheless, the beauty of the whole universe and the wonderful connection and order of all things in it do sufficiently declare that there is one first being, by whom all things are governed and from whom they draw their origin. St. Thomas has touched upon this argument in *Contra Gentiles*, Book 1, Chapter 13,[109] from [St. John] Damascene, *On Faith*, Book 1, Chapter 3,[110] and Gregory, in the *Moralia*, Book 26, Chapter 8,[111] and [St. John] Chrysostom, in the 4th *Homily on Genesis*.[112] And [Pseudo] Dionysius the Areopagite, in Chapter 7 of [his work] *On the Divine Names*, explicitly says that God is known from the most ordered disposition of all creatures;[113] which [St.] Augustine also used in his [work] *On the City of God*, Book 11, Chapter 4;[114] and Justin, when he is asked in Question 16 of his work, Gentium [*sic*]:[115] "From what can it be known whether there is any God at all?" answers elegantly and briefly: "from the concrescence, the nature, and the stability of those things which exist." Hence, in Book 7, Chapter 2 [*sic*] of his [work] On Preparation for the Gospel, Eusebius of Caesarea says very well: "Just as a house cannot be made without a craftsman or a cloth without a weaver, so neither can this universe [be made] without an author."[116] And Gregory Nazianzen, in his second sermon *On Theology*;[117] uses

---

109 Cf. *Opera*, vol. 13, p. 34.

110 Cf. *De fide orthodoxa*, ed. Buytaert, c. 3, nn. 3–4, pp. 18–19.

111 Suárez's reference here, which should be at *PL*, vol. 76, col. 359, does not check out. However, cf. XXVI, c. 12, *PL,* vol. 76, cols. 357–58.

112 Cf. S.P.N. Joannis Chrysostomi, *Homiliae in Genesin*, cap. I, *Homilia* IV, in *PG*, vol. 53, cols. 43–44.

113 Cf. S. Dionysii Areopagitae, *De divinis nominibus*, c. 7, *PG*, vol. 3, cols. 870–71.

114 Cf. S. Aurelii Augustini Hipponensis, *Ad Marcellinum de civitate Dei contra paganos, libri viginti duo* XI, c. 4, in *PL*, vol. 41, cols. 319–20.

115 For this, see: Pseudo Justin, *Quaestiones gentiles ad christianos, de incorporeo et de Deo et de resurrectione mortuorum*, Q. 3, in *Iustini philosophi et martyris, Opera subditicia*, ed. Car. Th. Eques de Otto, tom. III, pars 2 (Wiesbaden: Dr. Martin Sandig, 1969), pp. 338–39.

116 Eusebii Caesariensis, *Praeparationis evangelicae, libri quindecim*, VII, c. 3, in *PG*, vol. 21 (Paris, 1857), col. 511.

the example of a harp or of its harmony which is produced in a most orderly and beautiful way. For just as that cannot be understood without some author or craftsman, so neither can the most appropriate production of this universe [be understood] without God. Finally, the Philosopher has suggested this argument, in *Metaphysics*, Book 12 [*sic*], Chapter 2, in these words: "For in what way will there be order, if there is not something eternal, separate, and permanent?"[118] And he continues the same more at length in Chapter 10, where he also uses the example of a house and a rightly ordered family as well as the example of an army, which cannot be ordered without a leader.[119] And he touched on the same thing in Book 1, Chapters 3 and 4.[120]

8. *Evasions of the argument made.* – But in order that the force of this argument be better perceived, it must be more explained. For someone could say that from this effect it is at most inferred that there is one governor of all things, not one creator. Again, he could say that this [governor] is one not by nature or entity, but by consensus, as if several craftsmen would agree to construct one building. Again, this argument is not relevant to purely spiritual things, for in their regard it is not evident to us how much connection they have, either among themselves, or with other things of this visible world. Finally, if someone imagines that apart from this visible world there is another having no connection with this and that its creator is also uncreated but a distinct being from the one who created and governs this world, he could not indeed be convinced by the just given reasoning. Therefore, from the effects which we experience we cannot sufficiently prove that there is only one uncreated being, which is the principle of everything else which exists in reality, whether in this world or in another. Therefore, on the solution of these [objections] the force of the argument in question seems to depend, in order that it universally embrace all beings and conclude that among them all there is only one that is first and the source of the others. For this kind of being we call God.

The First Evasion Is Refuted and the Emanation of the Whole Sensible World Is Shown.

9. Therefore, to the first objection, or rather evasion, I am pleased to reply first of all in the words of Lactantius, in his *First Book: On False Religion*,

117 Cf. S.P.N. Gregorii Theologi, Archiepiscopi Constantinopolitani, *Oratio*, XXVIII – *Theologica* II, n. 6, in *PG*, vol. 36, cols. 33–34. For an English translation of this work, see A.J. Mason, *The Five Theological Orations of Gregory of Nazianzen* (Cambridge, 1899).

118 Cf. *Metaphysics* 11.2.1060a26–27.

119 Cf. *Metaphysics* 12.10.1075a11–22.

120 Cf. *ibid.* 1.3.984b15–20 and 1.4.985a18–21.

Chapter 2:[121] "No one is so uneducated, with so savage customs, who, raising his eyes to heaven, even if he does not know by the providence of which God all of this that he sees is ruled, still, from the very magnitude, the motion, the disposition, the constancy, the utility, the beauty, and the harmony of things, does not understand that there is some [providence]; and it is clear that what cannot happen except by a marvelous plan has been established with some greater counsel." In these last words he very well (*eleganter*) indicates that from governance creation is correctly inferred, because the universe can be governed only by him by whose counsel and power it has been created. For thus it clearly exists in a marvelous way and by plan and it is conserved with a striking connection and succession of things, because it has been so structured by a most wise craftsman, insofar as was necessary for such governance and conservation. In this way, therefore, from the connection and mutual operation of the things of the universe, not only is there inferred one governor of the universe, but also [one] maker.

10. This is further explained by going through all things of which this universe consists. And first of all, with respect to the species of all generable and corruptible things, it was shown above[122] that it cannot be thought that they have being from themselves by only a succession of one individual from another; but it is necessary that each species be produced by some superior cause in some individual. With regard at least to composites themselves and with regard to material forms, this becomes evident from what was said in the preceding Section. But as regards matter itself the argument made there is not cogent. However, a proof is derived from what was said above, in *Disputation* 22 [*sic*],[123] about creation, namely, since to exist from oneself is the greatest perfection, therefore, if this does not belong to a form or to a substantial subject much less can it belong to prime matter.[124]

11. *An Objection is Answered.* – Again, because if no substantial form is of itself innate in prime matter without any causation, neither can prime matter itself have from itself actual entity which is not received from some agent, since by its nature it requires a form and depends upon that. Hence, necessarily it exists only in a composite and under a form; therefore, of itself it cannot have being, but it waits for a form from an agent.

---

121 Cf. *PL*, vol. 6, col. 121a–b.

122 See Section 1, §§ 32–33, and 35, above.

123 Cf. *DM* XX, s. 1, nn. 17–20, 27, vol. 25, pp. 749–50, 753.

124 Prime matter is the pure passive potency which is basic in all corporeal substances. It is the totally unformed, i.e. undetermined and indeterminate, substrate of all bodies in the natural universe. Having of itself no form, it is receptive of all forms and subsequent privations. For Aristotle's most famous description, see *Metaphysics* 7.3.1029a20–21.

The consequence is plain, because, if it is of itself, it exists necessarily, even if no agent causes anything. However, it would be possible that an agent not cause a form, inasmuch as it may freely cause that [form], as we will afterwards say. Indeed, if matter were to have being from itself, it would necessarily be eternal. But an extrinsic agent could not from eternity induce some form of corruptible things into that [matter], unless perhaps through an infinite duration it would conserve in it the form it had from eternity induced into it, as is clear from what was said in the preceding Section. But no one of sound mind can imagine that the author of this inferior world (whoever that might be) was from eternity necessitated to induce into matter some particular form which he would conserve in that [matter] through an infinite duration. Nor has any philosopher, even from among those who have thought the world existed from eternity, imagined that this inferior corruptible world was eternal in such a way that in some one or more definite individuals it would have endured through eternity before generations and corruptions would have begun in it. If therefore, no form taken in a definite way is necessarily present in matter, therefore, none is necessarily caused in it by an agent, especially [caused] from eternity. Therefore, neither can that have from itself necessary and eternal being.

You will say that this argument is valid if we suppose that matter by its nature depends upon form: but this is not evident. I answer that even apart from any rigorous dependence, by the very fact that matter of its nature requires form and without that it cannot exist except in an extremely preternatural condition (which no one can deny), it is sufficiently inferred that it is completely foreign to the nature of matter to have being from itself and that it waits for a form from an agent. In this way, in the subject matter "On the Soul" (*materia de anima*),[125] philosophers teach that it is not natural for the rational soul to exist before the body, because by its nature it requires existence in the body, even though it does not depend upon the body. Hence, even though it can remain outside the body, it is however at that point in a preternatural condition. By this argument it is also correctly concluded that the rational soul does not of itself have necessary and eternal existence.

12. *From what has been said, a proof of the conclusion is drawn with regard to sublunar things.* – From all of this, therefore, it is correctly concluded that all things contained under heaven have been created by some superior author. Hence, first of all it is the case that the four elements[126] have been made by one and the same author – by him, namely, by whom they have been disposed and ordered in such a way as was appropriate for the conservation and governance of the whole universe. For just as they were created on account of this end, that is,

125 For this, cf. Suárez, *Tractatus de Anima* I, c. 5, n. 2, vol. 3, pp. 499–500.

126 That is, earth, air, fire, and water.

on account of the good of the universe and on account of the generations also of mixed bodies, as I will presently say, so they have been created in that proportion which would be consonant with that end. In a proportion, I say, not only of magnitude, but also of quality, and of natural similarity or diversity. Therefore, it was necessary that the same one be the author of all, otherwise that proportion and connection could not fall under one intention.

Then it is also inferred that the same one who was the creator of the elements was also not only the governor but even the creator of the mixed things[127] which are generated from the elements. It is not indeed necessary that all mixed things were immediately produced by the same author. Indeed, if that is understood about a production by a genuine and immediate creation, not only is it not necessary, but also it is not true. For even according to the Divine Scripture, God first produced mixed things from created elements,[128] which production could not properly be a creation, since it was from a presupposed matter. Rather indeed, with respect to the elements themselves, it is not evident that all were immediately created, or whether one was created first and the rest formed afterwards from that one. And although the first is more probable and more consonant with Sacred History, it cannot however be demonstrated by reason. Nor does it matter for what we are doing, as long as it is clear that there is one and the same author of all these things.

13. But if that is understood about mixed things in this way and with this extension – that is to say, with regard to [their] production, whether by a proper creation or from another body previously created – there is still need for distinction and an explanation. For it can be understood either about a production which is authored immediately by God alone or one which is effected through second causes. Again, among these mixed things, certain ones are imperfect, inasmuch as they can be made through a concourse of general causes apart from the concurrence of a cause which is particular and of the same nature. And in this way there are produced not only the mixed things which are properly called imperfect,[129] or meteorological things which are frequently generated in the second region of the air,[130] but also metals which are produced in the bowels of the earth

127 That is to say, compounds which are made from the four elements.

128 On this, cf. Suárez, *Tractatus de opere sex dierum* I, c. 10, esp. nn. 7–14, and 19; vol. 3, pp. 56–59, 61.

129 That is to say, mixtures which do not contain all of the four elements of earth, air, fire, and water or which contain them as imperfectly combined. For this and the next three notes I am drawing from W.D. Ross, *Aristotle: A Complete Exposition of his Works and Thought* (New York: Meridian Books, 1959), pp. 108–111.

130 The natural place of the sphere of air in the Aristotelian physics is below the sphere of fire and above the sphere of water; cf. *Meteorologica* 1.2.339a15–19; *ibid.* 3.340b19–23. The sphere of air itself is divided into two parts (*ibid.* b23–27): (1) the

by the power of the sun,[131] and many living things and imperfect animals.[132] And about all these things, it cannot (I think) be shown by any other evident argument that they are produced immediately by the first cause or the universal author, except that [argument] by which it has been shown above[133] that the first cause concurs immediately with second causes for all their actions and effects. For it is not necessary that the first cause employ a greater concurrence, since in created universal causes or in the concurrence of several causes there is sufficient power to produce these effects with the general concurrence of the first cause. But for the subject matter or the demonstration which we now intend this mode of emanation of these things from the same author by whom the elements have been made is enough. Indeed, in rigor it would be enough to demonstrate that these effects do not have another first author who is an uncreated being besides Him who created the elements and the other things of the universe, whether they proceed from Him immediately or mediately, that is, because the proximate cause of those effects has emanated from that first being.

14. But there are other mixed things which are so perfect that they cannot be made immediately by the heaven or by other general created causes without a proper and definite concurrence of a proximate cause of the same nature. For in this way a man is generated only by a man,[134] and a lion by a lion, and so with respect to other perfect animals, and in certain trees and plants we see the same thing happening. For wheat comes to be only from wheat, and in the perfect trees we seem to experience the same thing. Therefore, in the case of these things, their procreation much more evidently has to be reduced to some higher author, because neither the whole species can emanate from itself nor exist from itself, as has been shown above,[135] nor in all these visible causes is there power enough to introduce species of things of this kind into the universe.

Moreover, that the first author is the same for all these things, whether they are compared among themselves or with the elements, is evident from the connection of those things among themselves, whether by reason of matter or by rea-

---

lower which is the region in which are produced rain, clouds, mist, dew, frost, snow and hail; and (2) the upper part, which is the region in which are produced shooting stars, comets, aurora, and the milky way.

131 For this, see Aristotle, *Meteorologica* 3.7.378a26–b6.

132 In this last case, Suárez reflects the common ancient and medieval view that lower forms of life, e.g. worms and maggots, are generated by the sun from putrefaction. On this, also see *DM* XXII, s. 5, n. 15, vol. 25, pp. 841–42.

133 Cf. Section 1, § 25.

134 For Suárez on the Aristotelian doctrine that the sun and a man generate a man, cf. *DM* XXII, s. 5, n. 16, vol. 25, p. 842.

135 Cf. Section 1, §§ 32–33.

son of agent or of end.[136] For the elements are so created that these mixed things can be fittingly produced, nurtured, or conserved from them, to the extent that they are even changed somewhat from their natural places for the advantage and the benefit of mixed things.[137] And among those mixed things, certain ones serve others for food or other uses. And almost all serve man, because of whom that they have been immediately created, as can be especially understood from those things themselves and their different qualities and various properties most fitted for the use of men, which properties they have received from their first creation. This then is an evident sign that all these things are not only governed but have also been made by the same author.

Again, the beauty itself of the universe declares this, a beauty to which the so varied creation of mixed things is directed and disposed in such an orderly way, with the result that it could not by chance or by accident be made so by different authors, but only by a single universal author who intended this most beautiful machine of the universe.

15. *Whether heaven (caelum)*[138] *is animated and by what kind of soul?*[139] *[What] some have believed. – The assertion is proven with regard to the heavenly bodies.* – It remains to speak about the heavenly bodies, the origin of which seems to be naturally more obscure from the fact that they are incorruptible. Hence, many of the pagans have believed it clear that heaven did not have an origination, as Justin relates in the response to the fifth question proposed to the pagans.[140] However, that heaven also was made can be shown first of all from its imperfection. For heaven is a being which is more imperfect than man.

---

136 Here Suárez is referring to Aristotle's causal theory in which things that differ in form can be similar in their material, efficient, and final causality.

137 The natural order of the elements left to themselves, from the center of the universe out, would be earth, water, air, and fire. But under the action of the sun and the heavenly bodies they are mixed together in such ways that they move out of their natural places even though they never fly off far from those places. For example, the element of earth even when, as found in some mixture, it undergoes other motions nevertheless retains a natural tendency to move toward the center of the whole earth and to be at rest around that center.

138 While Suárez here uses the singular "heaven" (*caelum*), at other times he will use the plural (*caeli*) which corresponds to the more colloquial English usage of "the heavens."

139 On this, cf. St. Thomas, *Summa Theologiae*, I, q. 70, a. 3, in *Opera*, vol. 5, pp. 179–81, who like Suárez has given a negative answer to this question.

140 Cf. Pseudo Justin, Quaestiones christianae ad gentiles, Q. V, in *Iustini philosophi et martyris, Opera subditicia*, pp. 320–23.

Therefore, since man does not have being except from a superior cause, how can heaven be thought to have being from itself?

You will say first, that it is not sufficiently evident that heaven is more imperfect than man. For many people have thought that it is animated by an intelligent soul. The answer is that hardly any philosopher has thought that heaven is animated with a genuine animation through an information. For we find no indication or act of life in that [heavenly] body; since its illumination and its influences are all natural actions. But local motion by itself alone, and especially non-progressive [motion],[141] is not an indication of life, since it can be caused by either a natural or an extrinsic impetus.

Those therefore who say that heaven is alive or animated, have spoken thus because of an Intelligence moving heaven,[142] which, since it stands by it[143] and uses it in a certain way in order to act, by a kind of metaphor is called its soul. But those who in a more proper sense[144] have asserted that have spoken without proof. However, against him who would persist in that opinion, the argument that has been made would not be efficacious, but then we would have to philosophize in the same way about heaven as about dissimilar Intelligences, concerning which I will forthwith speak.

Thus we should answer in almost the same way, if someone says that man is superior to heaven only by reason of his intellective soul, and about this [soul] it is not sufficiently clear that it has been made. For that the intellective soul has been made must be said to be sufficiently evident, first from the general argument by which that can be shown with respect to the Intelligences. For since the soul is less perfect than the Intelligences, if these have been made, much more has it been made. Second, [it can be shown] by a special argument. For since it [the soul] is the form of a body and exists not so much on account of itself as on account of the whole composite, it can neither naturally exist before the body nor have existence from itself if that composite itself needs an efficient cause, as we explained a little before.[145]

16. Finally, someone can say, even though a heavenly body may be less perfect with respect to its grade of being, still it is in a way more perfect since it is incorruptible; and therefore it is possible that it may surpass man in the perfection of being from itself, even though it is itself surpassed in its essential grade.

---

141 Suárez is evidently alluding here to the fact that the heavens were thought to go forever roundabout in the same place.

142 That is to say, a separate Intelligence moving each heavenly sphere.

143 That is, that particular heavenly sphere which it moves.

144 That is, in a non-metaphorical sense.

145 See Section 1, §§ 27 and 40, above.

I answer: that is impossible and the nature of what is attributed to one is very different from that [which is attributed] to the other. For the fact that a thing is incorruptible can result either from its lack of a contrary, or from a condition of matter, or from a certain simplicity of that thing. Hence this property does not always indicate the supreme and maximum essential perfection of a thing.[146]

But being from oneself, and that unique necessity of being which results from an independence from every efficient cause, is an evident indication of a certain most eminent perfection, not only in some way but also in the grade of being itself. This is because through this perfection a being is more distant from nothing or from non-being than through any other which may prescind from this. Moreover, it is because such a being has the least potentiality, seeing that it cannot be in objective potency.[147] And finally such a being does not fall under the dominion of another. Hence, in a unique and supreme way, it is (if I may say so) "in charge of itself" (*sui juris*) and subject to no other.

Without doubt, all of this indicates a far more excellent perfection. Therefore, it is not possible that a thing which is inferior in its grade of being have this perfection which a superior thing cannot reach.

17. And from this is confirmed the following argument which is taken from the imperfection of heaven. For heaven is a material being, or (to speak beyond all opinion[148]) [one which is] corporeal, extended, and quantified, in which properties, namely, of quantity and extension, it has a similarity with inferior bodies which have the same character. And it is in passive potency, at least to motion and some accidental perfections. And it needs motion, at least in order that it can be applied to acting in various places. But indeed, it is unable to so move and apply itself unless it is moved by another. But then how is it credible that what lacks motion and cannot have it from itself could exist from itself? Therefore, such great perfection as to be an independent and necessary being without being in objective potency, is plainly incompatible with a being that has as many imperfections as are seen in the heaven. Accordingly, heaven is not an unproduced being, but one that has been made.

---

146 For a general division of what is incorruptible, see Suárez, *De Angelis*, I, c. 9, n. 1, vol. 2, p. 37; for an application of this to the heavens as contrasted with God, cf. *ibid.*, n. 4, p. 38.

147 By "objective potency" Suárez means "nothing else than to be capable of being an object of some power, or rather [an object] of the action or the causality of some power." But since a thing cannot be an object for its own power, or "cannot be made by itself, but rather by another, being in objective potency is said in relation to the power of another." cf. *DM* XXXI, 3, n. 4, vol. 26, p. 234.

148 That is, to speak with certainty.

18. But it remains further to be proven (and at the same time this will be confirmed) that [heaven] has the same author of its being which the elements and other inferior bodies have, which will easily be done by pursuing and applying the reasoning that was formulated about the connection and the proportion of these bodies among themselves.

For it is first of all evident that the celestial bodies have among themselves the highest proportion and due subordination, not only in their shape, their position, and their place, but (what is especially relevant) also in their motion and influence, insofar as is necessary or appropriate for the stability[149] and the good governance of the whole universe. This, therefore, is an evident sign both that all the heavens have been created by the same author and that he is not different from the creator of the whole universe or from him who created the elements and the other inferior bodies.

The consequence is proven with regard to the first part of the consequent,[150] because it cannot be understood either that this disposition and order of the heavens happened by chance or that the heavens were created first by some particular agents and were afterwards disposed and ordered by some superior agent who was concerned with the good of the whole universe. For the most beautiful and most fitting variety itself and the disposition of the heavens in size (*magnitudo*) evidently declare figuratively and virtually the wisdom of the creator, who for the purpose of some end and universal benefit has so disposed them. And the very stability and nature of the heavens sufficiently declare that they received that disposition not after but together with that nature itself. [This is so] especially as regards those four properties which we enumerated, namely, size, shape, position, and innate power to influence. For with respect to motion the reasoning is different since [motion] is necessarily posterior,[151] at least by an instant,[152] and it comes more from outside.

Therefore, the Maker of the universe should not be imagined in the manner of human craftsmen, who, in line with an end set up by themselves, order with regard to one another things which are already subsisting from elsewhere and in this way compose an artificial thing. But [the Maker should be thought of] as a

149 Here I accept Rábade Romeo's (*Disputaciones metafísicas* vol. 4, p. 289) reading of "stabilitatem," which is also that of Mainz, 1605 (vol. 2, p. 30) rather than the Vivès' "habilitatem."

150 That is: "that all the heavens have been created by the same author."

151 According to Aristotle (see *Physics* 3.1.200b32), whom Suárez reflects here, motion is never an absolute reality, but rather one which always presupposes a thing which is in motion.

152 This is not necessarily a temporal instant. It may be a moment of nature, causality, or being.

different kind of craftsman, who in creating the heavens, gave them a nature fitted to that kind of disposition and order which he simultaneously created with them.

19. From this it is easy to argue further for the other part of the consequent, namely: because of the same nature and the connection of those superior bodies with inferior ones, it is necessary to say that the creation of all is the same. This is further explained as follows.

The constitution of the universe from the heavens and sublunar bodies can be understood in two or three ways. First, that the heavens themselves, already existing either from themselves (which has before now been disproven) or from some agent, by their own power and efficacy created all inferior things and most appropriately fitted them for the constitution and the conservation of this inferior world. And this way is as such incredible:

One, because this inferior world cannot be made except by a creation. But, as was said above, [153] no corporeal thing has a natural power to create. Indeed, even if we were to imagine God to have first created matter, the heavens could not immediately from that have produced all the elements, as distinct and disposed as their nature or the utility and beauty of the universe require. For since the heavens act naturally and, insofar as [they act] of themselves, [they always act] in the same way, if they are applied with the same nearness or distance and with the same unhindered motion, they could not from the same matter, of themselves with equal indifference, cause so varied and so ordered effects. Therefore, it is evident that this was not the work of nature alone, but of an Intelligence having a most eminent and multiple power with regard to activity and the choice to operate for an intended end.

Two, [it is incredible] because the heavens by themselves alone can hardly do anything without the concurrence of the lower bodies. For they must first emit light or another influence proportioned to themselves and in order to achieve their effects they always require some cooperation of inferior causes. The argument for this is that the sun, which among all the stars is evidently the most efficacious, can in no way either create the harvests without rain and the preparation of the ground, or efficiently cause something similar by itself alone. Add the fact that there are some effects in these inferior things which cannot be produced by the heavens without univocal agents,[154] as was seen above.[155]

---

153 Cf. *DM* XX, s. 2, nn. 14–15, vol. 25, pp. 756–57.

154 On the distinction between univocal and equivocal causes or agents, cf. *DM* XVII, s. 2, n. 21, vol. 25, pp. 591–92.

155 Cf. this Section, § 14, above; also cf. Suárez, *Index locupletissimus*, VII, c. 8, q. 4, vol. 25, p. xxxv; and *DM* XXII, s. 5, n. 15, vol. 25, p. 841.

20. However, in a second way, it is possible to imagine that, with the heavens already existing and disposed as they are by their efficient cause, another completely distinct agent would have effected the lower world and would have disposed it in an acceptable and appropriate way, so that it could be cradled and governed by the superior world.

This way is also of itself impossible. For if it is understood that this was done by a kind of convention or agreement of both agents, that pertains to the second objection which will be treated presently.[156] But if it is being said (as is indicated in the words expressed) that the author of the heavens in so creating and disposing them was not looking in his mind and intention toward the advantage and benefit of the lower world, that is manifestly false, as can be clear enough from what has been said. For the very disposition and influence of the heavens proclaim that they have been created, as the Scripture says, "to help all nations."[157] This also is manifested by their most orderly motions, which by a certain uniform difformity[158] are so wonderfully distributed that they aid the inferior world for every necessary action, for example, for the variety of the seasons, for the generations and corruptions of things,[159] and finally "that they be for signs, and seasons, days, and years."[160]

Nor does it matter that these motions may have been added to the heavens after their creation and that (as is probable) they may be produced by movers which are distinct both among themselves and from the creator of the heavens, because even so the heavens have been created apt and proportioned to such motions, as their shape and influence declares. This, therefore, is a sign that they were created with that concern and intention. Hence, even though they have their proximate movers, these are not independent from the first Creator and Governor, and they move according to his command and intention, insofar as it is expedient for the good of the whole universe and the appropriate benefit of the lower bodies. Thus, from the making and the constitution of this universe, as well as the connection, the proportion, and subordination of its parts, it is in the best and most evident way deduced that there is one Author of the whole universe.

---

156 See § 21, immediately following.

157 Cf. *Deuteronomy* 4. 19.

158 Suárez here is evidently referring to the different speeds and angles at which the heavenly spheres were thought by Aristotle to move continuously.

159 Think here of the motion of the sun in the "oblique circle" or the ecliptic, which causes the different seasons as well as the generation and corruption of terrestrial substances. Cf. Aristotle, *De Generatione et corruptione* 2.10.336a31–b20 and *Meteorologica* 1.9.346b21–23.

160 *Genesis* 1. 14.

The Second Evasion Is Rejected and the True Unity of the First Author of the Whole Universe Is Shown.

21. But now we meet a second evasion. For this unity can be understood in two ways: first, as a natural and simple unity of the same cause; and second as an aggregation and consensus of several [causes]. We then intend the first unity, because it is needed in order to conclude that God exists. But the argument made, even though it shows unity, does not however appear to demonstrate that so perfect [unity]. For it is principally based on this, that the whole universe in the manner of one adequate effect must fall under the intention of one agent. However, this could be true even if several quasi-partial agents were to concur, as long as they were to agree in the manner of one [agent] to cause one adequate effect, just as several craftsmen [may agree to construct] one building. Therefore, in order to exclude this fiction and in order to show from this effect the true unity of the first agent, we must first of all suppose that a cause of this kind must of necessity be intellectual. This will be shown in an *a priori* way below[161] and it is evident from what has been said about the making and the disposition of the universe, and it is also evidently concluded from one effect, namely, man. Finally, even assuming that fiction, it is especially necessary. For two partial causes which lack knowledge, especially if they are of different natures, cannot by themselves intentionally agree to produce one adequate effect, unless they are subordinated to some higher cause, of which they are in a sense tools or instruments.

22. *How many absurd things follow from an assertion of several non-subordinated causes of this world.* – Hence, it should further be noted that this consensus of several partial causes in order to create the universe can be imagined in two ways. First, that they all are subordinated to one higher cause from which they have received existence. And this sense, although it contains false and erroneous doctrine, does not however pose any obstacle for, nor does it relate to, the matter we are now treating. For in that sense there is already admitted only one uncreated being from whom the rest have proceeded, and this whole world has primordially taken its origin from that being, which is enough for us to prove that God exists. For that first being we call God. But whether he has immediately by himself produced the world or through one or many inferior causes subordinated to himself, which is alluded to in the mentioned sense, pertains to another question about creation, which we have treated above[162] and which now occurs again.

Therefore, it can be understood in a second way, [namely], that several causes would have come together in order to produce this world, without any subor-

161 See Section 3, below.

162 Cf. *DM* XX, s. 2, vol. 25, pp. 766–69, where Suárez has denied that there are instrumental causes of creation.

dination either among themselves or to another higher [cause], but with a certain equality as regards their independence in being and acting, even though, perhaps, with regard to the production of the effects, one would concur more or would produce better effects than another, because necessarily one has made the heaven, another fire or water, or in some other similar way. And this is the sense of that error, which from its simple statement, without any refutation, of itself appears improbable and ridiculous. For those principles would be multiplied in vain and without necessity. And it is necessary that each of them be imperfect and insufficient for its own effect, or that the others be superfluous and consequently impossible.

23. *First*. – *Second*. – I argue then as follows. For either each of those causes requires the cooperation of the others, because without the others it is incapable of producing the whole universe, or because, even though as individuals they could produce the whole and of themselves would be equal in power, nevertheless they have decided to divide this effect among themselves.

If the first is said, it follows immediately that any one of the other causes taken by itself is very imperfect and limited in its power. From this, it follows next that it is also incapable [of producing] the effect that is attributed to it. For such an effect, for example, any heaven and even any element, could not come about except by a creation, which involves a total and primary production. However, it was shown above that in order to create in this manner of a primary cause, an absolutely infinite power is required.[163] It was also shown that a cause which has a primary power to create can create whatever is creatable.[164] But in the case of the causes in question the power is said to be limited and restricted to one or another effect. Therefore, that is not a creative power. Accordingly, neither is it sufficient for the first production of the universe even in part, unless before its action there would be presupposed a creation of matter. But if all matter were first created by some agent, some form was concreated with it, because matter is not produced by itself but with a whole[165] which is created. That [agent], therefore, is the first creator of the universe, whom we call God.

24. *Third*. – Third, it follows from this error that the aggregate of all those causes is limited in power, imperfect in wisdom, and changeable with the different wills [of the partial causes]. From this it further results that the providence and the governance of the world which depends upon that [aggregate] must be very imperfect, deficient in many ways, and very foreign to the infinite wisdom and power which the making and governance of the universe indicates well enough.

---

163 Cf. *DM* XX, s. 2, n. 40, vol. 25, p. 765.

164 *Ibid.*, n. 32, p. 762.

165 That is, a composite of form and matter.

The inference is explained: because, first of all, since the individual causes in that aggregate are of finite power, from all of them taken together no infinite power can emerge, unless perhaps those partial causes are said to be of an infinite number, which indeed cannot be said about those which have actually produced the things of universe. For since these things are finite in number, the number of causes cannot be infinite, unless it is said that several or even infinite [causes] concur simultaneously in order to produce individual things. But it is immediately evident how absurd and ridiculous that is.

Neither would it be less improbable to say that causes of this kind, which are able in this way to produce the things of the universe, are infinite, even if they are not all actually operating. For, to omit the common arguments which can be made against this infinity, again [it is improbable] because, if it cannot be deduced from any operation, it is imagined gratuitously and without basis. Again, [it is improbable] because that infinite multitude helps in no way for the creation of the universe insofar as it has been made, since the whole [multitude] does not concur for that. Besides all of this (I repeat), in that whole definite aggregate of causes there is no power of acting which is infinite and in every way perfect, because this perfection consists more in an intensity than in a multitude.[166]

25. Next, a similar argument can be made about wisdom, which is the most important perfection of an intellectual thing and is commensurate with perfection in being. But if a power is limited and imperfect, so also is the essence [in which that power is found]. Therefore, so again is the wisdom [which is commensurate with that essence]. Hence it could easily be thought about partial causes of this kind that any one of them is ignorant of many things, especially future things which depend upon the wills of the others. Therefore, of what kind could the providence be which comes from causes of this kind, even if they are imagined as all at one time consulting among themselves, and mutually helping one another, and one supplying for the imperfection and the weakness of another?

What can I say about their wills? For they would obviously be changeable, since they are finite. Therefore, they could easily disagree among themselves and one could act outside or against the will of another. Hence, directly to the matter about which we are treating, Justin Martyr, in his *Hortatory Speech to the Pagans*, said that a government of many is exposed to wars and disagreements, but the rule of one is free from these problems.[167] And in [support of] the same opinion, [St.] Athanasius, in his *Speech Against Idols*, has said: "Where there is

166 That is to say that the infinity involved here is intensive rather than extensive.

167 Actually, this is Pseudo-Justin. Cf. Pseudo-Iustinus, *Cohortatio ad Graecos, De Monarchia, Oratio ad Graecos*, edited by Miroslav Marcovich (Berlin/New York: Walter de Gruyter, 1990), *Cohortatio*, 17, ll. 19–22, p. 47.

no prince, there arises destruction; hence it is concluded that a multitude of gods is a negation of gods."[168] And [St.] Cyprian, in his book, *On the Vanity of Idols*, says: "Let us borrow from earthly things an example for Divine government: how the society of a kingdom has always begun with faith or how has it ceased to be without slaughter?"[169] And Plato, in the *Statesman*, after the middle [of the dialogue], said that the government of many is weak and infirm in all things.[170] For this reason, according to Aristotle, *Ethics*, Book 8, Chapter 10,[171] and the opinion of all philosophers, a monarchical regime is preferable to all the rest. On account of this, the same Aristotle, in Book 12 of his *Metaphysics*, concludes: "Beings do not want to be badly governed. A plurality of governments is not good. Therefore, there is one prince."[172]

Accordingly, governance and providence for the universe would be extremely imperfect, if it were to depend upon many heads and many finite and mutable wills without a subordination to some supreme power, supreme wisdom, and immutable as well as supremely good will.

26. Add that the things of the universe are so disposed and connected among themselves that some completely need others either for their own conservation or for pursuing their own activities. Also they all intend the integrity and the conservation of the whole universe, so much so that they sometimes abandon what is to their own advantage in order to preserve that. For example, water ascends in order to refill a vacuum,[173] and according to the more accepted opinion, earth, contrary to its own natural condition, occupies a higher place than water. But if (as others wish) water left to itself rises higher (*simpliciter eminet*), it is more wonderful that it always restrains its swelling floods, so as not to destroy the beauty of the earth and all its inhabitants. Which, therefore, of those partial causes will be sufficient for the protection and conservation of its own effect? Surely,

---

168 Cf. S.P.N. Athanasii Archiepiscopi Alexandrini, *Oratio contra Gentes*, n. 38, in *PG*, vol. 25, cols. 75–76.

169 Cf. S. Thascii Caecilii Cypriani episcopi Carthaginenis, *Liber de idolorum vanitate*, VIII, in *PL*, vol. 4, col. 576.

170 Cf. *Politicus* 297BC.

171 Cf. *Nichomachean Ethics* 8.10.1160a36–37.

172 *Metaphysics* 12.10.1076a3–4.

173 For the natural place of water next to earth and its ascent to fill a vacuum, cf. Aristotle, *De Caelo et mundo* 2. 4.287a32–b8. On water drawn up in a clepsydra, see *ibid.*, 13.294b20–21; or in heated vessels, *ibid.*, 4.5.312b13–14. For post-Aristotle discussion of experiments with clepsydrae, drinking straws, and siphons, showing how water fills a void, see Pierre Duhem, *Le système du monde: histoire des doctrines cosmologiques de Platon à Copernic* I, nouveau tirage (Paris: Librairie Scientifique Hermann et Cie, 1954), pp. 323–32.

none. But it would be necessary that the author of the mixtures and of the animals ask the lord of the waters to contain them lest they destroy his effects. And in this way each one would require the help of another, so that his effect could be protected and conserved. Similar problems and absurdities can easily be imagined because that which coalesces from many imperfect things must [itself] be imperfect. Therefore, the marvelous structure and the wonderful composition and order of diverse things cannot be conceived without one supreme architect.

27. But if someone were to choose the other side of the above-stated dilemma and say that there are indeed several first principles of the universe of things, but still each one is sufficient by itself, as well as equal in power and perfection, for the governance of the whole, etc.: against this first of all is the fact that it is said without foundation that causes of this kind have divided the production of the universe by parts among themselves. For from what effect is that deduced? Or, if it is not deduced, who has revealed it?

Again, the arguments made conclude simply that there is necessarily one adequate cause that by itself intends the whole universe, looking to its advantages, and that partial causes do not suffice, whether they are partial from impotence or from choice. Moreover, against him who would imagine that, reason enough should be that he would have introduced so many principles needlessly and without a sufficient motive. For, if each of those causes is supposed to be sufficient for the production and the conservation of the whole universe as it exists now and for every perfection that can be desired in it, what is the reason why several causes of this kind are imagined? Or from what effect can such a multitude be found or believed?

Perhaps someone may answer that such a multitude is not supposed on account of an effect, [that is] because it is necessary for such or so great an effect, but because by itself it pertains to the perfection of things that entities (*res*) that are so perfect be multiplied. But against this is the fact that the unity and singularity of its nature belongs to its and to others' perfection. This will have to be proven *ex professo* below when we treat of the unity of God,[174] and it will be mentioned also in a later paragraph of this Section. And now it is briefly explained by continuing the consideration of that first being under the concept of cause and according to its relation to this adequate effect which is the whole universe, into which consideration and conception we are now entering.

Therefore, if this universe were to have several principles, no one of them would have perfect dominion over the whole universe, and consequently no one of them could perfectly govern that universe. For, if one of them wanted to corrupt or annihilate something, he could not do so if another were unwilling, because it could not by him alone be sufficiently conserved. Likewise, if one of

---

174 Cf. *DM* XXX, s. 10, vol. 26, pp. 137–41.

them wished to stir up the wind or the rain, he could not do so if another were to resist, because they would at least be of equal power. And the same is true of other things. Therefore, it pertains to the perfection of such a cause, as it is the cause and master of its effect, and to the perfect governance of the same effect, that such causes, which are equal among themselves, not be multiplied. From this Aristotle, in Book 12 of his *Metaphysics*, correctly concluded in the words that were cited a little before.[175] From this also comes that well-known sentence of Homer, in Book 2 of the *Iliad*: "That many command is bad; let there be one king."[176]

28. Hence, Lactantius, in his *First Book: On False Religion*, Chapter 3,[177] has first correctly disproven a multitude of principles and governors of the universe, who divide tasks among themselves because they must be weak: "Since each of them without the help of the rest could not bear the governance of so great a mass." Then he proves that there cannot be several "such as the one we want, because the power of each" (he says) "will not be able to act, when the powers of the others oppose it; for it is necessary that each one cannot either cross its boundaries or if it were to cross it would expel another from its boundaries." And Jerome, in his *4th Letter to Rusticus*, with various examples, both natural and political, shows that two men cannot take possession of a kingdom and that power does not suffer sharing.[178]

29. One could just imagine and say that this is true in those [governors] who can have contradictory wills; but these governors or procreators of the world have entirely harmonious wills. He who, however, thinks this way in order to defend perfect dominion or rule over the universe, why does he not think there is only one will from which all things depend and by which they are governed? For as St. Thomas has said, in [*Summa Theologiae*] Part I, Question 103, Article 3[179]: "That which is essentially one can be a cause of unity more suitably than many things which are united; hence a multitude is better governed by one than by many."

Moreover, those wills would be concordant either from a necessity of nature or from free consent. The first cannot be understood unless those wills lack liberty and always operate from a necessity of nature, which cannot be thought

175 See § 24, this Section.

176 *Iliad* 2, l. 204. Cf. *The Iliad of Homer*, translated with an introduction by Richmond Lattimore (Chicago: The University of Chicago Press, 1951), p. 81.

177 Cf. *PL*, vol. 6, cols. 122b–24c.

178 For this, see Sancti Eusebii Hieronymi, *Epistola CXXV* (*ad Rusticum Monachum*), n. 15, in *PL*, vol. 22, col. 1080.

179 Cf. *Opera omnia*, vol. 5, p. 455.

about the first principle, as I will show below.[180] But what is assumed is clear, because if both wills are free and neither has power over the other, but each is absolute and independent, by what necessity of nature can it happen that what one wills the other is also going to will? Indeed, much less can that be certain and infallible through a free consensus, because there is no greater reason why one would consent to the other rather than conversely,[181] nor why one would initiate and the other would comply. Therefore, such a consensus will be happening in some way by chance, and for the same reason discord could often occur.

The Third Objection Is Answered and the Efficient Cause of the Intelligences Is Treated.

30. What we have said up to now, evidently (I think) follows with respect to that first being which is the cause of this visible universe that we experience, and from that therefore we can easily philosophize and reason.

But then there occurs a third objection, because from this effect and the unity of the universe we cannot prove that Intelligences and spiritual things do not have being from themselves or that they are created by the same author by whom the universe has been made. For from the effects of the visible universe we cannot show either that the Intelligences have been made or that they have some connection with other things of the universe by reason of which it is concluded that they were made by the same author by whom the universe or the heavenly bodies [were made]. In addition, for this reason some philosophers have thought the Intelligences to be essentially necessary beings that have been produced by no one. This opinion many, such as Gregory [of Rimini], in [his *Sentences* commentary] Book 2, Distinction 1, Article 1,[182] attribute to Aristotle and to the Commentator,[183] who however have not thought otherwise about the Intelligences than about the heavens, as we will say.

31. To this objection we must say that it is one thing to ask simply and without qualification whether the Intelligences are beings which are of themselves necessary and depending on another in their being and what can be demonstrated about this simply by natural reason; but it is another thing to ask what can be immediately deduced from these effects which we experience in the universe. And this second question is the only one that is relevant to the efficacy of the present argument.

---

180 See *DM* XXX, s. 16, nn. 20–56, vol. 26, pp. 189–203.

181 That is, that the other would consent to the one.

182 Cf. Gregorii Ariminensis, O.E.S.A., *Super primum et secundum Sententiarum*, reprint of the 1522 [Venetiis] edition (St. Bonaventure, N.Y.: The Franciscan Institute, 1955), II, q. 1, a. 1, vol. 2, fols. 1–3.

183 That is, Averroes.

For this we should first ask whether, in addition to the first substance which we have shown to be necessary for the production and governance of this visible world, we can, from natural effects, know that there are some substances which are separate and superior to all sensible things, and then whence they are or what origin they have. For indeed if there are no effects in nature from which such substances may be known, it will be impossible to deduce immediately from effects whether they are produced or unproduced. For let us grant that there are some substances of this kind, which have no operation on bodies which we experience, in what way then could we from effects immediately deduce whether such substances exist from the one first substance or not, and whether they are equal or inferior to that [first substance]? I am adding the word "immediately" because from the properties of God which we deduce from his effects, we can afterwards infer whether such properties are so proper to the one substance that they are incommunicable to others, and in this way indeed mediately from effects but proximately from the First it can be demonstrated that if there are other Intelligences besides the First, they exist by the efficiency of the First, and that the First alone is from itself – about which we will speak in the following Section.

32. Therefore, the general question as to whether such substances exist, will have to be treated afterwards in a special *Disputation* which we will craft about them.[184] Now I am saying briefly that merely from effects which we experience it is not evidently enough shown that they do exist. But if this is to be proven by a metaphysical means it will rather be from their cause than from their effect.[185] And thus in that way in which they are demonstrated to exist it is simultaneously demonstrated that they have received being from the First Being. Again, I affirm that from effects or from physical motion some conjecture is possible that substances of this kind do exist in reality from the fact that they may move the heavenly spheres. However, that is only a probable argument, not a demonstration, as I will show below.[186]

Finally, I say that in the way in which these substances can be investigated from effects they are not known as existing from themselves, but as having their origin effectively from the same First Cause that produced the universe. And in this way it is probable that Aristotle and other philosophers knew that the Intelligences were effectively from God. For St. Thomas, in [his *Sentences* com-

---

184 For this, see *DM* XXXV, vol. 26, pp. 424–77.

185 The thought here is that while there is no effect which leads to Intelligences short of God, it would be fitting for God to have caused such Intelligences between Himself and material things.

186 Cf. *DM* XXXV, s. 1, n. 14, p. 430.

mentary], Book 2, Distinction 1, question 1,[187] and [his commentaries on] *Physics*, Book 8,[188] and *Metaphysics*, Book 12,[189] suggests that Aristotle thought this way; [as] Scotus [also suggests in his *Sentences* commentary] Book 2, Distinction 2,[190] and his 7th *Quodlibetal Question*, near the end.[191] Moreover, Soncinas, in *Metaphysics*, Book 12, Question 16,[192] and Javellus, [in the same book], Question 28,[193] prove this explicitly; [as does also] Cajetan in [his commentary on] *De Ente et essentia*, Chapter 5, Question 10, where more directly he proves that this was the opinion of the Commentator.[194] Javellus, however, thinks that the Commentator erred in this and thought something different from Aristotle, [but something] which was of little consequence.[195] However, from the reasoning and the argument which we will presently make, perhaps it will be clear what of all this is more true.

Also Avicenna, in his *Metaphysics*, Book 9, Chapter 4, explicitly states that all things, both corporeal and immaterial, have emanated from the First Being, however not immediately, but that the first Intelligence flowed immediately from God and from the first Intelligence there flowed the second, and so on down to the last, by which the universe was proximately (*immediate*) made[196] – which doctrine is clearly Platonic,[197] and almost the same is presented under the name

187 Cf. S. Thomae Aquinatis, *Scriptum super libros Sententiarum Magistri Petri Lombardi*, II, d. 1, q. 1, a. 4, vol. 2, pp. 23–27.

188 Cf. S. Thomae Aquinatis, *In octo libros Physicorum Aristotelis expositio*, VIII, c. 1, l. 3, cura et studio P.M. Maggiòlo, O.P. (Taurini: Marietti, 1954), n. 996, p. 516.

189 Cf. *In duodecim libros Metaphysicorum Aristotelis expositio*, XII, c. 10, l. 12, ed. Cathala, no. 2662, p. 616.

190 Cf. *Ordinatio* II, d. 2, q. 1, in *Opera*, vol. 7 (1978), pp. 161–93.

191 Cf. Joannis Duns Scoti, *Quaestiones quodlibetales*, q. VII, a. 2, nn. 116–18, in *Obras* ... , ed. Alluntis, pp. 304–5. See John Duns Scotus, *God and Creatures: ...*, tr. Alluntis and Wolter, p. 194.

192 Cf. *Quaestiones* ..., XII, q. 16, p. 324.

193 Cf. Chrysostomi Iavelli Canapicii, *In omnibus Metaphysicae libris quaesita* ..., XII, q. 28; fol. 391rv.

194 Cf. Cajetan, *In De Ente et Essentia D. Thomae Aquinatis commentaria*, c. 5, q. 10, n. 94, ed. Laurent, p. 149.

195 Cf. Chrysostomi Iavelli Canapicii, *In omnibus Metaphysicae libris quaesita* ..., XII, q. 28; fols. 393r–94r.

196 Cf. Avicenna, *Liber de philosophia prima*, Tr. IX, c. 4, ed. Van Riet (1980), pp. 476–88.

197 That is, more properly, "neo-Platonic." For the probable immediate source of Suárez's judgment here, cf. note 198, just following.

of Aristotle in [the spurious work] *De Secretiore parte divinae Sapientiae*, Book 3, Chapter 2.[198] But just as that mode of emanation is so completely false, as easily is clear from what was said above about creation,[199] so also it has no evidence in all the effects or motions which we experience in the heavens or the elements or in ourselves. Therefore, we must now omit this doctrine, about which we have often spoken above[200] and we will say something in what follows.[201]

33. Therefore, the stated affirmation[202] is proven: because in the universe, besides the motion of the heavens, there is no effect or motion from which we can deduce that Intelligences exist. But this effect [of the motion of the heavens] with the same certainty or conjecture or probability by which it indicates that there are Intelligences, indicates them as subordinate and thus as caused by the same author of the universe; therefore.

The major premise is evident, first from Aristotle, in *Physics*, Book 8,[203] and in *Metaphysics*, Book 12,[204] where from the motion of heaven he ascends to the

198 For this cf. *Libri quatuordecim, qui Aristotelis dicuntur de secretiore parte divinae sapientiae secundum Aegyptios*. Qui si illius sunt, eiusdem metaphysica vera continent, cum Platonicis magna ex parte convenientia. Opus nunquam Lutetiae editum, ante annos quinquaginta ex lingua Arabica in Latinam male conversum: nunc vero de integro recognitum et illustratum scholiis, quibus huius capita singula cum Platonica doctrina sedulo conferuntur. Per Jacobum Carpentarium (Parisiis: Ex Officina Jacobi du Puys, 1571) [second edition: 1572], III, cap. 2 (p. 23rv). The interesting title page of this work translates as follows: *Fourteen Books, which are said to be from Aristotle, about the More Secret Part of Divine Wisdom* – which, if they do belong to him, contain his true Metaphysics, in great part agreeing with the Platonists. The work, never [before] edited at Paris, was fifty years earlier badly translated from the Arabic language into Latin; but now it has been completely revised and explained with scholia in which its individual chapters are carefully compared with Platonic doctrine, by Jacques Charpentier. At Paris: from the printshop of Jacques du Puys, 1571. For Charpentier's judgment that this order is most famously Platonic, cf. "Qui ordo apud Platonicos celeberrimus est, ..." *ibid.*, *Scholia* 1., p. 23v. For another reference by Suárez to this work, see *DM* XXI, s. 1, n. 15, vol. 25, p. 789, where he cites 8 lines from Book XII, c. 19.

199 Cf. *DM* XX, s. 2, vol. 25, pp. 754–66.

200 See, e.g. *DM* XV, s. 2, n. 9, vol. 25, p. 508; *DM* XVIII, s. 2, 4 and 18, vol. 25, pp. 594 and 598; *DM* XX, s. 2, nn. 1 and 27, pp. 754 and 761. Also cf. *DM* XXVIII, s. 1, n. 11, above.

201 Cf.: *DM* XXXV, s. 1, n. 14, vol. 26, p. 430; *ibid.* n. 23, p. 434; and *ibid.*, s. 6, nn. 2 and 8, pp. 468 and 470.

202 Cf. § 32, immediately preceding.

203 Cf. *Physics* 8.6.258b10–260a19.

204 Cf. *Metaphysics* 12.68.1073a14–b1.

contemplation of Intelligences; nor does he ever anywhere else find another way to show beings of this kind in the world, and almost all later philosophers have imitated him. Also [the major is evident] because, going through all the effects in the universe, there is not one for which beings of this kind are necessary. This is because for the production of the whole universe, the power of the first author is enough, both with respect to simple bodies and with respect to the perfect species of composites. But for alterations, generations and corruptions, as well as changes of the elements, there suffices the power of secondary proximate causes as well as universal or heavenly [causes], with the general concurrence of the first cause. Therefore, if in some thing these effects can depend upon Intelligences, it is only insofar as they depend upon the motion of heaven and, by the medium of that [motion], upon the mover of heaven.

34. To be sure, there do appear to be effects which men experience only in themselves and which can be called moral (*morales*) rather than physical, for the reason that they neither belong to nor are ordered to the physical generations and alterations which come to be in the universe, but to the customs (*mores*) of men. Moreover, of this kind are the interior voices (*locutiones*) or motions by which we are induced to good or evil, which by almost evident experience are known to come from some superior cause or spirit. And it also often happens that voices or apparitions of this kind are visible, about which many things are also found among the philosophers, who sometimes call these spirits "genies," sometimes "demons" and "gods."

However, this [kind of] effect either does not sufficiently show that there are superior spirits distinct from the souls of men and from the first cause, or, if it indicates that those exist, it at the same time indicates that they are created. For, first, it is not entirely evident that these interior motions or voices come immediately from some external intellectual agent and not rather from the internal power of the soul itself, by means of objects that occur to it. Second, even if we grant that sometimes motions of this kind are such or happen in such a way that, if they are correctly assessed, it can be sufficiently understood from them that they come from an external spirit, nevertheless, if the effect is good it can be immediately from God, and so it does happen frequently in the case of internal motions and voices. For, the fact that these may sometimes come from good angels is evident to us more by revealed doctrine than by reason. But if this did become known to some philosophers, perhaps they acquired it by some tradition or communication with the Faithful of their time, for example, with the Jews,[205] or perhaps through

205 This comes close to an opinion associated with the second century A.D. philosopher, Numenius, for whom Plato was just "an Atticizing Moses," that is to say, a Moses speaking Greek; cf. R. McL. Wilson, "Numenius of Apamea," *The Encyclopedia of Philosophy* (New York/London: Macmillan Publishing Co., Inc. & The Free Press, 1967), vol. 5, pp. 530–31.

a sufficient revelation by those same angels. This cognition then belongs to a certain human learning and faith, rather than to the discovery and knowledge from effects about which we are now treating.

But if the effect is bad or leading to a moral evil or to a deception, it cannot as such be immediately from God, who is supremely good. However, it is not evident that it cannot be from separate human spirits.[206] And, even if we grant that sometimes an effect [of this kind] is such that it may show that it is from a superior and more powerful spirit, nevertheless, at the same time it indicates that spirit to be created. For, since it is evil, it will be mutable and deficient in good inasmuch as evil is nothing more than the defect of good, as we have shown above.[207] But nothing is mutable and defectable except what is created. Therefore, these spirits have been created.

Again, from the evil itself of such spirits a very good deduction can be made, which Augustine, arguing against the Manichees, often suggests. For if these spirits become evil by defecting from the good, this very thing indicates the goodness of their nature. For it would not be an evil for them to defect from the good, unless that nature itself were good. However, it cannot be the supreme good, otherwise it could not turn away from the good. Therefore, it is good by participation. Therefore, it is effectively from the Supreme Good.[208]

Therefore, leaving aside this moral effect, which does not belong to either physical or metaphysical consideration, apart from the motion of heaven there is no natural effect that leads us to any cognition of Intelligences.

35. It remains to prove the second proposition which was asserted: namely, that just as from this effect[209] we infer that Intelligences exist, so we must also infer that they exist from the Creator of the universe.[210] First, because they are not less relevant to the make-up of this universe than are other things of which it consists, since without their activity this world cannot be naturally conserved nor could there be generations and corruptions in it. Therefore, this part of the universe is from the one from whom the whole exists.

Second, because an Intelligence moving a heaven moves it in such way as fits the good of the universe, and for this end it perseveres perpetually and without variation in that motion – therefore, this is a sign that this Intelligence moves on account of the end which is intended by the author of the universe, and con-

---

206 That is, souls separated from their bodies after death.

207 See *DM* XI, s. 1, n. 3, vol. 25, p. 356.

208 Cf. e.g. St. Augustine, *Confessiones* VII, 12, in *PL*, vol. 32, col. 743; *De natura boni*, 4–6, in *PL*, vol. 42, col. 553; *ibid.*, 12, col. 55; *ibid.*, 41, cols. 563–64.

209 That is, heavenly motion.

210 Cf. *DM* XXXV, s. 1, n. 5, vol. 26, pp. 426–27.

sequently it moves on account of the author himself of the universe, that is, either to obey his command, or to help or cooperate with him in order to pursue the goal intended by him, or to be like him in acting and doing well. Therefore it is a sign that this Intelligence is subordinated to that first cause itself and depends upon it and consequently that it has been made by that [cause]. And Aristotle in *Metaphysics*, Book 12, Text 36,[211] indicated this reasoning when he said there is one immobile mover on whom all the other Intelligences depend, because they all belong to the order of the universe and they are moved in this way by the first mover, at least as by a desirable end; but that itself is an immobile mover.

36. You will say that from this it is concluded only that the other Intelligences relate to the First as an end, but not as an efficient [cause].

The answer is that from a final cause there is inferred an efficient [cause], because whatever has a final cause also has an efficient [cause], as has been said above[212] and will come up again below.[213] Then it is said that in line with the reasoning which we have pursued in this whole argument, from the connection of these Intelligences with the universe there is inferred their emanation from the same author from whom the universe emanated. For we should not think that the author of the universe could not have created it whole and absolute with all its causes, among which these Intelligences hold the very highest place. Neither is it probable that after the creation of the heavens, he as it were called forth from somewhere else ministers which he would use to move them, and would not rather by his own force and power have brought those [ministers] from non-being to being, just as [he did] the heavens themselves. Finally, if the Intelligences were beings that would of themselves be as necessary as God, they would not be under his dominion and consequently they would not be subject to his command. Therefore, in what way could God effectively use them for necessary help with the universe? Accordingly, from a ministry of this kind it is correctly inferred that these Intelligences are creatures subject to the Author of the universe and produced by him.

The Fourth Objection Is Answered.

37. There was a fourth objection:[214] for apart from this universe there can be thought to be another that has been made by another first not-made being. To this the Philosopher perhaps would respond that it is impossible that there be anoth-

211 Cf. *Metaphysics* 12.7.1072a24–27.

212 Cf., e.g. *DM* XXVI, s. 3, n. 7, vol. 25, pp. 927–28.

213 Cf. Section 3, § 27, below.

214 See § 8, this Section.

er universe on account of the arguments which he makes in [his work] *On Heaven [and Earth]*, Book 1, Chapters 8 and 9.[215] However, those arguments must be of no importance for a Christian philosopher.[216] For there is no doubt that God could make many worlds, and that if he did make them, there would fail in that case all of Aristotle's conjectures, by which he wished to conclude either that in this universe there is all the matter of which simple or mixed things could consist, or that the elements of this universe cannot remain quiet in their places[217] if another universe were to exist.

However, he achieves nothing [with these arguments], for first of all there could be another universe consisting of simple bodies which would be diverse in species, either with respect to species or forms, or also (what is less certain) with respect to their physical genus or prime matter. Then, even though it is not evident that there is another matter besides that which is in this universe, because we have no indication of another matter, and therefore no philosopher can affirm that it exists, still in actual fact, and (so to speak) positively, there is no means by which to demonstrate that all the matter of corporeal things is in this universe.

Finally, with respect to the places or the motions of the elements, since these things must be derived from the natural order of those very bodies among themselves, the bodies of each world (if there were two) would remain quiet in their own places[218] and they would be moved naturally among themselves in order to preserve due order. But the bodies of distinct worlds would not have an order between them and therefore neither [a body in one world or another] would desire to be under another or over another [in a different world].[219] Therefore, it must be said that he who in order to vitiate the force of the argument which was made would imagine another world, would certainly say nothing impossible or entailing contradiction. However, (to leave out the error against the Faith[220]) he

---

215 Cf. *De caelo* 1.8–9.277b9–79a11.

216 Suárez, like many Catholic Scholastics before him, would probably have in mind here the famous and powerful condemnation by Stephen Tempier, Bishop of Paris, in 1277 of 219 propositions, of which one (n. 34) was: "That the First Cause could not make several worlds" (*Quod prima causa non posset plures mundos facere*."); for this, cf. Henricus Denifle, O.P., *Chartularium universitatis parisiensis*, vol. I (Paris, 1889/ impression anastatique, Bruxelles: Culture et Civilisation, 1964), annus 1277, n. 473, p. 543.

217 On the natural places of elements, see notes 130, 137, and 173, above.

218 *Ibid.*

219 That is to say the earth in one world would have no appetite to be under the fire in another world, nor would the fire in one world have any appetite to be over the earth in another world.

220 See note 216, just above.

would rashly affirm that which can come to be surmised from no argument or conjecture, and therefore, that subterfuge is not philosophical.

However, I confess that from this and the preceding objection I am convinced that the reasoning made to prove that there is only one unproduced being and that all the rest of beings have been made by that being does not conclude absolutely about all beings, but only about those which can fall under human cognition by way of natural reasoning or philosophy. Therefore, in order that the argument conclude universally, there necessarily must be employed a demonstration *a priori*, which we promised in the second place[221] and we will pursue in the following Section.

SECTION THREE

Whether in Some Way It Can Be Demonstrated A Priori *that God Exists.*

1. In order to expound the second way of proving the proposed truth, we must suppose that, simply speaking, God cannot be demonstrated to exist in an *a priori* manner. For God does not have a cause of his being, through which he might be demonstrated *a priori*. Or if he did have such a cause, God is not known so exactly and perfectly by us that we could follow him (so to speak) from his proper principles. In this sense, Dionysius, in chapter 7 of *On Divine Names*, said that we cannot know God from his proper nature.[222] But even though this is true,[223] nevertheless, after something about God has been demonstrated in an *a posteriori* way, we can from one attribute demonstrate another *a priori*. As an example: from [the Divine] immensity we may conclude to his local immutability. For I am supposing that in order to reason *a priori* in a human way a distinction of reason[224] among the [Divine] attributes is enough.[225]

---

221 Cf. Section 2, § 7, above.

222 Dionysius, *De divinis nominibus*, c. 7, *PG,* vol. 3, col. 870.

223 For Suárez in relation to the negative theology of Pseudo-Dionysius, cf. Goudriaan, *Philosophische Gotteserkenntnis* ..., pp. 148–55.

224 That is, a distinction not in things themselves but in our concepts of those things. For Suárez on distinctions of reason, see *DM* VII, s. 1, nn. 4–8, vol. 25, pp. 251–52.

225 With this compare the Prologue to the next Disputation, which treats the Divine Nature at length: "Up to now we have shown principally that God exists and have begun in part to explain what He is, since, as we said, in the knowledge [we have] of God these two things cannot be entirely separated. Now it remains to treat the rest of what directly pertains to knowing what God is. And at the same time we will explain of what kind (*qualis*) and how great (*quantus*) He is, because quality (*qualitas*) or greatness (*magnitudo*) in God are not other than his essence. However, we are presupposing that we cannot by natural reason know these things about God as they are in themselves, because that can only happen through a clear vision of Him, which is not natural for a man, as we will also show below. Neither can all these things be simply demonstrated *a priori* by us about God, since we can come to a knowledge of

The Resolution of the Question.

2. Therefore, as regards this way, one should say that having demonstrated *a posteriori* that God is a being which is necessary and self-sufficient (*a se*), from this attribute it can be *a priori* demonstrated that apart from him there can be no other necessary and self-sufficient being, and thus logically (*consequenter*) [it will be] shown that God exists.

You will say: therefore, from the known quiddity (*quidditas*)[226] of God it is demonstrated that God exists, because the essence of God is that he is a necessary and self-sufficient being. But this is obviously unacceptable, because the question "what is it?" presupposes the question "whether it is?" as St. Thomas, in [*Summa*], I, q. 2, a. 2, ad 2,[227] correctly noted as regards what is being proposed here (*ad hoc propositum*).

I answer: formally and properly speaking, the existence of God is not demonstrated through the quiddity of God as such. However, from a particular attribute, which in actuality is the essence of God but is conceived by us as a mode of a non-caused being, another attribute is inferred and in this way it is concluded that that being is God. Hence, in order to conclude in this way that God exists precisely as God (*sub ratione Dei*), it is presupposed that a certain essentially necessary being has been proven to exist, [i.e. proven] from effects and from the denial of an infinite regress. In this way, what is first proven about this being is existence, then necessary existence from within itself, and, from this, a unique existence in this character and way of being – and, therefore, the fact that it is God. In this way the question "whether it is?" is in some manner answered before the question "what is it?" However, as I said above,[228] in the case of God these questions cannot be entirely separated, for the reason that the existence of God is [the same as] the essence of God and the properties of that

---

Him only through effects. However, when we know one attribute of God from His effects, sometimes we can from that *a priori* infer another, according to our way of conceiving Divine things separately, and by eliciting one concept from another, as we touched upon in a Disputation above. And these two ways of demonstration should be noted and should be applied as far as possible to individual Divine Attributes. Therefore, the first foundation and principle, as it were, of all that is attributed to God is his being an essentially necessary being and his being by essence, which was demonstrated in the preceding Disputation. Therefore, the very being itself of God is His quiddity. But what may be included in this being or what may be inferred from this being by essence must now be seen." *DM* XXX, prol., vol. 26, p. 60.

226 Literally: "whatness" – that is, the essence.

227 Cf. *Opera*, vol. 4, p. 30.

228 Cf. this Disputation, Section 1, § 41.

existence, by means of which it can be shown that that existence is proper to God, constitute (so to speak) the quiddity and the essence itself of God.

Why There Can Be Only One Essentially Necessary Being: The First Demonstration.

3. It is, however, difficult to effectively deduce from the fact that there is one being [which would be] necessary from itself and through itself that there cannot be another [which would be] like it in that property. Soncinas, in his *Metaphysics*, Book 12, Question 17, proves this by the following argument: being belongs through itself and first (*per se primo*) to an unproduced being. But it cannot of itself and first belong to two things. Therefore, it can belong only to one unproduced being.[229]

The major [premise] seems self-evident, because an unproduced being does not have being in an accidental way (*per accidens*) but essentially, and it does not have being through another, since it is completely independent. Therefore, being belongs to that [unproduced being] through itself and first.

The minor is clear because that is said to belong to something through itself and first which belongs to it adequately in such a way that it always and essentially belongs to it and to no other except by it, either by reason of it or by means of it. Hence in the First Book of the *Posterior [Analytics]*, Text 2,[230] a predicate which belongs through itself and first is called universal, since it is not by another and it belongs adequately. This argument has been taken from St. Thomas, in *Contra Gentiles*, Book 2, Chapter 15,[231] although he uses different words and says that being belongs to God "insofar as God is Himself" (*secundum quod ipsum*). However [words aside], the matter is the same, as is clear from Aristotle, in the place cited.[232]

4. Yet, immediately it seems that in this argument there is a begging of the question. For when it is said that being belongs to God "essentially and first" (*per se primo*) the word "first" can be taken either negatively or positively. In the former way, the sense is that being belongs to God in such manner that it belongs to no other before. And in this way the proposition is self-evident, presupposing that God is by his essence his own existence. And it is only in this sense that the proposition is proven by the argument given, namely, that God has being not by accident and not by another. However, in this sense that principle is not sufficient in order to infer that no other being has being from itself, because, even though

229 Cf. Soncinas, *Quaestiones* ..., XII, q. 17, p. 326.

230 Cf. *Posterior Analytics* 1.1.71a17–28.

231 Cf. *Opera*, vol. 13, p. 295.

232 That is, *Posterior Analytics* 1.1.71a17–28.

[such other] may not exist before, nevertheless, it could have being in an equally first way.

Therefore, that principle must be taken in a second way. And the sense will be that being belongs to God before every other being, suchwise that it belongs to none in an equally first manner. And in this way, the question is begged in the argument. For this is the very thing that we are asking; and that proposition is not sufficiently proven in that sense by the reasoning [just] above. For from the fact that being belongs to God not by accident nor by another, at most it can be inferred that it belongs to no other before [it belongs] to him, but not that it belongs to him before it belongs to the rest.

Perhaps it will be said that this principle is taken in the prior sense, but that in a second proposition it can be assumed and proven that what belongs to something through itself and first cannot belong to another except through it.

5. But against this, there is a second and principal objection: for in all those terms, namely, "to belong through itself and first and through another," a major equivocation seems to be committed. For something can belong in two ways to many things by another which is prior. In one way, really and by a true efficient causality, as, for example, to enlighten can be said to belong to the sun through itself and first among all the stars; in a second way, by reason only and without any physical causality, but only in a metaphysical manner (*metaphysica tantum ratione*),[233] in which way being able to smile (*risibile*) belongs through itself and first to man, and then through that to Peter and Paul.

If, therefore, in the present instance, the proposition in question is taken in this second way, as in fact it is taken by Aristotle in the *Posterior Analytics*,[234] it is indeed true and rightly proven by the argument given there. However, this is not relevant, because here we are asking about the effective emanation of one thing from another; hence the prior proposition could be denied in a proportional sense, as I will say now.

But if that proposition is taken in the first sense, it will be found to be false, as is evident in the stated example of man, or in that of a triangle, which Aristotle gave.[235] For, even though having three angles equal to two right angles belongs through itself and first to a triangle, it does not efficiently belong through that to an isosceles [triangle].

---

233 Evident in this mode of expression is a conception of metaphysics as "essentialist," that is to say, concerned primarily with essences and their properties rather than with things as they actually exist. For such an understanding of Suárez's metaphysics, see Etienne Gilson, *Being and Some Philosophers*, 2nd edition (Toronto: Pontifical Institute of Mediaeval Studies, 1952), esp. pp. 96–105.

234 Cf. *Posterior Analytics* 1.1.71a17–28.

235 *Ibid.*

And in the same way, anyone who would think that there are two unproduced beings would say that indeed in reality (*secundum rem*) it belongs to both to be through itself and first, because it does not belong to either to be efficiently through the other nor to both [to be efficiently] through a third thing. And in this way it is not unacceptable that the same predicate belong to two things through itself and first, because it is not necessary that that predicate be universal or adequate with respect to all and each of the things to which it belongs in the said way, "through itself and first." However, he who would think like this would reasonably deny that being belongs through itself and first to God precisely as God, or as he is this particular being (*ut tale ens*), but [would allow that it so belongs] to an unproduced being as such, whose essence as it is understood (positing that hypothesis) would abstract from this or that unproduced being.

Hence, when, in this reasoning, being by another is said not to belong to God, if it is understood: that is, [not to belong] by an efficient cause, this is true and is rightly proven from the fact that he is an unproduced being. But if it is understood: that is, not through another more abstract concept according to an intellectual precision, in this way that proposition will be denied by him who will have posited two unproduced beings. And in that sense it cannot be proven from the argument that was made.

6. To state the problem more fully: in order that the argument may proceed without prejudice or equivocation, we must speak with proportion about [1] being (*esse*) and [2] a being (*ens*) or that which is. Therefore, either we are talking about a particular determinate being which exists in reality or [we are talking] about being (*esse*) itself as abstractly conceived.

In the first way it is true that this particular being which is in God belongs first to God as he is God, and it adequately belongs to him and it is formally in no being except in him, or in that individual subject which is God, and it is by participation in no [other] being except through him. However, from this it cannot be cogently inferred that no other being (*esse*) can belong to another being (*ens*) through itself first. For something else (*aliud*)[236] can be thought which is really distinct from the being (*esse*) of God and not participated from him.

236 Here Suárez's word, "*aliud*," is ambiguous. Translated as "another," on its face it could be abstract being (*esse*) or a concrete being (*ens*). From the context, it seems plain that it should be taken in the former sense, that is, not as a concrete being but rather as an abstract "being itself" which is a being that is commonly possessed by but not restricted to any concrete being. In connection, we may note Suárez's refusal to allow any real distinction in creatures between existence and essence; for this see: *DM* XXXI, vol. 26, pp. 224–312, translated by Norman J. Wells: *Francis Suárez, On the Essence of Finite Being as such, On the Existence of that Essence and their Distinction*, Milwaukee: Marquette University Press, 1983. What Suárez is talking about in the present context is not a distinction between existence and essence but

Neither, from the argument that was made, does it appear how this is proven to be impossible.

But if we are talking about being (*esse*) as such and as conceived abstractly, in this way it will be denied that its subject or the quasi-subject, to which it is adequately related and [to which] through itself and first it belongs in an *a posteriori* manner, is this singular being which is called God. For it is not necessary that a common concept be said through itself and first about a singular thing. Hence, if being is taken most abstractly as it is something analogous with respect to unproduced and produced being, it does not seem to belong through itself and first to God, or to an unproduced being, but to being as such, as it is something analogous with respect to being by essence and participated [being]. If however being is taken less abstractly[237] – for unproduced being, in this way it will now be said to be something common according to concept, and therefore it will not relate through itself, first, and adequately to this being which is this God, but to unproduced being which is also supposed to be common, indeed even univocal,[238] according to concept to many unproduced beings, if we proceed logically according to this hypothesis. And although this [hypothesis] is false, and

rather between a particular being and a common being. The latter may be viewed on three levels. At first, it may be identical with the adequate object of understanding itself (cf. Suárez, *De Anima* IV, c. 1, n. 9, vol. 3, p. 715); second, it may be identical to the common objective concept of real being which is the object of metaphysics (cf. *DM* I, s. 1, n. 26, vol. 25, p. 11); and third, it may be restricted to a common concept of unproduced being. In the present context, Suárez is concerned only with the latter two levels.

237 That is, still abstractly but less so.

238 Note this: there are different ways in which we may conceive being in relation to its inferiors. Between God and creatures, it is analogical in the manner indicated above in *Disputation* 28, Section 3. Between substance and accidents it is also analogical. However, at various levels, for example, among substances themselves as such, or accidents as such, or here in the conjectured case of a number of unproduced beings, it will be univocal. On all of this, cf. e.g.: "... nothing prevents being from being univocal with respect to some things,..." *DM* XXVIII, s. 3, n. 5, vol. 26, p. 14; *DM* XXVII, s. 1, n. 11, vol. 25, p. 952; *DM* XXXII, s. 2, n. 24, vol. 26, p. 326; *ibid.*, no. 21; *DM* XXXIX, s. 3, n. 15, vol. 26, p. 528. At the same time, note again that, strictly speaking, *being is not a genus,* cf. *DM* II, s. 5, n. 10, vol. 25, p. 96; *ibid.,* s. 6, nn. 10, 12, pp. 101–2; *DM* XXXII, s. 2, n. 1, vol. 26, p. 323; and *DM* XXXIX s. 3, n. 18, vol. 26, p. 529. In this last view, Suarez differs from some later seventeenth-century authors whom he has profoundly influenced on other metaphysical questions; cf., e.g., the Dutch Calvinist, Franco Burgersdijk, *Institutionum Metaphysicarum, Libri Duo, Opus Posthumum* (Lugduni Batavorum: Apud Hieronymum de Vogel, 1640), II, c. 2, n. 14, p. 18; and his fellow Jesuit, Roderigo de Arriaga, S.J., *Cursus Philosophicus* (Lugduni, 1669), *Logica*, disp. XI, sec. 9 (Vol. 1, p. 187a).

similarly those things are false which follow on this [hypothesis], nevertheless, that does not seem possible to prove by this argument about whose efficacy we are now asking.

7. Perhaps it will be said that in that argument being (*ens*) is presupposed to be analogous, and therefore being (*esse*) itself cannot be reduced to a common nature (*ratio*), to which it "essentially and first" (*per se primo*) belongs, but [rather it is reduced] to some singular thing. And from this it cannot be logically (*consequenter*) inferred that it belongs through that [singular thing] to other things formally and according to a nature (*secundum rationem*), and therefore, it is rightly concluded that it belongs through that [singular thing] efficiently (*effective*). Likewise, it can be said (what almost amounts to the same thing) that that argument supposes that in God it is not possible to abstract a common quasi-generic and specific [character], as well as a particular character, and therefore that something belongs in the same manner to God, either as he is a particular being or as he is unproduced being.

However, this response does not seem to bring efficacy to the argument that was made, nor to be satisfactory – for two reasons. The first is because (omitting what is said in this opinion about the analogy of being, which is enough to weaken the force of the demonstration) that analogy of being rightly explained supposes an emanation and a dependence of all things upon God, as is clear from what was said above[239] about the analogy of being with respect to God and creatures.

The second reason is because, even positing analogy, it is not proven from analogy that there follows an emanation, but only an inequality.[240] Hence, it could easily be said that although being, according to its principal and primary significate, through itself and first belongs to God, nevertheless, according to some less principal concept (*ratio*) it belongs to other unproduced beings, because it is not necessary that among analogates that which is secondarily signified flows from what is primarily signified.

Finally, because even though being is analogous with respect to uncreated and created being, or [with respect] to substance and accident, nevertheless, one could reply that it is univocal with respect to several unproduced substances, just as *de facto* it is univocal with respect to created substances when they are compared only among themselves.[241] Hence, what was said, namely, that in God there is neither a common nor a particular character, is false if it is understood about a common character that is analogous and able to be abstracted by our reason. But if [it is understood] about a univocal character, even though in reality it

239 That is, *Disputation* 28, Section 3.

240 This should be noted as indicating the relationship which Suárez sees between proving the existence of God and the general analogy of being.

241 Cf. note 238, just above.

may be true, still perhaps it might be denied by one who would state that there are a number of unproduced beings. Therefore it should not be presupposed in the argument under discussion, lest there be a begging of the question.

A Second Argument Why There Cannot Be Several Beings by Essence.

8. To all of this it is possible to reply by adding a proof from St. Thomas, *Contra Gentiles*, Book 1, Chapter 42, Point (*ratio*) 7,[242] where he argues as follows: "If there are two things, both of which must necessarily exist, it is necessary that they agree in the concept of necessity of existing. Therefore, it is necessary that they be distinguished by something which is added either to both or to one of them. And thus it is necessary either that one or both of them be composite. However, no composite thing is of itself necessarily existing." And in this way he concludes that there cannot be several things of which each necessarily exists.

But this reasoning also is very problematical. For if it proves anything it would also prove that there is not one concept of being or of substance which would be common to God and to creatures. Again, the whole reasoning can be applied to the three Divine Persons, insofar as they agree in the concept of person. For by a similar argument one could conclude that these [Persons] would be composed from a common character of person and something added by which they are distinguished. But if, admitting the number of the three Persons, anyone were to deny that there is a concept of person which is common to them, for the same reason, even though there be admitted several unproduced beings, there will be denied a concept of necessary being which is common to them.

Or, contrariwise, if (what is more probable) the Divine Persons are understood to agree in a common concept of person and to be distinguished in what is proper to each of them, without a composition which will destroy their simplicity, because that community exists through a mental abstraction and precision, and the determination does not exist by a proper composition even of concept, but by a simple quasi-transcendental modification, so we could speak in the same way about two unproduced beings, insofar as they agree in a common character of necessary being and would be distinguished in their own proper entities.

Indeed, even if it were admitted that either both or one of those beings is properly composed by a composition of concept (*ratio*), such a composition does not seem to be formally incompatible with a necessity of being, because it does not include a proper real potentiality nor the real dissolubility of those things from which such composition results. For, since they are distinguished not in reality but only in concept, they are in reality properly not united but rather one. Hence, neither are they separable in reality, but they can be prescinded only by the mind – which is not incompatible with a necessity of being.

---

242 Cf. *Opera*, vol. 13, p. 118.

And in this way and by the previously mentioned example of the agreement and distinction of Divine Persons, there seem to be weakened many arguments which are usually made in this matter and are touched upon by St. Thomas, in the previously cited places and in many others in the First and Second Books of the *Contra Gentiles*, which [arguments], although they are very subtle as well as metaphysical and apt to persuade an intellect which is well disposed, are nevertheless hard to prove to a stubborn and recalcitrant person.

The Third Argument for the Same Thing.

9. Of the same type seems to be that argument which St. Thomas gives in the tenth place, in Chapter 42, of Book 1, of the *Contra Gentiles*,[243] namely: A being which is essentially (*per se*) necessary has a necessity of being insofar as it is this singular thing. Therefore, it is impossible that there be many essentially necessary beings. Therefore, there cannot be many unproduced beings. Accordingly, whatever exists takes its origin from one unproduced being.

The first consequence is clear, because the singularity of a thing is not communicable to another thing, and therefore what belongs to something insofar as it is this definite singular thing cannot be multiplied. The rest of the inferences are self-evident. But the antecedent is proven: because if a necessary being does not have a necessity of being insofar as it is this singular individual, then this singularity is not essentially required for a necessary being as such. Therefore, it depends upon some other thing or originates from elsewhere. But this involves contradiction. For an essentially necessary being must above all be such insofar as it is singular, because it is not actually a being except insofar as it is singular. Therefore, singularity itself must most of all belong to it from an intrinsic necessity and not from elsewhere nor in dependence upon another. But if singularity belongs to it from an intrinsic necessity of being, it cannot be multiplied, just as, if man from the intrinsic nature of man necessarily were to bring with itself the singularity of Peter, it could not be multiplied.

10. This is certainly an excellent and subtle argument. However, someone in keeping with prior responses could respond that this singular being which is unproduced has a necessity of being with respect to its whole singular entity and that as such is not communicable to another; but nevertheless the opposite cannot be said, nor must a necessary being as such require this singularity; but it is possible to have several necessary singular beings and for each to have its singularity necessarily, not from elsewhere nor in dependence upon another, but from its intrinsic entity and nature, not as common but as proper. For that community or agreement, which is only according to concept, can often be based in those

243 *Opera*, vol. 13, p. 119.

singular entities themselves and in properties which they have as they are singular. In this way, to be by nature an incorruptible being belongs to an angel even according to each [angel's] singular nature, although that does not arise from its singularity alone, but absolutely from the whole nature or essence. Therefore, the same could be said about several unproduced and singular beings with regard to the necessity of being absolutely.

The Fourth Argument to Prove the Same Thing.

11. Nevertheless, very probative for me is an argument which I propose in the following way: for wherever a common character is multipliable in respect to diverse singular natures, granted that it is not necessary that singularity be distinguished in actual reality from the common nature, it is however necessary that it be in some way outside the essence of such a nature. For, if it were essential to that [nature], in fact such a nature would not be multipliable, as was said above when we were treating of the principle of individuation.[244] But in an unproduced being it cannot be understood that singularity is outside its nature. Therefore, it is impossible that such a nature be capable of being multiplied.

The minor [premise] is proven: because in an unproduced being it is necessary that the very being itself of existence (*ipsum esse existentiae*)[245] be of its essence. For the intrinsic necessity of [its] being consists in this that it has being by virtue of its own essence, in such way that it is essentially its own being. But being belongs only to a singular thing inasmuch as it is singular. Therefore, it is necessary that the singularity of such a nature belong also to its essence, and consequently a nature of this kind not be multipliable. And this indeed is what St. Thomas says:[246] [i.e.] that a being which is unproduced, or which is absolutely necessary, or which is essentially its own being, is not this singular being through something which is outside its essence, even according to concept. For unless it would include singularity in its own essential concept, it would not include necessity of being in its own essential concept, because to be in act entails being singular.

12. *An Objection of Aureoli against the proposed argument of St. Thomas.* – You will say (as Aureoli objects in [his Questions on the *Sentences*] I, Distinction

---

244 On this, see *DM* V, s. 2, vol. 25, pp. 148–61. For an English translation of *Disputation* V, cf. Jorge J.E. Gracia, in *Suárez on Individuation* (Milwaukee: Marquette University Press, 1982).

245 For this and related terms, cf. *DM* XXXI, s. 1, n. 2, vol. 26, pp. 224–25; tr. Wells, p. 45. Also, cf. J. Owens, "The Number of Terms in the Suarezian Discussion of Essence and Being," *The Modern Schoolman*, 34 (1957), pp. 147–91, esp. 151–52.

246 Cf. *Summa contra Gentiles* I, c. 42, in *Opera*, vol. 13, p. 119.

3):[247] by this argument at most there is proven that there cannot be two unproduced beings that are distinct only in number. But it is not proven that they cannot be distinct in species or essentially. For in this way many Thomists say that angelic natures are essentially individual and therefore cannot be multiplied numerically and, nevertheless, they can be multiplied according to species.

I answer: first of all it is most probable that no nature which properly is specific and has a genus in common with another [specific nature] is essentially individual. This is first because by the very fact that it is a specific nature it is of itself potential, and therefore there is no reason why it is incompatible with those [natures] to be multiplied in number. Second [it is most probable] because if a composition of genus and specific difference is not incompatible with that [nature], there is no reason why a composition of species and individual difference would be incompatible with it.

Next it is said that from the argument made, when it is applied proportionately, the conclusion is that there is incompatibility between an intrinsic, essential necessity of being and the multiplication of such a nature, as St. Thomas has indicated in the same Chapter [42 of *Contra Gentiles* I], Argument 8.[248] For just as in the essential concept of that nature which exists of necessity there is included singularity, there is also included the whole essence of such a singular nature. Therefore, it is impossible that this essence of a necessary being be other and other (alia et alia), either in singularity or in its essential nature (*ratio*). Hence, just as it cannot be understood that such a nature may become singular through something added which is outside its essence, even according to concept (*ratio*), so it cannot be understood that it be, so to speak, constituted in such a species by something added to this common character (*ratio*) of necessary being, which is even according to concept (*ratio*) outside its essence as such. For, by the very fact that it is understood to be a necessary being, just as it is necessarily understood to be a singular being, so also it is understood as having an essence which must be entirely necessary. Therefore, it cannot be constituted in such or such an essential character (*ratio*) by something added, even according to concept (*ratio*).[249] Therefore, an essentially (*per se*) necessary being cannot be truly conceived as common – either specific, generic, or analogous – but only as singular. Therefore, in no way can it be multiplied.

247 Cf. Peter Aureoli, *Scriptum super primum Sententiarum*, ed. Buytaert, I, d. 3, a. 3, p. 661, n. 131.

248 Cf. *Opera*, vol. 13, pp. 118–19.

249 The interplay in this paragraph between "*ratio*" translated as "concept" and "*ratio*" translated as "character" is an example of ambiguity which obtains not just in Suárez but in just about every other Latin philosophical writer as well.

13. *From this last argument the first [argument]*[250] *is strengthened.* – But if this argument is solid, as indeed it is, the first argument draws strength from it, [the first argument] which is based on the fact that being belongs to God or to a necessary being "through itself and first" (*per se primo*)[251] or according to itself. For it is understood to belong to that [being] through itself and first not under some common character (*ratio*), but as it is this singular being, in such way that when being is said to belong to this being not accidentally (*per accidens*) nor by another, the sense is not only: not by another [thing], that is, not by another efficient cause but also not through some other character which is common or abstracting from singularity.

But that this is true has been sufficiently proven by the reasoning above. And certainly it seems evident from the proper nature of being itself; for first and through itself it belongs to a singular and not a common thing. Hence, even in those things or natures which have a received being, being cannot be communicated through itself and first to a nature that is common, but rather to [one that is] singular. Therefore, that thing which has being, essentially and insofar as it is, has that [being] as it is a certain singular thing and not according to some common character (*ratio*). Therefore, being belongs through itself and first to such a being, excluding every medium, whether that be an extrinsic agent or a common formal character because of which, taken abstractly and according to itself, the necessity to be may belong to it.

14. But from this principle so explained it is very easily inferred that being can belong to some being only by an effective emanation from the first unproduced being. For although that condition (*habitudo*) or predication "according to what that thing itself [is]" does not always require this relation of efficient causality between that which is such "through itself and first" and the rest which are such by means of that, nevertheless, when that First Thing is a singular thing and is entirely distinct from other things and extrinsic to these, there cannot be imagined another way of mediation or of participation.

And therefore no difficulty is posed by the examples of common characters by which something belongs through itself and first, such as, for man to be rational or for a triangle to have three angles equal to two right [angles]. For those are like a formal medium, because a common nature is related as a form to an individual. But, in the present instance, a being by essence, to which it belongs through itself and first to be, is a certain singular being, which cannot be a formal medium nor a form of other things. And therefore being cannot belong through that to the rest, except as through an efficient medium. For the character

250 Cf. § 3, this Section.

251 Here and elsewhere another translation of the phrase, "*per se primo*," might be "essentially and immediately."

of an end is not by itself sufficient, because an end does not immediately give being, but it metaphorically moves an agent to give being.[252] And therefore its causality by itself alone is not enough in order that those things which are being in a secondary way have being by the medium of that which has being through itself first and according to what it itself is. And from all of this it is easy to answer the difficulties mentioned with respect to the previously stated arguments.

The Fifth Argument.

15. We can add, finally, another argument, which is both enough by itself and which also confirms the preceding argument, namely: if there were two unproduced beings, either they would be of the same or of a diverse species. But neither can be said; therefore.

The first part of the minor [premise] is proven: because a supremely abstract[253] being cannot be multiplied numerically. For every numerical multiplication is done through matter or in relation to that.

However, this proof is not convincing. For that is true with respect to a physical and natural multiplication of individuals, but it is not true absolutely about every possible or entitative multiplication of singular things.

A better proof is one that is taken from the preceding reasoning: for a nature which is essentially singular cannot be numerically multiplied. But the nature of God or of a being which is necessary through itself is essentially singular. Therefore.

There can be a second proof that should not be contemned: because a multiplication of individuals is by accident, and where it is possible, it can, of its own nature, proceed to infinity. For it is not a greater contradiction that there exist these two individuals rather than three or four, or of any number at all. For there is no reason necessarily to stop in some one, since they keep no order by themselves, but for each of them the multiplication of another is accidental. If therefore two unproduced beings distinct only in number were possible, so also would three, four, and so on up to any number.

But as many as would be possible, the same amount would be necessary. For in these things that axiom is most of all true: "In eternal things, being and being able to be are the same."[254] For if they are essentially necessary beings there is

---

252 On the metaphorical movement of the end, cf. *DM* XXIII, s. 4, nn. 8–9, vol. 25, pp. 861–62. For a brief indication of the ramifications of this doctrine, see Vernon J. Bourke, *Will in Western Thought: An Historico-Critical Survey* (New York: Sheed and Ward, 1964), p. 178.

253 Separate, that is, from matter.

254 Cf. Aristotle, *Physics* 3.4.203b30.

in them no "able to be" but only actual being. We could not, therefore, stop in some finite number of such beings. To be sure, in those individuals that have a cause, although of themselves they can be multiplied to infinity, a stop is made in some certain number with regard to actual being, either from the will of a cause, or from the power and manner of acting successively, or on the basis of matter. But in these beings which have being from themselves without a cause, in no way could we stop at a certain number, because a greater number would not be more contradictory than a lesser one, and by the fact itself that it would not be contradictory, it would be actual. However, no one would admit that there is an actual infinity of unproduced beings. Therefore, a stop must be made in one single particular unproduced being.

16. The second part, about specific diversity, has already been proven, in responding to Aureoli and cxplaining the force of arguments above.[255] But now it should be proven with another dilemma. For either those beings would be equal in perfection, or not. Neither can be said. Therefore.

The first part of the minor can be proven first from the common opinion of the philosophers, that there cannot be two essences that are specifically distinct and equal in perfection. For as Aristotle says, in *Metaphysics* Book 10, Text 5 [*sic*],[256] differences dividing a genus are always related as privation and possession (*habitus*), because always one is less perfect and in that way it is compared to a privation.[257] From this also there arose the axiom that the species are like numbers.[258] But the argument seems to be that if they are equal beings, they are equally distant from non-being and from what then can they have essential diversity or dissimilarity? And certainly in all things essentially diverse which we experience this inequality seems to be found. And therefore that principle[259] is extremely probable.

However, it is not evident. For although two things may be equally distant from non-being, it seems that they can be dissimilar in nature. For a relation of equality is different from a relation of similarity. Hence in the instance of the Divine relations: Paternity and Filiation, inasmuch as they are relations, are dissimilar or (as they say) "disquiparant"[260], and nevertheless in perfection and rel-

255 Cf. §§ 12–13 in this Section.

256 Possibly: Text 15.

257 See Aristotle, *Metaphysics* 10.4.1055a33–38.

258 Cf. *Metaphysics* 8.3.1043b33.

259 That is, that species are like numbers.

260 This is now an obsolete word in English. But see: *The Compact Edition of the Oxford English Dictionary* (Oxford: Oxford University Press, 1971), vol. 1, p 499, where disquiparancy is described as: "The relation of two correlates which are heteronymous, i.e. denoted by different names, as father and son." Also the source is given as

ative entity as such they are thought to be equal, not only insofar as they include the [Divine] essence, but also according to the proper features in which they are distinguished. Therefore, in this way someone could contend that it is not contradictory that there be two unproduced essences which would be dissimilar and equal.

17. Nevertheless, (let us say this incidentally) the argument here is very different in cases of relatives and absolutes. For relations have diversity from their formal termini together with the feature (*ratio*) on which they are founded. And, therefore, in them diversity can more easily be understood to be together with equality, because equality arises from a degree of entity, while diversity [comes] from [their] mutual relation (*habitudo*).[261]

But in absolute beings, such as those unproduced beings would be, it can hardly be conceived in what they would be dissimilar if they were equal and, as regards all that which they would have in themselves, essentially necessary.

And in the case of these [absolute] things there is also a special argument, because to be a being by oneself or [to be] necessary and independent formally and according to the precise concept [of such] is the greatest of all perfections. Indeed, it necessarily in some way includes every other perfection, as will be explained below.[262] But each of those beings according to its proper and, as it were, specific nature (*ratio*) includes this perfection, which necessarily would be of the same character (*ratio*) in each. Therefore, in them there cannot be understood a diversity of perfection together with equality.

Here also is relevant the argument that was made about an infinite multitude of such natures. For if they would be equal and dissimilar, they would also have no order among themselves. But they would equally divide whatever conceivable character would be common to them. Therefore, if they could be multiplied in some number, they could also be multiplied in any number. For there would be no reason to stop at some definite number, nor could we point to any contradiction on account of which that number could not be increased. Therefore it would be necessary that the multitude of such natures be infinite.

18. Neither is it difficult to apply these and similar arguments in order to prove the other side of the dilemma,[263] namely, that those beings cannot be many and unequal in perfection. First, because by the very fact that such beings by their

---

a 1697 translation of F. Burgersdijk's *Logic* I, 7, 22. This is interesting in view of the fact that Burgersdijk, a Dutch Calvinist, was much influenced by Suárez.

261 Suárez's thought here seems to be that in, for example, the relation of two white things, there is a sameness on the level of their being white but a diversity inasmuch as each of them is a distinct terminus for the relation in the other.

262 Cf. *DM* XXX, s. 1, n. 2, vol. 26, pp. 60–61.

263 Cf. This Section, § 16.

proper natures agree in the supreme perfection of being from themselves, which formally or eminently includes all others, as I will show below,[264] no inequality among them is intelligible. Second, because either among them there would be one supreme being which would be absolutely and simply more perfect than the others, or not. If not, then there is no limit in that multitude, but it is evidently infinite. And still with that posited and actually existing, it is plainly unintelligible that there be in it no being which is more perfect than all the rest, since they are all said to be unequal in perfection.

Again, it necessarily follows from this that any one of those beings is finite in entitative perfection, because each would be surpassed by another, indeed even by infinite others. Therefore, that whole multitude would also be imperfect, because it comes together from imperfect things, and in that whole [multitude] there cannot be an infinite intensive perfection, but only an infinite multitude of finite perfections. But it is inconceivable that there not be in things something of infinite intensive perfection, as was touched upon above when treating of creation,[265] and we will also speak of it below.[266]

To be sure, this argument taken from infinity would suffice in order to demonstrate what we intend. However, we are putting it aside, because it assumes two principles which must be proven below, namely, [1] from the fact that a being is sometimes from itself and essentially its own being, it follows that it is simply infinite in the genus of being[267] and [2] infinite beings of this kind cannot be multiplied – which two things must be demonstrated in the following Disputation[268] treating of Divine attributes.

19. But if in that multitude there is one which is supremely perfect and surpassing the rest, that still would not be infinite, both because the arguments already made are valid and also because no argument can be given as to why beyond that [one being] there could not be another more perfect essentially necessary being. For why will the whole range of beings be limited at that finite grade?

Add the argument that was made above about the multiplication of such beings to infinity. Even if they were essentially diverse and unequal in perfection, there would be no reason to stop at some finite number. For although there would seem to be some essential order among their distinct essences, nevertheless, there

264 Cf. *DM* XXX, s. 1, n. 9, vol. 26, p. 63.

265 Cf. *DM* XX, s. 2, vol. 25, pp. 754–66.

266 Cf. *DM* XXX, s. 2, vol. 26, pp. 64–72.

267 See note 66, in Disputation 28, above.

268 That is, *DM* XXX, vol. 26, pp. 60–224. This is the longest of all the Disputations in the *Disputationes metaphysicae*. It is also one of the richest in terms of content and is waiting for its English translation.

could also be a progression to infinity in this order, as is evident in the case of possible creatures. It is necessary, therefore, that in the whole range of beings there be one which is infinite and more perfect than all the rest. Therefore, that supreme being, more perfect than the rest and absolutely infinite, we call God, and from this same perfection of that [being] the inference is that all other beings which are counted with that [being] have come to be effectively from that infinite being.

[This is] first, indeed, because infinity belongs immediately to that being by the very fact that it is actually a being by its essence. For it results from this that in some way it includes and contains all being, because it does not have anything by which it would be limited, nor from which it would participate this part of being (so to speak) rather than another. Therefore, conversely, from the very fact that other beings do not have the supreme perfection and totality of being (if I may say it so), we have an obvious sign that they are not beings by essence which are entirely unproduced, but rather beings by participation, receiving their being from that First Being.

20. [This is] second, because in this way there is understood to be an essential order in the whole range of beings, either by their subordination among themselves or at least by the reduction of all to one, with the result that they may not be rashly and haphazardly so multiplied to infinity.

This is very well explained by a theological example (by which we are at the same time answering the philosophers, lest they think that the arguments by which we are proving the unity of the uncreated being disprove the trinity of Persons). For in matters pertaining to God, even though the Catholic Faith states [that there is] a multitude of Persons, [this is] not, however, without the order which they call "of origin," in such way that by ascending we stop at some entirely unproduced Person which is the source of the Others, and in descending there is some character (*ratio*) based in the very nature of such a being because of which there ensues a multiplication up to the number of three and not farther. This is doubtless because in a purely intellectual nature there is no other way of internal operation or emanation except by intellect and will.[269]

However, if in God unproduced persons could be multiplied, plainly an infinite number of persons could be multiplied. Therefore, Faith does not admit that there be many unproduced persons and neither does reason permit them or many beings in any way without a reduction to one First, from whom the others flow.

21. Third, the same thing can be proven from the efficient causality of the first infinite being. For, if it is first and infinite, it will be the cause of the rest, in line with the common axiom which is believed to be taken from Aristotle, in

269 On this, cf. Suárez, *De sanctissimo Trinitatis mysterio, libri duodecim* I, c. 9, n. 6, vol. 1, pp. 561–62.

Metaphysics, Book 2, Text 4: "The maximum in each genus is the cause of all things which belong to that genus."[270] This is especially understood with respect to the efficient cause, when in that most perfect thing there is sufficient power to effect the rest.

But in this proof, first of all, the text of Aristotle from which that axiom is said to be taken is not correctly adduced. For, as we noted in the Index[271] with regard to that text, Aristotle did not say that what is most of all such a being is the cause of the rest, but conversely: that which is in some order the cause of the others is most of all such.[272] But from this principle there cannot be inferred the other,[273] because a universal affirmative proposition is not simply convertible.[274] Therefore, even though that which is the cause of the rest inasmuch as they are such is itself most of all such,[275] it does not follow that every thing which is most of all such is the cause of the rest.

Again, that axiom taken in itself is not so evident that a demonstration can be constructed from it. Indeed, Durandus [of Saint-Pourçain], in [his *Sentences* commentary] Book 2, Distinction 15, Question 3,[276] and Aureoli, as related by [John] Capreolus, in [Capreolus's *Defensiones*], Book 1, Distinction 3, Question 1,[277] taught that it is not true. For [they reason] man, even though he is the most perfect of all the animals, is not on that account the cause of the rest; nor is whiteness the cause of the other colors, even though it is the most perfect color.[278] Hence, Cajetan also [in his commentary on the *Summa Theologiae*] Part 1, Question 2, Article 3,[279] thinks that that axiom is neither necessary nor true when it is understood with respect to a proper and especially an efficient cause. But others explain it [as being] about a cause said broadly, as it includes an extrinsic

270 Cf. *Metaphysics* 2.1.993b24–25.

271 That is, the *Index locupletissimus* II, c. 1, q. 6, vol. 25, pp. v–vi.

272 That is, the cause of the others in an order most of all possesses that which is the base of the order among them.

273 That is, the converse.

274 Suarez says: "is not simply converted" (*non convertitur simpliciter*).

275 For this, cf. Aristotle, *Posterior Analytics* 1.2.72a29–30.

276 Cf. D. Durandi a Sancto Porciano, O.P. et Meldensis episcopi, *In Petri Lombardi Sententias Theologicas commentariorum libri IIII* (Venetiis: Ex Typographia Guerraea, 1571), II, d. 15, q. 3, ad 2, fol. 158vb, n. 14.

277 Cf. Johannis Capreoli, *Defensiones theologiae divi Thomae Aquinatis* I, d. 3, q. 1, tom. 1, p. 166.

278 Cf. Aristotle, *De sensu et sensato* 3.439b14.

279 Cf. *Commentaria Cardinalis Caietani [In Summam Theologiae]*, I, q. 2, a. 3, § VII, in Sancti Thomae Aquinatis, *Opera*, vol. 4, p. 33.

exemplar, which can be called a measure rather than a cause, in the way that Aristotle, in *Metaphysics*, Book 10, said that the first thing in any genus is the measure of the rest.[280] But according to this interpretation from that axiom it could only be inferred that since among beings some are more and others are less perfect, there is some one which is most perfect which is the measure of the others by the fact that they are reckoned to be more or less because of their approach to or recession from that. From this, however, it could not be concluded that only that being is unproduced and is the efficient cause of all the others.

The Same Truth Is Confirmed from the Opinion of Aristotle.

22. For this reason, Aristotle, in the cited passage,[281] rather assumes that there is some being which is the cause of the rest and concludes from this that that being is the truest and most perfect – which should be noted in passing so that it is clear that Aristotle did come to this truth. For he plainly says that the First Being is not only the cause of corruptible and contingent things, but also of those which exist always, under which he seems to include the heavens and the Intelligences.

Neither can that passage be explained [as being] only about final or exemplar causality, as [John of] Jandun, in that place, Question 5,[282] and Gregory [of Rimini], in [his *Sentences* commentary] Book 2, Distinction 1, Question 1,[283] contend – both because Aristotle explicitly gives an example regarding an efficient cause, and also because even in the present context final causality is not separated from efficient [causality], as has been mentioned above[284] and will presently be more fully explained.[285]

Neither also is it a problem that Aristotle seems to speak about effects which univocally participate the nature of their cause; for this is what he says: "The cause of that is something the same and it agrees in name and nature,"[286] where

280 Cf. *Metaphysics* 10.1.1052b18–19.

281 *Metaphysics* 2.1.993b24–25.

282 Cf. Ioannis de Ianduno, Philosophi perspicaccissimi, *Acutissimae Quaestiones in duodecim libros Metaphysicae* II, q. 5 (Venetiis: Apud Hieronymum Scottum, 1560), pp. 132–38.

283 Cf. Gregorii Ariminensis, *Super primum et secundum Sententiarum*, II, q. 1, a. 2, vol. II, fols. 3–6.

284 See Section 2, § 36, above.

285 Cf. §§ 27, 28, 30, this Section.

286 Cf. *Metaphysics* 2.1.993b 24–25. Suárez's Latin here is: "cuius causa aliquid, idem et nomine et ratione convenit." With this cf. Fonseca: "cuius causa caeteris et nomine et ratione convenit." in Petri Fonsecae, S.J., *Commentariorum in libros Metaphysicorum Aristotelis Stagiritae, tomi quatuor*, II, text. 4 (Coloniae: Sumptibus Lazari Zetzneri, 1615), vol. 1, col. 384.

the other translation has: "according to which there is present a univocity with other things."[287] This, I say, is not a problem, but rather from this passage is derived the fact that the analogy of being between the first being and the rest does not exclude some unity of character (*ratio*) or concept together with a unity of name. And, therefore, by the Greeks sometimes it was included under synonyms, as Fonseca also has noted in that place.[288] Therefore, Aristotle adds that phrase only to exclude equivocal effects, which in no way agree with their cause in name and nature. For in those it is not necessary that the cause be most of all such formally, but [it may be such] eminently.

23. *Aristotle's passage is explained.* – The only thing that could prompt doubt or hesitation is the fact that Aristotle concluded in the plural: "the principles of those things which always exist are most true."[289] Hence, he seems to think that there are many first unproduced principles of eternal things, as Jandun and Gregory, as cited above,[290] explain and attribute to Aristotle. By "those things which always exist," they understand the motions of the heavens; while by "the principles of those things" [they understand] all the separate substances, which they think are according to Aristotle unproduced. But that certainly cannot be derived from that passage. For Aristotle also first spoke in the singular saying: "that is most true which is the cause for those coming after to be true, and each one is most of all such which is a cause for the others, etc."[291] – which was said because of the first cause, as the Commentator has remarked.[292] And immediately and without qualification or discrimination he [i.e. Averroes] says: "those things which always exist have their origin from a first principle."[293] But that expression in the case of the doctrine to be treated amounts to a universal. Therefore, it is without cause limited by some to the heavenly bodies, in such

287 Cf. "secundum quod aliis univocatio inest." *Metaphysica* 2.1, as translated by Cardinal Bessarion, in *Aristotelis opera cum Averrois commentariis* (Apud Junctas, 1562), vol. 8, fol. 29vK.

288 See Fonseca, *Commentariorum* ..., II, text. 4, note o, vol. 1, col. 384. A point of interest is that in this place Fonseca supports his translation and interpretation from the earlier translation of John Argyropoulos (ca. 1415–1487). On Argyropoulos, see *The Cambridge History of Renaissance Philosophy*, edited by Charles B. Schmitt and Quentin Skinner (Cambridge: Cambridge University Press, 1988), p. 808.

289 *Metaphysics* 2.1.993b28–29.

290 Cf. § 22, just above.

291 *Metaphysics* 2.1.993b27.

292 See Averroes, *In Metaphys.* II, t. 4, in *Aristotelis opera cum Averrois commentariis*, vol. 8, fol. 30rC.

293 Cf. Aristotle: "and so it is necessary that the principles of eternal beings be eternally most true." *Metaphysics* 2.1.993b28–29.

way that Aristotle would have thought that the heavens, even though they are eternal, have a cause not only of their motion but also of their being, while the Intelligences are said to be a number of unproduced principles. This, however, is refuted by the same arguments and also, because for Aristotle the nature of a heavenly body and of the Intelligence which moves it is the same in this regard, because they have between themselves a maximum correlation in eternity or necessity of being. Likewise, because, according to Aristotle, the heaven is absolutely unable to be generated.

Therefore, others think that Aristotle spoke in the plural because of prime matter, which they think according to Aristotle was unproduced and in its own genus a principle of other things. But this is not correctly said, otherwise Aristotle would have had to also conclude that prime matter is most of all being and that it is the principle of everything which exists always. But both points are false and against his doctrine.

Therefore, Aristotle stated that plural in place of the singular either because of the eminence of the first cause, or because in the first cause the many first kinds (*rationes*) of causes come together. For it is the first final, efficient, and exemplar cause. Therefore, by the name of "principles" he understands these causes, which however in reality are only one first cause.

These things have been noted in passing with regard to that opinion of Aristotle. But now in the present context we will try to prove that in the case of the First Being it rightly follows from the fact that he is the greatest being that he is the cause of the rest, granted that that does not follow in every case. This, then, we will show in the reasoning which ensues.[294]

Whence It Follows[295] that What Is the Greatest Being Is the Cause of the Rest.

24. Therefore, let there be another argument. A first unproduced being is supreme and infinite in perfection; hence, it is most powerful in acting; therefore, it produces all things which are, and there is nothing besides that being which is unproduced.

The first antecedent is taken from preceding arguments, by which it was shown that we must come to some unproduced being which is more perfect than the rest. But the fact that this being is infinite has been partly proven because [what is] "being itself by essence" (*ipsum esse per essentiam*) does not have anything from which it would be limited; and it can be partly taken from what was

294 A small point of style: Suárez actually here uses three forms of the same word, "*sequor*." I have translated these twice with "follows" and then a third time by "ensues."

295 Once more, Suárez uses a form of *sequor*.

said above about creation,[296] which we have shown to be possible for the first being and for which there is required infinite power. And in that way the first consequence[297] is also proven.

But the second [consequence][298] is usually proven in this way: because every [active] potency has some adequate object, and the higher and more universal a potency is, the more universal an object it has. But the active potency of the first being is the highest and most universal which can exist, since it is proportionate to the perfection of that being. Therefore, it includes in its object all being. Therefore, all being is producible by that potency, and consequently there is no possible being which is not producible by that potency. Therefore, there is no essentially necessary being besides that first being. For it is contradictory that a necessary being be producible by some potency.

25. But against this argument it is possible to object that it is not of the nature of an active potency, however much supreme and infinite, that it include all being under its object – otherwise, it would also include the first being itself. Therefore, some limitation must be added from the side of that potency itself, which is not sufficiently stated by saying that its object is possible being. For either that "possible" is taken only in a positive way, or as it includes the necessary under itself, and in this way it also includes God; for, according to the rules of the logicians, what is can be.[299] Or it is taken as it includes the privation of the necessity of being, and in this way the question is begged when it is said that every being which is other than the First Being is possible. For this is what is in question, namely, whether there is something necessary. He, therefore, who would imagine such intrinsically necessary beings besides the First, will logically (*consequenter*) say that the adequate object of this potency is producible being. For what productive potency can be imagined more universal than that which extends itself to every producible thing? But such a potency would not be extended to necessary things, because they are not producible.

26. *The stated argument is defended.* – But nevertheless, the stated argument, which has been taken from St. Thomas, the *Contra Gentiles*, Book 2, Chapter 15,[300] can be defended in many ways from the doctrine of the same [St.

---

296 Cf. *DM* XX, s. 2, vol. 25, pp. 754–66.

297 That is: "it is most powerful in acting."

298 That is: "therefore, it produces all things which are, and there is nothing besides that being which is unproduced."

299 That is, "from being to possibility the inference is valid" (*ab esse ad posse valet illatio*). For example, cf. John Buridan (d. ca. 1360), *Tractatus de consequentiis* II, concl. 15, ed. Hubert Hubien (Louvain: Publications Universitaires, 1976), p. 74.

300 Cf. *Opera*, vol. 13, pp. 294–95.

Thomas], especially arguments 3, 4, 6, and 7 [of Chapter 15].[301] First, indeed, because it belongs to the perfection of the First Being that it virtually[302] or eminently[303] contains all entity. Therefore, the First Being which exists of itself is able to efficiently cause every entity which is distinct from itself. Therefore, it is incompatible with the perfection and the omnipotence of the First Being that besides itself there be anything which is unproduced and completely necessary. Hence, even though it is true that the adequate object of Divine potency is creatable or producible being, nevertheless it simultaneously belongs to the perfection of that potency that it is not itself producible by itself, like something contained eminently in itself.

This can be explained by its opposite: for it belongs to the perfection of the potency of that thing that it can reduce to nothing any thing at all which is distinct from itself, otherwise, it would not have full dominion over all things. Therefore, it is incompatible with the perfection and the universality of that potency that some being outside it be absolutely necessary and independent.

This is confirmed and explained from the side of those beings themselves which are distinct from the First, whatever they are. For it has been shown that no being which is distinct from the First can be equal to that [First] in perfection and essence, but it is necessarily inferior to that – and from this it necessarily results that every such being is finite and imperfect. Therefore, on that account it is not contradictory that every such being be producible, because the imperfect always draws its origin, insofar as it has perfection, from something more perfect. And in like manner, participated being draws its origin from a being by essence, and no reason can be given why it is incompatible with such a being to be producible. Indeed, this is much more in conformity with its limitation and imperfection than that it be an absolutely necessary being. Hence, every being of this kind is included under the object of the effective power of the First Being, and, therefore, there is no necessary and uncreated being apart from it.

A Last Argument – From the Causality of the End.

27. A last argument can be taken from the causality of the ultimate end. For among things there is one most perfect being which is the ultimate end of all the others; therefore, that same thing is the first efficient principle of the rest, and therefore that alone is uncreated and the true God.

Almost all philosophers admit the antecedent. For at least in the genus of end they do not deny that there is an order between the Second Intelligences and the First. And the argument is the same with respect to any other beings; for all

301 *Ibid.*

302 That is: in its "power" (*virtus*).

303 That is: in its essence in a higher way.

things imitate that same First Being and they strive to be like it. And those which can attain it in some way, such as intellectual beings, have their happiness placed in that.[304] And they do not rest until they come to that, as we experience in ourselves. Finally, there would be a great imperfection and confusion of things, if there were no order among them. Therefore, it is necessary that all things be related to some one ultimate end. But if there is some ultimate end of the rest of things, it can only be the First and Highest Being. About this subject I have said many things above in *Disputation* 24.[305]

But the first consequence[306] is proven: because whatever has a final cause also has an efficient [cause]. For, as Aristotle attests, the end is that on account of which something is effected. For the end moves the efficient cause to action.

28. An *"evasion" (evasio) which weakens the previous argument.* – However, someone could respond that it is one thing to have an end and another thing to have a final cause. For an end as such entails only the character (*ratio*) of a terminus. But a final cause entails the character of a principle and a mover. Moreover, it can be understood that some thing may have an end in the first way but still not properly and rigorously [have] a final cause. And in that case the consequence from an end to an efficient cause will not be valid. And some philosophers seem in this way to have understood the character of an end between the proximate movers of the world and the first immobile mover – without any effective emanation. For even though they thought that Second Intelligences exist of themselves and necessarily, nevertheless, they still believed that they were carried by a kind of natural impulse toward the First Intelligence[307] as toward an end or terminus of their own natural perfection.

But if someone continues to object: that it is contradictory to have this relation to another as to an end without [having] dependence on that thing; but every dependence is incompatible with necessity of being, because if one thing depends upon another, then if that [other] is completely removed this [thing] also will be taken away,[308] and consequently it is not absolutely and intrinsically necessary – they[309] answer that from the relation of one thing to another as to a ter-

304 Cf. *Nichomachean Ethics* 10.8.1178b23–24.

305 Cf. vol. 25, pp. 890–99.

306 That is: "that thing is the efficient principle of all else."

307 That is the First Intelligence after the First Being, cf. § 32, Section 2, above.

308 Suárez's grammar is weak here. The problem is with the antecedents of the pronouns "illa" and "haec." Grammatically "illa" should be equivalent to "the former" and "haec" should mean "the latter." But if we were to give them these meanings, Suárez's sentence would read: "if that one [dependent thing] were destroyed, the other [independent thing] would also be destroyed" – which, of course, is the opposite of what is wanted.

309 That is, the "some philosophers" just mentioned.

minus or an end there does not follow a genuine dependence, but there follows only a necessary connection of the one thing to the other. Such is usually the case between a relation and a terminus without a genuine dependence of the one upon the other as we are obliged to affirm between the Father and the Son in the case of God.

Nor is that conditional, "if one is destroyed, the other is removed," contrary to an intrinsic necessity of being when the second thing in that conditional[310] is also supposed to be intrinsically necessary. For, although the conditional may be true, nevertheless, just as the antecedent is impossible, so also is the consequent, and, therefore, the opposite of both can be absolutely and intrinsically necessary.

29. *This is refuted.* – But although this evasion has a certain appearance of probability, nevertheless, in actual fact it is not probable. First, because it involves contradiction that some thing be from itself and through itself and yet not on account of itself but rather on account of something else. For it is not a lesser perfection to be from itself than to be on account of itself. Therefore, the first perfection is unreasonably attributed to something to which the second is denied.

Likewise, [it is not probable] because a nature which has being from itself is an entirely absolute thing and one which needs no [other] thing in order to be. Therefore, in its being it cannot include a relation toward another thing as toward an end.

Finally, this [improbability] is shown *a posteriori*: for a thing which is terminated at another thing as at an ultimate end loves itself and its whole being on account of that end. But there is no reason that a thing which has being from itself would relate that being to another on account of which, only or principally, it would love itself.

In addition, from the response here an occasion is taken to deny all final causality and operation on account of an end. For someone could similarly say that all things tend by a natural inclination toward their ends, as toward certain termini, without any causality of an end. But this is most absurd. For although all things have these natural inclinations toward their ends, nevertheless, this same condition of those things proclaims that they are not from themselves, but have been created by and have received these inclinations toward their ends from a higher agent.

30. Still someone could say: granted that it is true that whatever has a final cause [also] has an efficient cause, nevertheless, these causes do not always coincide in the same thing. For health is the end of walking, for example, and nevertheless it is not its efficient principle. Therefore, in this way God can be the end of the Intelligences even if he is not their efficient cause. [This is true] for that reason or, most of all, because it can be said that secondary Intelligences do not

---

310 That is, the subject of the consequent.

so much exist, but rather operate, on account of the first as on account of an end. Thus, not so much their substance, but rather their operation, has a final cause and also has an efficient cause. But these are not the same thing. For the efficient cause of the operations is the substance of the operating Intelligence, but the final cause is the higher and first Intelligence.

Beginning with this last part, the answer is that that evasion has no standing according to the opinion of the philosophers, who say that the Intelligences are beings which are necessary of themselves. For, following from that (*consequenter*), they say that the operation of an Intelligence is its substance. For they think, and indeed logically (*consequenter*), that [Intelligences] are pure acts, since they think that they are their own being by their essence. Therefore, if the operation of an Intelligence is ordered toward God as toward an end and its operation is its substance, it is necessary also that its substance be ordered to an end. But if the operation necessarily has an efficient cause, because it has a final cause, necessarily the same must be said about the substance. Moreover, just as the substance cannot be the efficient cause of itself, so neither [can it be the efficient cause] of its own operation, since the substance is said to be its own operation.

Finally, if we suppose the true opinion that in secondary or created Intelligences operation is distinguished from substance, we must necessarily say that if the operation of an Intelligence is on account of God as an end, its substance also is ordered to the same end – both because such a substance exists on account of its own operation and also because it does not achieve or attain its end except through its operation. Therefore, not only the operation but also the substance itself has been ordained for such an end.

31. And from this it results that it cannot be related to itself as to an efficient cause, in the way that its operation is [related] inasmuch as operation presupposes a being from which it can effectively flow. But being itself does not presuppose itself, nor does substance. Accordingly, the conclusion then is that that substance must be reduced to another efficient cause, which can be other only if it is the First Being itself to which [that substance] is ordered as to an ultimate end.

Accordingly, although the thing which is the end is not always also an efficient principle, especially when the end itself must be produced by an action and it is the "end by which" (*finis quo*) or "for the sake of which" (*cujus gratia*), nevertheless, often the end and the efficient cause do coincide in the same thing, especially when the end is "the end for which" (*finis cui*) or "which" (*qui*). For, in this last way, everything which operates, operates in some way for itself and consequently it is at once both efficient cause and end of its own operation.[311]

In the present case, therefore, from the fact that God is the ultimate end, it is

311 For light on the complex doctrine of "end" see e.g. *DM* XXIII, s. 2, vol. 25, pp. 847–51.

very well inferred that he is the first principle of all. [This is], first, because he is an end which is not to be efficiently caused but rather obtained, imitated, and honored by his effects. Also, second, because the ordination of things toward such an end cannot be attributed to any other cause. For either that cause would be within the order of things effected, and as such produced on account of that end, and then its cause will have to be sought; or it is outside that order, and thus it cannot be other than the ultimate end itself.

And this is by itself compatible with reason, because God is not the "end for which" (*finis cui*) some advantage is sought by [his] action, but which (*qui*) intends to communicate its own goodness to other things and which all other things in some way desire to pursue or to imitate, as St. Thomas rightly says, [in *Summa Theologiae*] Part 1, Question 44, Article 4.[312] Therefore, God is an end only as the first cause which operates in order to communicate its own goodness. And in this way, the end very well corresponds and is proportionate to the principle. For the order of agents follows the order of ends, and therefore to the supreme agent there corresponds also the supreme end. And so in the present context from the fact that all things are ordered to God or to the First Being as to an ultimate end, it correctly follows that he is the first principle of them all.

32. *The conclusion from all that has been said.* – From all of this, therefore, it has been sufficiently demonstrated that God exists.[313] For although, perhaps, some arguments from among those which have been given, taken by themselves or individually, may not convince the intellect to the degree that an obstinate man or one who is badly disposed could not find evasions, nevertheless, all the arguments are efficacious and especially when they are taken together they most sufficiently demonstrate the stated truth. To these [arguments] we will add others below[314] from those by which the unity of God is usually shown.

But if someone attentively considers just the arguments offered, he will find that also in their regard there is relevant what was said in the first Section,[315] namely, that just as the task of proving that there is some uncreated being belongs to the metaphysician, although the physicist in some way begins and prepares the way, so also to prove that unproduced being is only one, that it is the principle of all other things which exist, and that therefore it is the true God, is certainly the task of the metaphysician.

Indeed in the second way of proceeding, which we have said is in some way *a priori*, this is self-evident, since the most potent, and almost the entire, force of the demonstration is based upon the perfection of that being by essence. However, in the first kind of demonstration, since it appears to be taken from sen-

312 Cf. *Opera*, vol. 4, p. 461.

313 Note this clear claim that by this point the existence of God has been demonstrated.

314 Cf. *DM* XXX, s. 10, vol. 26, pp. 137–41.

315 Cf. Section 1, § 41, above.

sible effects, something seems to be received or taken from natural philosophy and, therefore, in that also it is true that [natural] philosophy prepares the way and helps in that mode of demonstrating. But the proper medium of that demonstration in fact is metaphysical, namely, the unity of end and the mutual connection or subordination which is found among all things which exist in nature. For this is a most abstract and universal argument and therefore it essentially belongs to metaphysics, although [that discipline] often uses the help of [natural] philosophy in order to apply that [argument] to individual things.

The Second Opinion Reported in the Preceding Section Is Rejected.

33. Lastly, from all that has been said it can be clear by, so to speak, a certain most evident experience how far from truth is the opinion reported above[316] which asserted that the existence of God is so self-evident that, for that reason, it could not be demonstrated. For it is clear from what has been said that there is need for great consideration and speculation in order to efficaciously prove this truth. Therefore, how can this truth be thought to be self-evident?

Wisely, then, St. Thomas [in *Summa Theologiae*] Part 1, Question 2, Article 1,[317] supposing the distinction which is given and extensively explained in Book 1 of the *Posterior [Analytics]*[318] about a self-evident proposition as either in itself only or in itself and also for us, affirms that "God exists" is self-evident in itself, because to be through himself and without a medium belongs to God and is contained in the primary concept and character of God. But he denies that it is self-evident for us, because we do not conceive the essence of that being as it is in itself, nor is it evident to us from the terms themselves that in the order of effects and causes we must stop at some uncreated being – and it is less self-evident that a being of this kind can only be one.

Hence, many pagans have been in doubt about this truth or have even denied it. And up to the present day, many, not only pagans but also heretics, after having heard the word of the Gospel, labor under the same foolishness and are atheists. And even some faithful and learned [persons] deny that truth to be evident. But none of this occurs in the case of things which are self-evident for us. And in this opinion, besides Hervaeus [Natalis],[319] Capreolus[320], and other

316 Cf. Section 2, § 3, above.

317 Cf. *Opera*, vol. 4, p. 27.

318 Cf. *Posterior Analytics* 1.2.71b35–72a6.

319 Cf. Hervei Natalis Britonis, O.P., *In quatuor libros Sententiarum commentaria* I, d. 3, q. 2 (Parisiis: Apud viduam Dionisii Moreau, 1647), p. 34–37.

320 Cf. Johannis Capreoli, *Defensiones theologiae divi Thomae Aquinatis* I, d. 2, q. 2, a. 1–2, vol. 1, pp. 144–50.

Thomists[321] – St. Thomas [in his *Sentences* commentary], Book 1, Distinction 3,[322] Durandus, [ibid] Question 3,[323] and Richard [of Middleton], Question 2,[324] agree.

34. But others, even though they embrace the second part of this opinion[325] – which is enough for us – nevertheless, deny the first part, because they do not admit that distinction nor [do they admit that there is] any proposition self-evident in itself which is not self-evident for us, for example: Scotus, in [his *Sentences* commentary] Book 1, Distinction 2, Question 2;[326] Ockham [ibid.], Distinction 3, Question 2 [*sic*];[327] Gabriel [Biel] [ibid.], Question 4,[328] and Henry [of Ghent] in his *Summa*, Article 22, Question 2.[329]

However, the mentioned authors have for no reason labored over a logical question, about which in fact there can hardly be any controversy. For who doubts that there are certain truths that are in themselves immediate, which we

321 See e.g.: Cajetan, *In Summam Theologiae* I, q. 2, a. 1, in S. Thomae Aquinatis, *Opera omnia*, vol. 4, pp. 28–29; Ferrara, *In Contra Gentiles*, I, cc. 10–11, in S. Thomae Aquinatis, *Opera*, vol. 13, pp. 24–28; and Domingo Bañez, O.P., *Scholastica commentaria in primam partem ...*, Q. II, a. 1, Commentarium, ed. Urbano, pp. 102–7.

322 For this, cf. *Scriptum super libros Sententiarum* I, d. 3, q. 1, a. 2, ed. Mandonnet, vol. 1, pp. 93–94.

323 Cf. Durandi a Sancto Porciano, *In Petri Lombardi Sententias* I, d. 3, q. 3 (ed. Venetiis, 1571), fol. 22ra, n. 5.

324 Cf. Ricardi de Mediavilla, O.M.Conv, *Super quatuor libros Sententiarum Petri Lombardi quaestiones subtilissimae* I, d. 3, a. 1, q. 2 (Brixiae, 1591; reprint: Frankfurt: Minerva, 1963), vol. 1, pp. 40–41.

325 That is: "there is need for great consideration and speculation in order to efficaciously prove this truth."

326 Cf. Duns Scotus, *Ordinatio* I, dist. 2, pars 1, qq. 1–2, in *Joannis Duns Scoti Opera omnia*, vol. 2 (Civitas Vaticana: Typis Polyglottis Vaticanis, 1950), p. 136, nn. 22–23.

327 Cf. Guillelmi de Ockham, *Scriptum in librum primum Sententiarum ordinatio, Distinctiones II–III*, ed. Stephanus Brown, O.F.M. adlaborante Gedeone Gál, O.F.M. (St. Bonaventure, N.Y., 1970), d. 3, q. 4, pp. 432–42. For a readable and scholarly comparison here between Scotus and Ockham, see Armand Maurer, *The Philosophy of William of Ockham in the Light of its Principles* (Toronto: Pontifical Institute of Mediaeval Studies, 1999), pp. 159–67.

328 Cf. Gabrielis Biel, *Collectorium circa quattuor libros Sententiarum*, Prologus et Liber primus, collaborantibus Martino Elze et Renata Steiger, ediderunt Wilfridus Werbeck et Udo Hofmann (Tübingen: J.C.B. Mohr (Paul Siebeck), 1973), *In Sent.* I, d. 3, q. 4, aa. 1–3, pp. 221–25.

329 Cf. Henrici a Gandavo, *Summae quaestionum ordinariarum*, a. 22, q. 2 (Parisiis: In aedibus Iodoci Badii Ascensii, 1520), fol. 130vR–31vY.

can understand only through some medium? Certainly, for example, that quantity is an accidental entity, if it is true, is true without any medium between the predicate and the subject, and yet it is not known by us except through media and even extremely extrinsic [media].[330] Therefore, since a self-evident and an immediate proposition are the same, it cannot be doubted that many things are self-evident in themselves which are not self-evident for us.

But if Scotus and others say that they are not speaking about things but rather about propositions, which intrinsically entail an order to our concepts which [concepts] cannot be distinguished as according to themselves and with respect to us, we will reply that they are laboring over something equivocal, because we are not dealing with signs themselves but with the thing signified, nor with formal concepts, but rather with objective [concepts], and the given distinction falls very well on these.[331] For often those things which are objected to our formal concepts have an immediate and therefore self-evident connection, even though, as they are objected to our formal concepts and are denominated from those, their connection is not immediately known to us. Therefore, that distinction is very good and is most fittingly applied to the present question, as has been well enough explained.

35. Nevertheless, I would add that although strictly it is not known as totally evident to us that God exists, it is however a truth which is so consonant with natural reason (*lumen*), and with the consensus of all men, that it can scarcely be unknown by anyone. Hence, [St.] Augustine, in his *Treatise 106 on [the Gospel of] John*, treating the words: "I have manifested thy name to men," says: "Not that name of yours by which you are called 'God' but that by which you are called my Father. For this name by which he is called God could not have been in every way unknown to every creature and to all nations, before they believed in Christ."[332]

---

330 While "quantity is an accident" is a self-evident statement, we come to know its truth through the experience of spatial extension, divisibility into parts, motion, and inferences from these. A further thought might be that while quantity is an accident which intrinsically affects its subject, i.e. substance, it does so through the medium of matter; cf. *DM* XXXIX, s. 2, n. 13, vol. 26, p. 513. We come to know matter only by the medium of change, especially local motion. But such is extrinsic to the thing which is changed or moved, which can be what it is without a particular change or motion.

331 Note the richness of this sentence which tells us something about the semiotic theory of Suárez in relation to formal and objective concepts as well as distinction in general and the present distinction in particular.

332 Cf. S. Aurelii Augustini Hipponensis, *Tractatus in Joannis Evangelium* CVI, in *PL*, vol. 35, cols. 1909–10.

However, this knowledge of God can be understood in two ways. In one way: under some common and confused concept (*ratio*), for example, under the concept of a certain higher deity which could help us or make us happy or something similar – which concept, although it would belong to the true God, could still be applied to false gods. And perhaps in this way Cicero, in Book 1 of his *On the Nature of Gods*, said: "There is no nation which has not some 'precognition' (praenotio) that God exists."[333]

In a second way, it can be understood about the knowledge of the true God, through the concept of the supreme being, than whom there cannot be a greater being and who is the principle of the rest. And it is in this way that Augustine seems to be speaking in the place cited.[334] Hence he adds: "For this is the power of the true Divinity, that to a rational creature which is now using its reason he cannot be completely and utterly hidden. For with the exception of those few in whom nature is extremely depraved, the whole human race confesses that God is the author of this world."[335] And Tertullian, in his *Apology*, Chapter 17, has spoken in the same sense,[336] and [St.] Cyprian, [in his work] *On the Vanity of Idols*, [says]: "The supreme sin is to be unwilling to know Him who cannot be unknown."[337] And in the same way, others, whom we have cited above,[338] have said that knowledge of the true God has been naturally implanted in men.

36. However, this knowledge comes to all men neither from a demonstration, because not all are capable of that, nor simply from the evidence of the terms.[339] For, even if we grant that by the name of God there is signified an essentially necessary being, than whom a greater cannot be thought, as Anselm wants[340] and as he took from Augustine, in [his work] *On Christian Doctrine*, Book 1, Chapter

---

333 Suárez's quotation is not exact; but for the thought, cf. Cicero, *De Natura deorum* I, n. 43, ed. Pease, vol. 1, pp. 294–96. The word that Cicero actually uses, and ascribes to Epicurus (d. 270BC), in this place is "prolepsis" which in I, n. 44 he equates with "praenotio;" on this see Pease's note, pp. 296–97.

334 That is: *Tractatus in Joannis Evangelium*, CVI.

335 See *PL*, vol. 35, col. 1910.

336 Tertulliani, *Apologeticus adversus gentes pro christianos*, c. 17, in *PL*, vol. 1, cols. 376a–77a.

337 Cf. S. Cypriani Carthaginensis, *Liber de idolorum vanitate*, IX, in *PL*, vol. 4, col. 577a.

338 Cf. Section 2, § 3, above.

339 That is the terms in the proposition, "God exists."

340 Cf. Section 2, note 95, above.

7,[341] it is still not immediately evident whether what is signified by that name is some true thing or is only something contrived or imagined by us.

Therefore, this knowledge could have arisen from two sources. First, from the very great proportion which this truth has with the nature of man. For when this truth has been proposed and its terms have been explained, although it does not immediately appear to be completely evident, however it does by itself immediately appear to be consonant with reason and it is most easily shown to a man who is not completely ill disposed. For there appears to be nothing in that truth which would make it unacceptable or difficult to believe. Conversely, there are many things which immediately incline one to the acceptance of that truth. Many things (I say) not only metaphysical or physical, but also moral, not only external, but also internal. For if a man reflects on himself he knows he does not exist from himself, nor does he suffice for himself for his own perfection, nor do all the creatures which he experiences satisfy him. Indeed, he recognizes in himself a nature more excellent than those [creatures], even though [that nature is] on its own level imperfect since both in knowing the truth and in loving the good he knows himself to be weak and infirm. Hence most easily a man is persuaded that there must be a higher nature from which he may draw his origin and by which he may be ruled and governed.

37. Second, this general knowledge is founded on the tradition and education of [our] predecessors, both [the education] of children by parents and of ignorant persons by those more learned. From this also there has grown and has been accepted a general feeling among all nations that God exists. Hence this knowledge for the most part seems to have come by way of human faith, especially among the common people, rather than from the evidence of the matter. However, it does seem to have come with a certain practical and moral evidence, which could have been enough to oblige [men] to assent to this truth that God exists and also to worship Him. And in accord with this, all things are easily understood which the [Scholastic] Doctors say about a naturally implanted knowledge of God.

---

341 Cf. S. Aurelii Augustini Hipponensis, *De doctrina christiana, libri quatuor*, I, c. 7, in *PL*, vol. 34, col. 22.

Dramatis Personae

Abulensis (Alfonso Tostado de Madrigal [d. 1455]) – Bishop of Avila, Commentator on the Bible.

Albert the Great, St., O.P. (ca. 1200–1280) – Dominican theologian, Bishop of Regensburg, and teacher of St. Thomas Aquinas.

Alexander of Aphrodisias (fl. ca. 200) – Commentator on the works of Aristotle.

Alexander of Hales, O.F.M. (ca. 1186–1245) – Franciscan theologian at the University of Paris.

Anselm, St. (1033–1109) – Theologian, Archbishop of Canterbury, author of *Proslogion* and *Monologium*.

Aquinas, St. Thomas (1225–1274) – Dominican and foremost philosopher-theologian of the Middle Ages.

Argyropoulos, John (ca. 1415–1487) – A translator of Aristotle from Greek to Latin.

Aristotle (384–322 BC) – Greek philosopher, disciple of Plato, called "The Philosopher" (*Philosophus*) by the Latins

Athanasius, St. (293–373) – Theologian, Bishop of Alexandria, Father of the Church, played leading role at Council of Nicaea. Opponent of Arianism.

Augustine of Hippo, St. (354–430) – Bishop of Hippo, most important Latin theologian and Church Father.

Averroes (*aka* Ibn Rushd [1126–1198]) – Arabic philosopher, commented on Aristotle's works for which he was called by the Latins "the Commentator" (*Commentator*).

Avicenna (*aka* Ibn Sina [980–1037] – Arabic philosopher, renowned for learning and medical skill; author of numerous scientific, religious, and philosophical works, including an original presentation of Aristotelian metaphysics.

Bañez, Domingo, O.P. (1528–1604) – Spanish Dominican theologian, holder of the *Catédra de prima* in theology at Salamanca, commented on the *Summa Theologiae* of St. Thomas.

Basil, St. (ca. 329–379) – Greek Father of the Church, Bishop of Caesarea, brother of St. Gregory of Nyssa, combatted Arianism.

Bessarion, Cardinal Joannes (c. 1403–1472) – Byzantine theologian, Archbishop of Nicaea, titular Patriarch of Constantinople, co-founder (with Gemistus Plethos) of the Platonic Academy in Florence, translated Aristotle's *Metaphysics* into Latin.

Biel, Gabriel (1410?–1495) – Philosopher and theologian at Tübingen, follower of Ockham's nominalism.

Boethius, Anicius Manlius Severinus (ca. 480–524/5) – Christian Latin philosopher and theologian, translated and commented on logical writings of Aristotle, author of "On the Consolation of Philosophy" (*De consolatione philosophiae*).

Buridan, John (ca. 1300–1360) – Scholastic philosopher. Taught in the Faculty of Arts at Paris, where he was twice (1327 and 1340) Rector of the University. Commented on Aristotle and especially worked in logic and physics.

Cajetan (*aka* Tommaso de Vio, O.P. [1469–1534]) – Cardinal, theologian, Master General of the Dominicans, and principal commentator on the *Summa Theologiae* of St. Thomas Aquinas

Capreolus, Joannes, O.P. (1380–1444) – Thomistic commentator, known as the "Prince of Thomists" (*Princeps thomistarum*).

Chrysostom, John, St. (ca. 347–407) – A Doctor of the Church; Archbishop of Constantinople, famous for his preaching, author of very influential homilies, letters, and commentaries on Scripture.

Cicero, Marcus Tullius (106–43 B.C.) – Roman Senator, orator, and author of philosophical treatises.

Clavius, Christopher, S.J. (1538–1612) – Jesuit mathematician and astronomer. Taught at the *Collegium Romanum* and was the principal author of the 1582 reform of the Julian calendar under the auspices of Pope Gregory XIII.

Cyprian, St. (d. 258) – Theologian, Bishop of Carthage, Christian martyr.

Damascene, St. John (d. 780) – Christian archbishop of Damascus, theologian, author of "On the Orthodox Faith" (*De fide orthodoxa*).

Diagoras (fifth cent. B.C.) – Greek Sophist, called "the Atheist."

Dionysius the Areopagite (aka Pseudo-Dionysius (sixth cent. A.D.) – Unknown author of important and influential treatises in theology, mistakenly identified with St. Paul's convert at the Areopagus (*Acts of the Apostles*, c. 17, v. 34).

Durandus of Saint Pourçain, O.P. (ca. 1275–1334) – Dominican theologian, Bishop of Meaux, important figure in early 14th century theology at Paris.

Eusebius of Caesarea (ca. 260–ca. 339) – Theologian and Church historian.

Ferrara (*aka* Franciscus de Sylvestris, O.P. [1474–1525]) – Theologian, Master General of the Dominicans, and principal commentator on the *Summa contra Gentiles* of St. Thomas Aquinas.

Ficino, Marsilio (1433–1499) – Italian Renaissance figure, philosopher and Greek scholar, translated and commented on Plato and various neo-Platonists.

Fonseca, Pedro da, S.J. (1548–1599) – Jesuit philosopher, edited and translated the *Metaphysics* of Aristotle. He was himself known as "the Portuguese Aristotle."

Gregory Nazianzen, St. (ca. 330–389) – Greek Father of the Church, called "Gregory the theologian," an opponent of Arianism.

Gregory of Rimini, O.S.A. (d. 1358) – Theologian, Minister General of the Augustinians, influenced by nominalism.

Henry of Ghent (1217?–1293) – Belgian, secular master of theology at Paris, influenced by St. Augustine and Avicenna, opposed on many points by Duns Scotus.

Hervaeus Natalis, O.P. (*aka* Hervé Nédélec [d. 1323]) – Dominican theologian, Master General of his Order, author of various works including a "Treatise on Second Intentions" (*Tractatus de secundis intentionibus*).

Hilary of Poitiers, St. (ca. 315–366) – Theologian, Bishop of Poitiers, Church Father, fought against Arianism.

Javelli, Chrysostom, O.P. (d. ca. 1538) – Dominican philosopher and theologian.

Jerome, St. (ca. 347–419) – Latin Church Father, Biblical translator (author of the *Vulgate*) and commentator.

John of Jandun (ca. 1286–1328) – French philosopher, author of influential commentaries on Aristotle, defended Averroism.

John of St. Thomas, O.P. (*aka* John Poinsot [1589–1644]) – Portuguese Dominican, a Thomist, and a major figure in late Scholastic philosophy and theology.

Justin Martyr, St. (ca. 100–ca. 165) – Greek theologian, a philosopher, and then a convert to and an apologist for Christianity, opened first Christian school in Rome.

Lactantius (ca. 240–320) – Latin Christian writer, rhetorician, called "the Christian Cicero" because of his elegant style.

Lychetus, Francis (d. 1512) – Franciscan philosopher and theologian, commentator on the works of Duns Scotus.

Maimonides, Rabbi Moses (1135–1204) – Jewish philosopher, author of *The Guide for the Perplexed*.

Michael of Ephesius (eleventh–twelfth cent.) – Byzantine bishop of Ephesus, probable author of part of the *Metaphysics* commentary attributed to Alexander of Aphrodisias.

Ockham, William of (ca. 1285–1349). Most important philosopher of the 14th century. Principal medieval nominalist.

Petrus Aureoli (ca. 1280–1322) – Franciscan, Archbishop of Aix, regarded as nominalist precursor of Ockham.

Pico della Mirandola, Giovanni (1463–1494) – Italian humanist.

Plato (428–348 BC) – Greek philosopher, disciple of Socrates, and teacher of Aristotle.

Pseudo-Alexander of Hales (Alessandro Bonini, O.F.M. [ca. 1270–1314]) – Author of a commentary on Aristotle's *Metaphysics* which was published at Venice in 1572 erroneously under the name of Alexander of Hales.

Peter d'Ailly (*aka* Petrus de Alliaco [1350–1420]) – Cardinal, Bishop of Cambrai, theologian, prominent at Councils of Pisa and Constance.

Peter the Lombard (ca. 1095–1160) – Bishop of Paris, author of the "*Sentences*," which became the standard text for theological instruction at medieval universities. As a condition for graduation all Masters of Theology were required to write commentaries on the *Sentences* of Peter the Lombard.

Richard of Middleton, O.F.M. (ca. 1249–1300/8) – Franciscan theologian.

Scotus, John Duns (1266–1308) – "The Subtle Doctor," the most important Franciscan philosopher and theologian. Influenced by Avicenna.

Soncinas, Paul, O.P. (d. 1494) – Dominican philosopher, author of a much cited "Metaphysical Questions" (*Quaestiones metaphysicales*).

Soto, Domingo de, O.P. (1494–1560) – Dominican philosopher and theologian.

Tertullian (ca. 155–ca. 220) – Early Christian writer. One of the "Apologists."

Theodoretus of Cyr (ca. 393–ca. 466) – Bishop of Cyr, theologian, and controversial Greek Father of the Church. Mistakenly cited by Suárez as "Theodosius."

Bibliography

General Bibliographies

Iturrioz, J., "Bibliografía suareciana," *Pensamiento*, numero extraordinario (Madrid, 1948), 603ff.

Santos-Escudero, C., "Bibliografía suareciana de 1948 a 1980," *Cuadernos Salmantinos de Filosofía*, 7 (1980), 337–75.

Latin Edition Principally Used in this Work

Suarez, Franciscus, S.J., *Opera omnia*, 26 vols., Paris: L. Vivès, 1856–1866; plus two volumes of indices, 1878.

Disputationes Metaphysicae, ed. Carolus Berton, in Vols. 25–26 of *Opera omnia* (Vivès), reprinted: Hildesheim: G. Olms, 1965.

Latin Edition Secondarily Used

R.P. Francisci Suarez, S.J., *Metaphysicarum disputationum*, 2 vols., Moguntiae [i.e. Mainz]: Excudebat Balthasarus Lippius, Sumptib. Arnoldi Mylii, 1605.

Edition and Spanish Translation of Disputationes Metaphysicae

Francisco Suárez, *Disputaciones metafísicas*, 7 vols., edición y traducción de Sergio Rábade Romeo, Salvador Caballero Sánchez y Antonio Puicerver Zanón, Madrid: Editorial Gredos, 1960–1966. Disputations 28 and 29 are contained in vol. 4 (1962) of this work.

English Translations of Various Metaphysical Disputations

Suárez, Francisco, *Disputatio V: Individual Unity and its Principle*, tr. Jorge J.E. Gracia, in *Suárez on Individuation*, Milwaukee: Marquette University Press, 1982.

_________, *On Formal and Universal Unity* (*Disputatio VI*), tr. James F. Ross, Milwaukee: Marquette University Press, 1964.

_________, *On the Various Kinds of Distinctions* (*Disputatio VII*), tr. Cyril Vollert, Milwaukee: Marquette University Press, 1947.

_________, *The Metaphysics of Good and Evil according to Suárez: Metaphysical Disputations X and XI and Selected Passages from Disputation XXII and Other Works*, Translation with Introduction, Notes, and Glossary, by Jorge J.E. Gracia and Douglas Davis, München: Philosophia Verlag, 1989.

_________, *On the Essence of Finite Being as Such, on the Existence of that Essence and their Distinction* (*Disputatio XXXI*), translated with an Introduction by Norman J. Wells, Milwaukee: Marquette University Press, 1983.

_________, *On Efficient Causality: Metaphysical Disputations 17, 18, and 19*, tr. Alfred J. Freddoso, New Haven: Yale University Press, 1994.

_________, *On Creation, Conservation, and Concurrence: Metaphysical Disputations 20, 21, and 22*, Translation, Notes, and Introduction by Alfred J. Freddoso, South Bend, Ind.: St. Augustine's Press, 2002.

_________, *On Beings of Reason (De Entibus Rationis): Metaphysical Disputation LIV*, translated with an Introduction and Notes by John P. Doyle, Milwaukee: Marquette University Press, 1995.

Some Other Primary Sources

General

Migne, J.-P. (Jacques-Paul), *Patrologiae Cursus Completus ... Series Latina*, 221 vols., Paris: J.-P. Migne, 1844–1891.

_________. *Patrologiae Cursus Completus ... Series Graeca*, 161 vols., Paris: Garnier, 1855–1891.

Specific

Alphonsi episcopi Abulensis, *Prima pars super Exodum*, Venetiis: In aedibus Petri Liechtenstein, 1528.

Albert the Great, St. *Opera omnia*, Cura ac labore Augusti Borgnet, Parisiis: Apud Ludovicum Vivès, 1891; and *Opera omnia*, Lugduni: Sumptibus Claudii Prost, et al, 1651.

Alexander of Aphrodisias, *In Aristotelis Metaphysica Commentaria*, ed. M. Hayduck, in *Commentaria in Aristotelem Graeca*, vol. 1, Berolini: Typis et Impensis Georgii Reimeri, 1891.

Alexander of Hales, O.M. [actually, Alessandro Bonini], *In duodecim Aristotelis Metaphysicae libros dilucidissima expositio*, Venetiis: Apud Simonem Galignanum de Karera, 1572.

Anselm, St., *Opera omnia*, ed. F.S. Schmitt, O.S.B., Edinburgh: Apud Thomas Nelson et Filios, 1946.

Aristotle, *Aristoteles graece*, Ex recensione Immanuelis Bekkeri, 5 vols, Berolini: Apud Georgium Reimerum, 1831.

________, *The Basic Works of Aristotle*, Edited with an Introduction by Richard McKeon, New York: Random House, 1941.

Arriaga, Roderigo de, S.J., *Cursus philosophicus*, Lugduni, 1669.

Athanasius, St., *Oratio contra Gentes*, in *Patrologia Graeca*, vol. 25.

Augustine, Aurelius, St., *De diversis quaestionibus 83*, in *Patrologia Latina*, vol. 40.

________, *Confessionum libri tredecim*, in *Patrologia Latina*, vol. 32.

________, *De doctrina christiana*. ed. Fr. Balbino Martín, O.S.A., in *Obras de San Augustin*, Tomo XV, Madrid: Biblioteca de Autores Cristianos, 1957; and in *Patrologia Latina*, vol. 34.

________, *De Trinitate*, ed. L. Arias, O.S.A., in *Obras de San Augustin*, Tomo V, Madrid: Biblioteca de Autores Cristianos, 1956; and in *Patrologia Latina*, vol. 42.

________, *De Civitate Dei*, ed. José Moran, in *Obras de San Augustin*, Tomo XVI, Madrid: Biblioteca de Autores Cristianos, 1964; and *Ad Marcellinum de civitate Dei contra paganos, libri viginti duo*, in *Patrologia Latina*, vol. 41.

________, *Contra literas Petiliani Donatistae Cirtensis episcopi, libri tres*, in *Patrologia Latina*, vol. 43.

________, *Tractatus in Joannis Evangelium*, in *Patrologia Latina*, vol. 35.

________, *Contra mendacium*, ed. P. Ramiro Flórez, O.S.A., in *Obras de San Augustin*, Tomo XII, Madrid: Biblioteca de Autores Cristianos, 1954.

Aureoli, Petrus, *Scriptum super primum sententiarum*, ed. Eligius M. Buytaert, O.F.M., Book II, Distinctions II–VIII, St. Bonaventure, NY: The Franciscan Institute, 1956.

Averroes, *In Libros Metaphysicorum Aristotelis*, in vol. 8, *Aristotelis Opera cum Averrois commentariis*, Venetiis: Apud Junctas, 1562–1574.

________, *In Libros de Coelo Aristotelis*, in vol. 5, *Aristotelis Opera ....*

________, *Sermo de substantia orbis, nuper castigatus, et duobus capitulis auctus*, in vol. 9, *Aristotelis Opera ....*

________, *Destructio destructionum philosophiae Algazelis*, in ibid.; and *Destructio destructionis, In the Latin Version of Calo Calonymus*, ed. Beatrice H. Zedler, Milwaukee: Marquette University Press, 1961.

Avicenna, *Liber de philosophia prima sive scientia divina*, édition critique de la traduction latine médiévale, par. S. Van Riet, 2 vols., Louvain: E. Peeters – Leiden: E.J. Brill, 1977 and 1980.

Bañez, Domingo, O.P., *Scholastica commentaria in primam partem Summae Theologiae* I, q. 2, a. 3, ed. P. Luis Urbano, Madrid: Editorial FEDA, 1934.

Basil, St., *Adversus Eunomium*, in *Patrologia Graeca*, vol 29.

Biel, Gabriel, *Collectorium circa quattuor libros Sententiarum*, Prologus et Liber primus, collaborantibus Martino Elze et Renata Steiger, ediderunt Wilfridus Werbeck et Udo Hofmann, Tübingen: J.C.B. Mohr (Paul Siebeck), 1973.

Boethius, Ancius Manlius Severinus, *Opera theologica: Quomodo Trinitas unus Deus ac non tres dii*, in *Patrologia Latina*, vol. 64.

Bonaventura, St., *In libros Sententiarum*, in, *Opera Theologica Selecta*, editio minor, Quaracchi: Ex Typographia Collegii S. Bonaventurae, 1934.

Burgersdijk, Franco, *Institutionum metaphysicarum. libri duo, Opus posthumum*, Lugduni Batavorum: Apud Hieronymum de Vogel, 1640.

Cajetan (*aka* Tommaso de Vio, O.P.), *In De Ente et Essentia D. Thomae Aquinatis commentaria*, ed. P.M.H. Laurent, Taurini: Marietti, 1934.

_________, *Commentaria in Summam Theologiae*, in *Sancti Thomae Aquinatis Opera*, vols. 4–12, Romae, 1888–1906.

Capreolus, Johannes, O.P., *Defensiones theologiae Divi Thomae Aquinatis*, de novo editae cura et studio RR. PP. Ceslai Paban et Thomae Pègues, Turonibus: Sumptibus Alfred Cattier, 1890.

Chrysostom, St. John, *Homiliae XXI de statuis ad populum Antiochenum habitae*, in *Patrologia Graeca*, vol. 49.

_________, *Homiliae in Genesin*, in *Patrologia Graeca*, vol. 53.

Cicero, M. Tullius, *De Natura deorum,* liber primus, ed. Arthur Stanley Pease, Cambridge: Harvard University Press, 1955.

Clavius, Christophorus Bambergensis ex Societate Jesu, *In Speram Ioannis de Sacro Bosco commentarius, nunc quinto ab ipso auctore hoc anno 1606, recognitus, et plerisque in locis locupletatus. Accessit Geometrica, atque uberrima de crepusculis tractatio*, Romae: Sumptibus Io. Pauli Gellii, 1607

Cyprian, St., *Liber de idolorum vanitate*, in *Patrologia Latina*, vol. 4.

D'Ailly, Peter, *Questiones magistri Petri de Alliaco Cardinalis cameracensis super primum tertium et quartum sententiarum*, Parisiis: Impressae arte et industria Iohanis Barbier, expensis honesti viri Iohanis Petit, n.d.

Damascene, St. John, *De fide orthodoxa*, versions of Burgundio and Cerbanus, ed. E.M. Buytaert, O.F.M., St. Bonaventure: Franciscan Institute, 1955.

Descartes, René, *Oeuvres de Descartes*, ed. Charles Adam and Paul Tannery, Paris: L. Cerf, 1897–.

Dionysius the Areopagite, *De divinis nominibus*, in *Patrologia Graeca*, vol. 3.

_________, *De mystica theologia*, in *Patrologia Graeca*, vol. 3.

Durandus a Sancto Porciano, O.P., *In Petri Lombardi Sententias Theologicas commentariorum libri IIII*, Venetiis: Ex Typographia Guerraea, 1571.

Eusebius of Caesaria, *Praeparationis evangelicae, libri quindecim*, in *Patrologia Graeca*, vol. 21.

Ferrara (*aka* Franciscus de Sylvestris, O.P. [1474–1525]), *Commentaria Ferrariensis in Summam contra Gentiles*, in *Sancti Thomae Aquinatis Opera*, vols. 13–15, Romae, 1918–1930.

Fonseca, Pedro da, S.J., *Instituçiõnes dialécticas: Institutionum dialecticarum libri octo*. Introdução, estabelecimento do texto, tradução e notas por Joaquim Ferreira Gomes, Coimbra: Universidade de Coimbra, 1964.

_________, *Commentariorum in libros Metaphysicorum Aristotelis Stagiritae, Tomi I–IV*, Coloniae: Sumptibus Lazari Zetzneri, 1615; reprinted Hildesheim: Georg Olms, 1964.

Gregory of Rimini, O.E.S.A., *Super primum et secundum Sententiarum*, reprint of Venice, 1522 edition, St. Bonaventure, N.Y.: The Franciscan Institute, 1955.

Gregory, St., Romanus Pontifex, *Moralium libri, sive expositio in librum B. Job*, in *Patrologia Latina*, vol. 76.

Gregory Nazianzen, St., *Oratio, – Theologica* in *Patrologia Graeca*, vol. 36; and A.J. Mason, *The Five Theological Orations of Gregory of Nazianzen*, Cambridge, 1899.

Henry of Ghent, *Summae quaestionum ordinariarum*, Parisiis: In aedibus Iodoci Badii Ascensii, 1520.

Hervaeus Natalis, O.P., *In quatuor libros Sententiarum commentaria*, Parisiis: Apud viduam Dionisii Moreau, 1647.

Hilary of Poitiers, St., *De Trinitate, libri duodecim*, in *Patrologia Latina*, vol. 10.

Jandun, John of, *Acutissimae Quaestiones in duodecim libros Metaphysicae*, Venetiis: Apud Hieronymum Scottum, 1560.

Javelli, Chrysostom, *In omnibus Metaphysicae libris quaesita testualia metaphysicali modo determinata. In quibus clarissime resolvuntur dubia Aristotelis, et Commentatoris, eaque ut plurimum decisa habentur iuxta Thomisticum dogma*, Venetiis: Apud Haeredes Ioannis Mariae Bonelli, 1576.

Jerome, St. (*aka* S. Eusebius Hieronyimus Stridonensis presbyterus), *Commentariorum in epistolam ad Ephesios, libri tres*, in *Patrologia Latina*, vol. 26.

_________, *Commentaria in Ephesios*, in *Patrologia Latina*, vol. 26.

_________, *Commentarii in librum Job*, in *Patrologia Latina*, vol. 26.

_________, *Epistola CXXV* (*ad Rusticum Monachum*), in *Patrologia Latina*, vol. 22.

John of St. Thomas, O.P. (*aka* John Poinsot), *Cursus philosophicus Thomisticus*, ed. B. Reiser, O.S.B., 3 Vols., Taurini: Marietti, 1930–37.

John Duns Scotus, *Opera omnia*, ed. L. Wadding, 12 vols., Lugduni: Sumptibus Laurentii Durand, 1639.

_________, *Opera omnia*, Civitas Vaticana: Typis Polyglottis Vaticanis, 1950–.

_________, *Quaestiones quodlibetales*, in *Obras del Doctor Sutil Juan Duns Escoto, Cuestiones cuodlibetales*, edicion bilingüe, introducción, resúmenes y versión de Felix Alluntis, O.F.M., Madrid: Biblioteca de Autores Cristianos, 1968.

_________, *Obras del Doctor Sutil Juan Duns Escoto*, edicion bilingüe, *Dios uno y trino*, versión de los Padres Bernardo Aperribay, O.F.M., et al., Madrid: Biblioteca de Autores Cristianos, 1960.

Lactantius, Lucius Caecilius Firmianus, *Divinarum institutionum, liber primus: De falsa religione deorum*, in *Patrologia Latina*, vol. 6.

Lychetus, Franciscus, *Commentaria in Io. Duns Scotum: super primo, secundo et tertio sententiarum*, in *Joannis Duns Scoti, Opera omnia*, ed. L. Wadding, vols. 5, 6, and 7, Lugduni: Sumptibus Laurentii Durand, 1639.

________. *Commentaria in Io. Duns Scoti, O.M., Quaestiones quodlibetales*, in *I.D. Scoti, Opera omnia*, ed. Wadding, vol. 12, Lugduni: Sumpt. L. Durand, 1639.

Moses Maimonides, *The Guide for the Perplexed*, translated from the original Arabic text by M. Friedlander, 2nd edition, seventh impression, London: George Routledge and Sons, 1947.

Petrus Lombardus, *Sententiae in IV libris distinctae*, Quaracchi: Apud Collegium S. Bonaventurae, 1971–81.

Pico della Mirandola, Giovanni, *De hominis dignitate, Heptaplus, De ente et uno, e scritti vari*, ed. E. Garin, Firenze: Vallechi, 1942; *On the Dignity of Man* (tr. Charles G. Wallis); *On Being and the One* (tr. Paul J.W. Miller); *Heptaplus* (tr. Douglas Carmichael), with an Introduction by Paul J.W. Miller, Indianapolis/New York: The Bobbs-Merrill Company, 1965.

Pseudo-Augustine (?), *Cognitio vitae seu de cognitione verae vitae liber unus*, in *Patrologia Latina*, vol. 40.

Pseudo Justin, *Quaestiones gentiles ad christianos, de incorporeo et de Deo et de resurrectione mortuorum*, in *Iustini philosophi et martyris, Opera subditicia*, ed. Car. Th. Eques de Otto, vol. 3, Wiesbaden: Dr. Martin Sandig, 1969.

________, *Cohortatio ad Graecos, De Monarchia, Oratio ad Graecos*, edited by Miroslav Marcovich, Berlin/New York: Walter de Gruyter, 1990.

Richard of Middleton, O.M.Conv., *Super quatuor libros Sententiarum Petri Lombardi quaestiones subtilissimae*, Brixiae, 1591; reprint: Frankfurt: Minerva, 1963.

Sacrobosco, Joannes de, *Tractatus de spera Magistri Iohannis de Sacrobosco*, in Lynn Thorndike, *The Sphere of Sacrobosco and its Commentators*, Chicago: The University of Chicago Press, 1949.

Soncinas, Paulus Barbus, O.P., *Quaestiones metaphysicales acutissimae*, Venetiis, 1588; reprinted: Frankfurt: Minerva, 1967.

Soto, R.P. Dominicus, O.P., *Summularum aeditio secunda*, Salmanticae: Excudebat Andreas a Portonariis, 1554; reprint: Hildesheim: Georg Olms, 1980.

Tertullian, *Apologeticus adversus gentes pro christianos*, in *Patrologia Latina*, vol. 1.

Theodoretus of Cyr, *Graecarum affectionum curatio*, in *Patrologia Graeca*, vol. 93.

Thomas Aquinas, St., *Summa Theologiae*, in *Opera omnia*, iussu impensaque Leonis XIII P. M., vols. 4–12, Romae: Ex Typographia Polyglotta S.C. De Propaganda Fide, 1888–1906.

________, *Summa Contra Gentiles*, in *Opera omnia*, vols. 13–15, Romae: Typis Riccardi Garroni, 1918–1930.

________, *Quaestiones disputatae de veritate*, ed. P. Fr. Raymundi Spiazzi, O.P., Taurini: Marietti, 1953.

________, *Scriptum super libros Sententiarum*, ed. R.P. Mandonnet, O.P. et R.P. M.F. Moos, 4 vols., Paris: Lethielleux, 1929–1947.

________, *Quaestiones disputatae de potentia Dei*, Cura et studio R.P. Pauli Pession, Taurini: Marietti, 1953.

________, *In duodecim libros Metaphysicorum Aristotelis expositio*. Ed. M.R. Cathala, O.P., Taurini: Marietti, 1950.

________, *In Librum de Causis expositio*, Pt. I, lect. 1, ed. C. Pera O.P., Taurini: Marietti, 1955.

________, *De fallaciis*, in *Opera omnia*, vol. 43, Romae: Editori di San Tommaso, 1976.

Viñas, Miguel, S.J., *Philosophia Scholastica*, tribus voluminibus distincta, ... in alma S. Jacobi Regni Chilensis Universitate, ... Genuae: Typis Antonii Casamarae, 1709.

William of Ockham, *Scriptum in librum primum Sententiarum ordinatio, Distinctiones II–III*, ed. Stephanus Brown, O.F.M. adlaborante Gedeone Gál, O.F.M., St. Bonaventure, N.Y., 1970.

Further Reading

Burns, J. Patout, "Action in Suarez," *The New Scholasticism*, 38 (1964), pp. 453–72.

Copleston, Frederick, S.J., *A History of Philosophy*, vol. 3: *Ockham to Suarez*, Westminster, Md.: Newman Press, 1953.

Courtine, Jean-François, *Suarez et le système de la métaphysique*, Paris: Presses Universitaires de France, 1990.

Cronin, Timothy, S.J., *Objective Being in Descartes and in Suarez*, Rome: Gregorian University Press, 1966.

Doig, James C., "Suarez, Descartes, and the Objective Reality of Ideas," *The New Scholasticism*, 51 (1977), pp. 350–71.

Doyle, John P., *The Metaphysical Nature of the Proof for God's Existence according to Francis Suarez, S.J.*, unpublished Ph.D. dissertation, University of Toronto, 1966.

_________, "Suarez on the Reality of the Possibles," *The Modern Schoolman*, 44 (1967): pp. 29–40.

_________, "Suarez on the Analogy of Being," *The Modern Schoolman*, 46 (1969): pp. 219–49; 323–41.

_________, "Heidegger and Scholastic Metaphysics," *The Modern Schoolman*, 49 (1972): pp. 201–20.

_________, "The Suarezian Proof for God's Existence," in *History of Philosophy in the Making: A Symposium of Essays to Honor Professor James D. Collins on his 65th Birthday*, ed. Linus J. Thro, Washington: University Press of America, 1982, pp. 105–17.

________, "*Prolegomena* to a Study of Extrinsic Denomination in the Work of Francis Suarez, S.J.", *Vivarium*, 22 (1984), 2: pp. 121–60.

_________, "Suarez on Beings of Reason and Truth", *Vivarium*, 25, 1 (1987): pp. 47–75; 26, 1 (1988): pp. 51–72.

_________, "Suárez, Francisco," *Routledge Encyclopedia of Philosophy* (London/New York: Routledge, 1998), vol. 9, pp. 189–96

Duhem, Pierre, *Le Système du monde: histoire des doctrines cosmologiques de Platon à Copernic*, 8 vols., Paris: Librairie Scientifique A. Hermann et Fils, 1916.

Ferrater Mora, José, "Suárez and Modern Philosophy," *Journal of the History of Ideas*, 14 (1953), pp. 528–43.

Fichter, Joseph, *Man of Spain: Francis Suarez*, New York: Macmillan, 1940 (A readable biography in English).

Gilson, Etienne, *Being and Some Philosophers*, 2nd edition, Toronto: Pontifical Institute of Mediaeval Studies, 1952.

Goudriaan, Asa, *Philosophische Gotteserkenntnis bei Suárez und Descartes in Zusammenhang mit der niederländischen reformierten Theologie und Philosophie des 17. Jahrhunderts*, Leiden/Boston/Köln: Brill, 1999.

Grabmann, Martin, "Die 'Disputationes Metaphysicae' des Franz Suarez in ihrer methodischen Eigenwart und Fortwirkung," in *Mittelalterisches Geistesleben*, vol. I, München: Hueber, 1926.

Gracia, Jorge J.E., editor, *Francisco Suárez*, special issue, *American Catholic Philosophical Quarterly*, 65 (1991): 3 (Contains articles on various aspects of Suárez's work.)

Guthrie, Hunter, S.J., "The Metaphysics of Francis Suarez," *Thought*, XVI (1941), pp. 297–311.

Guy, Alain, "L'analogie de l'être selon Suarez," *Archives de Philosophie*, 42 (1979), pp. 275–94.

Hellin, José, S.J., *La analogia del ser y el conocimiento de Dios en Suárez*, Madrid: Gráficas Uguina, 1947.

_________, "Sobre el transito de la potentia activa al acto segun Suárez," *Razón y fe*, 138 (1948), pp. 353–407.

________, "El ente real y los posibles en Suárez," *Espiritu*, X (1961), pp. 146–63.

________, "Obtenación del concepto del ente, objeto de la metafísica," *ibid.*, 17 (1961), pp. 135–54.

________, "El concepto formal según Suárez," *Pensamiento*, 18 (1962), pp. 407–32.

Hoeres, W., "Francis Suarez and the Teaching of John Duns Scotus on Univocatio entis," in *John Duns Scotus (1265–1965)*, ed. J.K. Ryan and B.M. Bonansea, Washington, DC: Catholic University of America Press, 1965.

Iriarte, Joaquín, S.J., "La proyección sobre Europa de una gran metafísica, o Suárez en la filosofía de los dias del barocco," *Razón y fe*, 138 (1948): pp. 229–65.

Iturrioz, Jesús, S.J., *Estudios sobre la metafísica de Francisco Suárez*, Madrid: Ediciones Fax, 1949.

Jansen, Bernhard, S.J., "Die Wesenart der Metaphysik des Suarez," *Scholastik*, 15 (1940), pp. 161–85.

________, "Der Konservatismus in den *Disputationes Metaphysicae* des Suarez," *Gregorianum*, 21 (1940), pp. 452–81.

Junk, Nikolaus, *Die Bewegungslehre des Franz Suarez*, Innsbruck/Leipzig: F. Rauch, 1938.

Marion, J.-L., "Entre analogie et principe de raison: la *causa sui*," in J.-M. Beyssade and J.-L. Marion (eds), *Descartes. Objecter et répondre* (Paris: Presses Universitaires de France, 1994), pp. 305–34.

Mesnard, P., S.J., "Comment Leibniz se trouva placé dans le sillage de Suarez," *Archives de Philosophie*, XVIII (1949), pp. 7–32.

Neidl, Walter M., *Der Realitätsbegriff des Franz Suarez nach den Disputationes Metaphysicae*, München, 1966.

Noreña, Carlos G., "Ockham and Suárez on the Ontological Status of Universal Concepts," *The New Scholasticism*, LV (1981), pp. 348–62.

________, "Suárez on the Externality and Internality of Relations," *Cuadernos Salmantinos de Filosofía*, X (1983), 183–95.

________, "Heidegger on Suárez: The 1927 Marburg Lectures," *International Philosophical Quarterly*, 23:92 (1983), pp. 407–24.

________, "Suárez and Spinoza: the Metaphysics of Moral Being," *Cuadernos Salmantinos de Filosofía*, 12 (1985), 163–82.

________, "Suárez and the Jesuits," *ibid.*, pp. 267–86.

Owens, Joseph, C.Ss.R., "The Conclusion of the *Prima Via*," *The Modern Schoolman*, 30 (1952–53), pp. 33–53, 109–21, 203–15.

________, "The Number of Terms in the Suarezian Discussion on Essence and Being," *The Modern Schoolman*, XXXIV (1956–57), pp. 147–91.

Rast, Max, S.J., "Die Possibilienlehre des Franz Suarez," *Scholastik*, 10 (1935), pp. 340–68.

Robinet, A., "Suarez dans l'oeuvre de Leibniz," *Cuadernos Salmantinos de Filosofía*, VII (1980), pp. 269–84.

________, "Suárez im Werk von Leibniz," *Studia Leibnitiana*, XIII (1981), pp. 76–96.

Roig Gironella, Juan, S.J., "La analogía del ser en Suárez," *Espiritu* (Barcelona), 36: 95 (1987), pp. 5–47.

Ross, W.D, *Aristotle: A Complete Exposition of his Works and Thought*, New York: Meridian Books, 1959.

Schmutz, Jacob, "La doctrine médiévale des causes et la théologie de la nature pure," *Revue Thomiste*, 101 (2001), pp. 217–64.

Schneider, Marius, O.F.M., "Der angebliche philosophische Essentialismus des Suarez," *Wissenschaft und Weisheit*, 24 (1961), pp. 40–68.

Scorraille, Raoul de, S.J., *François Suarez de la Compagnie de Jesus*, 2 vols., Paris: Lethielleux, 1912–13. (The definitive biography of Suárez).

Seigfried, Hans, *Wahrheit und Metaphysik bei Suarez*, Bonn, 1967.

Varii, *Suárez en el cuarto centenario de su nacimiento (1548–1617), Pensamiento*, 4, numéro extraordinario, Madrid, 1948.

Weisheipl, James A., O.P., "The Principle *Omne quod movetur ab alio movetur* in Medieval Physics," *Isis*, 56 (1965), pp. 26–45.

Wells, Norman J., "Suarez, Historian and Critic of the Modal Distinction between Essential Being and Existential Being," *The New Scholasticism*, 36 (1962): pp. 419–44.

_________, "Old Bottles and New Wine: A Rejoinder to J.C. Doig," *The New Scholasticism*, 53 (1979–80), pp. 515–23.

_________, "Suarez on the Eternal Truths, I and II," *The Modern Schoolman*, 58 (1980–81): pp. 73–104, 159–74.

_________, "Material Falsity in Descartes, Arnauld, and Suárez," *Journal of the History of Philosophy*, 22 (1984): pp. 25–50.

Werner, Karl, *Franz Suarez und die Scholastik der letzten Jahrhunderts*, 2 vols., Regensburg, 1889.

Index of Names

Subject Index